Criminal Defence and Procedure

The College of Law
Braboeuf Manor
Portsmouth Road, Guildford
Surrey GU3 1HA

Criminal Defence and Procedure

Comparative Ethnographies in the United Kingdom, Germany, and the United States

Thomas Scheffer
Humboldt Universität zu Berlin, Germany

Kati Hannken-Illjes
Friedrich Schiller Universität Jena, Germany

Alexander Kozin
Freie Universität Berlin, Germany

First published 2010 by
PALGRAVE MACMILLAN

Palgrave Macmillan in the UK is an imprint of Macmillan Publishers Limited, registered in England, company number 785998, of Houndmills, Basingstoke, Hampshire RG21 6XS.

Palgrave Macmillan in the US is a division of St Martin's Press LLC, 175 Fifth Avenue, New York, NY 10010.

Palgrave Macmillan is the global academic imprint of the above companies and has companies and representatives throughout the world.

Palgrave® and Macmillan® are registered trademarks in the United States, the United Kingdom, Europe and other countries.

ISBN-13: 978–0–230–23022–4 hardback

This book is printed on paper suitable for recycling and made from fully managed and sustained forest sources. Logging, pulping and manufacturing processes are expected to conform to the environmental regulations of the country of origin.

A catalogue record for this book is available from the British Library.

A catalog record for this book is available from the Library of Congress.

10   9   8   7   6   5   4   3   2   1
19   18   17   16   15   14   13   12   11   10

Printed and bound in Great Britain by
CPI Antony Rowe, Chippenham and Eastbourne

Contents

List of Figures

1
Introducing Procedure

In this book we would like to offer a comparative ethnomethodological study of the criminal defense work in three legal settings: German, American (US), and English. The study is based on the programmatic ethnomethodological premise that in order to fully understand how lawyers work, one needs to examine all the law-relevant activities (for example, dealing with the client, identifying, selecting, and assembling paperwork in the file, conducting interviews, and carrying out arguments in the court) in the course of their procedural path. Importantly, while law-relevant activities are defined in terms of case-making, procedure serves as the condition for the possibility of making a case in the first place. Thus, we presume that by examining case-making, we can understand procedure and its effects on the administration of justice, which in the case of ethnomethodology means "doing law". With the latter emphasis, this study joins a growing area of law-in-action. As an emergent subdiscipline of the sociology of law, law-in-action does not show clearly delineated boundaries, demanding that we begin by first explaining the law-in-action program and second establishing its operational relation to ethnomethodology.

An overabundance of the studies that focus on the rule of procedure tends to overshadow other important issues concerning procedure, including the relationship between procedure as a legal rule and procedure as an observable and explainable activity. In this book, we focus precisely on this relationship. This focus demands a trans-sequential approach that undertakes *procedure* both synchronically and diachronically, in its multi-faceted and multi-sited unfolding. We pursue this thesis empirically with several comparative analyses of ethnographic data. An extensive ethnographic fieldwork allowed the authors to access the dual nature of the procedure in a series of procedural events.

In the following chapters we approach these events as individual studies.[1] At the same time, all the studies in this book belong to a more general frame that can be called "procedural order". In order to understand the manner in which individual studies relate to each other within this order, we find it necessary to preview our analyses by identifying the role of procedure in the discipline of law-in-action.

Furthermore, we suggest that one should approach law-in-action not only as an emergent discipline but also as an interdisciplinary platform for the study of legal practice in the broadest sense of the word. Various contributions made by sociology, psychology, anthropology, ethnology, political studies, communication studies, translation studies, and women's studies, for example, justify this characterization.[2] Regardless of a specific academic affiliation however, all the law-in-action research belongs to the category "basic and qualitative". A common ground for this kind of research is the methodological focus on the local and participant constitution of meaning in and through purposive actions and activities performed by various actors in the legal process (for example, judge, attorney, police officer, plaintiff, witness, or defendant) who relate various legal settings (for example, court, law firm, jail, police station) to each other via the procedural order.

Ethnomethodological law-in-action

The participation of ethnomethodology in the law-in-action research is endemic to the method's objectives. These objectives were predefined by Talcott Parsons and refined by the founder of ethnomethodology, Harold Garfinkel, and Harvey Sacks. It is important to note that all three sociologists had a direct relationship to law by both academic training and legal practice. It is common to credit Parsons with a renewal of sociology which he accomplished by insisting that 'social facts must be understood on the basis of a theory that would rise from the actual circumstances of their production' (Heritage, 1984, p. 9). Known as "Parsonian backdrop" or "bottom up approach", this way of (anti)theorizing posed a challenge to the grand theories of human behavior inherited from the sociological thought of the nineteenth century. The main difference between the two approaches lay in Parsons' view of the human subject as both an active and passive participant in the creation and transformation of his or her environment. This is not to say that normative complexes based on habitualized behaviors did not matter any longer; however, habit was no longer considered as the only adhesive matter that could hold a social order together. As Parsons claimed, and Garfinkel came to demonstrate, in order for the things to proceed as usual, the participants must utilize various locally constituted means of articulation, which underlined, as it were, explicitly stated social rules of various behaviors. This view contrasted sharply with the instrumentalist approach, which presupposed a passive adherence to the common purpose in question.

At the time, Parsons' theory did not appear to be entirely sound. Its critics would call it voluntaristic metaphysics, insisting that it showed human action to be unpredictable and selfish. In his defense Parsons indeed admitted allowing for certain indefinable vagrancies of human actions, but he also insisted on the normative character of those actions. Apparently a contradiction, the dual property of action will form the backbone of the ethnomethodological method. From this perspective, sociology of law would focus on how 'law's structure matches law's functioning in the modern societies' (Parsons, 1949, p. 370). In his own study of law, Parsons focused on the key actor of any post-industrial legal system, an attorney. For him, the lawyer was a paradigmatic figure because he both represented and manipulated the prescribed legal rules and norms of a juridical system. This might explain the reason why the original ethnomethodological research selected this figure for such a close scrutiny. As someone who stands at the edge of the court system, the attorney fits only too well the ethnomethodological profile of a semi-voluntaristic actor. At the same time, the ethnomethodological emphasis on relational structures clearly stated that the situated order of a social institution could not be understood without taking into account all the relevant activities on the part of all the participants, and not just an attorney.

This insight was advanced by Harold Garfinkel, who began his sociological career with the study of different institutional orders (for example, suicide prevention center and the jury room) in terms of their dealing with various everyday problems. In his pioneering study of jury deliberations Garfinkel showed how legal rules were being employed for practical purposes in an ad hoc manner, following the principle 'if the interpretation makes good sense, then that's what happened' (1967, p. 106).[3] As a result, he managed to reformulate the status of the person (defined as always a member and participant) and the nature of the social world for this person (constituted in situ vis-à-vis other members) by suggesting the existence of a discrete system of locally enacted (ethno) methods. With this reformulation, the social order appeared as a stratified system which is based on some collective activity. The study of collective activity seemed particularly opportune in the legal setting, which features 'a modified system of the basic rules used in the everyday life' (ibid., p. 104). For the study of law-in-action, this premise meant a continuous focus on the distinction between 'maintaining, elaborating or transforming circumstances of actors' actions' and 'reproducing, developing or modifying the institutional realities which envelop these actions' (Heritage, 1984, p. 180). At the same time, Garfinkel's sociological innovations spawned some well-grounded critique, which we address at a later point in this chapter. Indeed, although undoubtedly Garfinkel pioneered a new perspective on law, he failed to develop a straightforward and relatively clear analytical frame. It is Harvey Sacks, a disciple and close associate of Garfinkel's, who should be credited with this achievement.

The contribution of Sacks to the ethnomethodology lies in his streamlining and therefore reducing the social world at large to one of its most common expressions, that is, conversation or talk. The latter is based on the orderly sequential turn-by-turn production governed by 'a certain procedural rule' (1992, p. 4). Hence, Sacks' treatment of law which exhibited a strong investigative focus on: 'a) management of routinization in their everyday activities and b) management of continuity in court' (1997, p. 43). The first activity focuses on the attorney who suspends the taken-for-grantedness of everyday activities for a problem which can be solved only by nontraditional means. According to Sacks, these means are derived from the everyday immersion in the ordinary. They include emphasis on the written form, coherence, clarity, and so on. By doing so, the lawyer creates a particular legal product that would have otherwise, under ordinary circumstances, not been created. Not that we live in a problem-free world but rather that we do not attempt to solve our problems in a specifically created social environment that brings those features to prominence: 'The legal system provides a complete set of features, which are defined in terms of the particular type of interaction' (ibid., p. 44).

We consider Garfinkel and Sacks to be the stalwarts of the ethnomethodological approach to law. Although their individual contributions to the emergent discipline could only be called indicative, the fact that the legal institution and its actors were deemed a significant subject by the founders of ethnomethodology helped to establish a certain methodological tradition. For our concern with law-in-action, this approach offers several advantages. First, it considers law as what is being enacted, used, and performed in courts, law firms, or judicial chambers. Second, ethnomethodology shifts the concern of the jurists from the normative evaluation of the law's effects toward the practical (interactional) constitution of law. The question about how laypeople and professional lawyers alike call law into existence moved the analysis inside certain interactions: lawyer–client conferences, plea bargaining sessions, and, most prominently, court hearings. These encounters were approached as what was sequentially produced and therefore subjected to analysis in terms of their sequential production "here and now". The empirical bases for these detailed micro-studies were formed by empirically obtained data: recordings and transcripts of legally defined or legally relevant events. The choices of events for our studies were in part motivated by the main themes of the empirical law-in-action. Below we would like to mention the main themes of the law-in-action research beginning with the study of the courtroom.

The first comprehensive study of the courtroom can be attributed to Atkinson and Drew (1979). The two authors designed their project on the basis of comparing natural talk (or everyday talk) and pre-structured, as in institutional settings, talk. A court, in this view, pre-allocates speech-positions, pre-defines certain rituals and conventions. In reverse, this institutional structuration changes the tasks allocated for the participating members. In the court of law, the latter collaborate differently: some bring stories, others construct cases and deliver arguments and counter-arguments; the common ground for all is based on the pre-established rules of institutional communication. Relying on the transcribed tape-recorded proceedings and field-notes, Atkinson and Drew investigated courtroom activities with an emphasis on the interactional mechanics that 'comprises both the topic and resource in formalizing, specifying and analyzing court procedures' (1979, p. 7). With the help of a mixed ethnomethodological, conversation analytic, and ethnographic methodology they probed those question–answer sequences that could be defined as the most characteristic for the court order. They showed, for example, that the attorneys of both sides managed those in a sequential manner as in soliciting 'shared attentiveness' (ibid., p. 85). This work is undoubtedly seminal for the interactive perspective on law-in-action. At the same time, the examination of the court proceedings can be deepened, expanded, and diversified, especially along the comparative lines, as was proposed by the above authors themselves. For the study of procedure, courtroom research indeed appears to be most promising since procedure is simultaneously actualized and vocalized there. As the primary legal setting, the court of law also appears to be the very place for the study of procedural justice. In addition, as a public venue, the courtroom lends itself easily to an empirical examination.

The public trial in the context of the common law is a case in point. The sheer performativity of the multi-party body interactions, such as witness testimonies and closing speeches, make a public trial appear to be both an event of drama and the source of truth in the last instance. Among the classical ethnomethodological studies of the court as a social order we find several distinct foci: (a) general studies of the social organization of trials in traffic courts (Pollner, 1979), civil courts (Pomerantz, 1984), or – mainly – criminal courts (Feeley, 1992; Komter, 1998; Martinez, 2005); (b) court-related communication events, such as informal mediation (Maynard, 1982; Atkinson, 1992; Garcia, 2000), pre-trial communications (Lynch, 1982), examination of eyewitnesses (Wolff and Müller, 1994; Harris, 2001), especially cross-examination (Drew, 1997; Sidnell, 2004), or expert testimony (Peyrot and Burns, 2001; Shuy, 2001; Burns, 2008); (c) principal players in the courtroom, for example, professional judges (Bogoch, 2000), lay judges (Machura, 2001), defense lawyers (Philips, 1998), and jurors (Musterman, 1986; Manzo, 1993; Diamond and Vidmar, 2001; Hans *et al.*, 2003); and (d) legal language and discourse, for example, verbal deception and formulations (Stygall, 1994; Lebaron, 1996; Matoesian, 1997). Obviously, this list is merely suggestive: the study of courtroom interaction involves many diverse phenomena and components. At the same time the list is fairly representative of courtroom studies insofar as it demonstrates a priority for phenomena that are available for the researcher in terms of recorded speech or talk.

In the wake of the foundational essay on lawyering by Parsons, the figure of the attorney solicited a lot of attention from both Garfinkel (2005) and Sacks (1997), who also addressed the profession of lawyering at the outset of their respective careers, thus laying the ground for a separate subfield of law-in-action. The courtroom studies often touch upon the figure of the attorney; and it is unavoidable considering that he or she is a major player behind both the case and the trial. At the same time, the attorney is often investigated as an actor of his own, outside of the courtroom. The studies of the legal profession involve several themes: (a) running a law firm (for example, Flood, 1981; Flood, 1987; McIntyre, 1987; Travers, 1997; Flood, 2006); (b) managing lawyer–client relations (for example, Hosticka, 1979; Cain, 1983; Flemming, 1986; Griffiths, 1986; Abel, 1997; Hallsdottir, 2006); (c) evaluating attorneys' casework (Kritzer, 1998; Colbert *et al.*, 2002); (d) discussing social functions of private attorneys such as doorkeeper (Danet *et al.*, 1980a; Erickson and Schultz, 1982); or (e) dealing with the ethical implications of lawyering such as altruism (Mungham and Thomas, 1983), responsibility (Felstiner and Sarat, 1992), power (Felstiner, 1998), honesty (Lubet, 2001), or social distance (Heinz *et al.*, 2003). Two general observations follow from this overview. Firstly, research in a common law environment shows some preference for the attorney and his or her law firm.[4] Secondly, by focusing on the attorney, the scholars cannot help but consider casework.

The criminal case, though, starts earlier than this. This is why the study of the police in the ethnomethodological register is complimentary to the study of both the courtroom and the law office. Both Garfinkel (1967) and Sacks (1972) wrote on the practices of policing, focusing on the ways the police assess potentially volatile situations. As what precedes the public execution of justice, police activities instigate the works of law, as it were, juxtaposing the performative side of law as it is being witnessed in the courtroom with its investigative, secret side. The ethnomethodological studies of the police and its practices include such themes as (a) patrolling and arrest (Black, 1971; Williams, 1991); (b) police interviews and interrogations (Emerson, 1994; LeBaron and Streek, 1997; Komter, 2003; Benneworth, 2007); (c) police and surveillance technology (Meehan, 1993); (d) citizen-police communications (Zimmerman, 1984; Williams and Whalen, 1990; Meehan, 1992; Edwards, 2006). In this strand of law-in-action, the legal matter bifurcates even further. It is considered by law-in-action research before it is set: as upshots of labeling or stigmatizing processes.

Finally, one more research theme needs to be mentioned: record-making has often figured as an essential issue for all the legal settings; it has also been designated as one of the most problematic issues of ethnomethodological inquiry (Zimmerman, 1974; Walker, 1986; Smith, 2005). The significance of creating "records" for law-in-action lies in transforming spoken discourse that belongs to a nonprofessional, that is, the client, and, by default, the realm of the ordinary and mundane, in accordance with the institutional rules of documentation and remembrance (Garfinkel, 1967; Benson and Drew, 1978; Travers, 1997; Komter, 2006). Empirical studies that focus on the activities of documentation and archiving show the capacity of record-making to shape, reshape, and thus alter oral discourse by way of literalizing its "core" for specific purposes of the legal establishment (Lemert, 1969; Jönsson and Linell, 1991; Scheffer, 2003). There are more subthemes that concern ethnomethodological law-in-action research, such as the relation between regulation and legal facts (Goodrich, 1984; Damaska, 2003), records and evidence (Lemert, 1969; Benson and Drew, 1978; Jönsson and Linell, 1991; Matoesian, 1999; Komter, 2006), or problem groups and police statistics (Meehan, 1993). Although seemingly peripheral to the court studies, the research on the organization of memories turned out to be instructive to our perspective on lawyers' casework.

This brief overview could show how prolific and instructive ethnomethodological law-in-action research actually has been until today. However, there are serious shortcomings that we wish to address in this introduction because they lie at the heart of our own study on *doing procedure*. Firstly, most ethnomethodological law-in-action research abstains from comparative legal studies as can be illustrated by the ethnological and ethnographic tradition (Nader, 1965; Nader and Yngvesson, 1973; Starr and Goddale, 2002) or legal anthropology (Rüschemeyer, 1973; Bohannan, 1997; Perry, 2001; Dupret, 2005). This research tends to carry out case studies focusing on one type of court, one type of lawyer, or one type of police. As a consequence, law-in-action studies tend to underrate differences among court hearings, defense work, or the police.[5] The other concern of the ethnomethodological law-in-action research deals with the tendency to focus only on specific procedural components, while bracketing out others. Court hearings, lawyer–client conferences, plea bargaining sessions, and so on, are analyzed as if they were separated social encounters. Ethnomethodological scholars restrict the prehistory of the encounter under study to concise background information ("after the offence was introduced by … ") or a vignette ("in the case of manslaughter, we … "), not unlike the ex post accounts offered by lawyers to the ethnographer in the field. Over-generalization and thematic fragmentation are persistent shortcomings of ethnomethodological law-in-action research. We would like to address these problems with this book by firstly providing an in-depth ethnomethodological comparison of certain activities and secondly by introducing procedure as an analytical meaning-producing frame that evolves from the proximity of interaction.

Integrating procedural events, activities, and roles can be seen as another attempt to 'radicalize ethnomethodology' (Arminen, 2008). Our literature review shows that some innovation came about by way of combining the above themes into a whole of extensive longitudinal studies. Several methodological innovations, such as 'multi-sited ethnography' (Marcus, 1998), 'circulating reference' (Latour, 1999), and 'dialogical networks' (Nekvapil and Leudar, 2006), stand out in that respect. The need to reconfigure ethnomethodology rises from certain self-imposed restrictions common to the method. By restricting their analyses to the management of the "here and now" of (institutional) talk, (pre-structured) conversation, or ambiguous social situations, ethnomethodologists refuse to deal with complex conceptualizations, bringing upon themselves the critique of excessive empiricism. This omission prompted sociologists to re-evaluate the dependence on the empirical examinations as well as the relationship between the black letter law and law-in-action.

As far as the former is concerned, there have been attempts to move the boundaries of law-in-action farther away from the immediately accessible matters (Maynard, 1989; Burawoy, 1991; Burns, 2005) toward the formation of facts and cases in legal discourse. As for the latter, the most radical example in that regard is the study by Lynch and Bogen (1996). The two scholars investigated the Iran-Contra hearings in the course of many months by using the recordings from live televisual coverage. In a postscript to their minute analyses of the broadcasted examinations, they criticized the analytical focus of ethnomethodological law-in-action studies. They identified a "talk bias" and an orthodox self-restraint toward the verbal (or gestural) interaction. The preference for direct interaction and conversation seemed insufficient for answering the members' (framing) questions of "what is going on here?" Alternatively, Lynch proposed a "post-analytical" turn in ethnomethodology, with an emphasis on conversation analysis. For one, they claimed that the frame of analysis should not be preset. The sense-making machinery should not be restricted to the "proximity" of human interaction. Post-analytical ethnomethodology implies an expansion away from the tight focus on the turn-by-turn exchange. This expansion could lead toward creating various chains of action, inter-textual fields, or dialogical networks.

Lynch's "post-analytical ethnomethodology" leaves open the question of how exactly the researcher can divert from the turn-by-turn sequence in accordance with the members' references and activities. What other frames do members attend to and what other frames help the researcher to make sense of the members' moves? Bogen and Lynch call for eclectic debates to overcome the diagnosed conversation analytical reductionism. Their debates crisscross conversation analysis, discourse analysis, and semiotics. The authors offer explanations in reference to an "inter-textual field", using press coverage, official reports, parliamentary debates, forensic evidence, rhetorical *Gestalt*, procedural rules, and so on. From our micro-ethnographic perspective, these post-analytical extensions seem to be chosen in a random manner. Their explanations of Oliver North's responses, his lies, his forgetfulness, and his counterstrategies resemble intelligent speculations with as little as a hint of some empirical evidence. What is lacking is something complementary to the orthodox conversation analysis: another tight, definite, and controlled frame of reference. This frame of reference, we suggest, could be procedure. Procedure, next to direct interaction, provides law-in-action research with a solid analytics of what members orient toward, how they do it, and to what effects. In short, what is said here and now might be a pair completion (for example, a yes-or-no-answer), a contribution to the case (for example, an answer in accordance with former instructions or versions), and an anticipation of ensuing procedural stages (for example, a specification that can be quoted in the final sentencing hearing).

In sum, our review of ethnomethodological law-in-action showed the importance and diversity of this research, its relation to law-in-action research as well as the need and the possibility to simultaneously expand and refine ethnomethodology of law. Procedure serves as the key for this refinement. From the point of view of participation, procedure provides, next to the proximities of direct interaction, a meaning producing frame demarcated by beginning and ending, by relevant and irrelevant themes, by admissible and inadmissible facts, and so on. Before we utilize this meaning producing and interpretative frame, the concept of procedure should obtain some analytical modulation in contrast to its common identification with rule, ceremony, ritual, or pattern. Therefore, in the following section we would like to consolidate various senses of procedure into a working definition. In order to construct this definition, we review the very basic sociological sources that could help us outline approximate boundaries of that phenomenon.

The sociological foundations of procedure

For the roots of procedure we would like to return to the nineteenth century which is rightfully considered as the century of jurisprudence. The original focus of jurisprudence was the interpretation of the legal rule. At first sight this focus appears to be antithetical to the law-in-action program and seems to provide little ethnomethodological value for the understanding of procedure. We would like to argue, however, that there is not only an evolutionary link to law-in-action, but more importantly that one cannot fully apprehend the structure and meaning of procedure without taking jurisprudence into account. The importance of jurisprudence for law-in-action consists in establishing the first connection between the idea of law and empirical research. Granted, originally scholastic, this kind of research privileged the exactitude of expression and the narrow range of interpretability. The empirical basis for the study of legal doctrine was provided by legal statutes and codes. An examination of those was conducted vis-à-vis individual cases and judicial verdicts. Generally, the study of the black letter law, as it became known today, was aimed at improving the effectiveness of law. One way of achieving this task was seen in measuring the effects of legal reforms by two social processes: (a) execution of justice and (b) prevention of deviant behavior. The role of procedure in both processes lay in approaching the written law from the perspective of its execution. Both emphases were imported into the twentieth century under the name of criminology. In the twentieth-century criminology developed into an independent field; however, it did not become the only or even a proper discipline for the study of law. Instead, it was the union of jurisprudence and the critical sociological theory that led to the understanding of law as action.

Several sociological figures contributed to this reorientation. Karl Marx, Emile Durkheim, and Max Weber are the classical trio of scholars who not only predicted the advances of modernity and, with it, the capitalist society, but took great interest in the legal institution as it appeared to be serving the capitalist ideology directly, in a systemic manner (Morrison, 1995). Due to his critical approach, Marx could be named the most vocal critic of capitalism and its governing bodies, including law. For him, law was a means of implicit control designed and maintained with the purpose of serving the bourgeois morality. The stronger the capital, the greater the crime, the more effective the law: 'The criminal produces not only crimes but also criminal law [...] the whole of the police and of criminal justice' (Engels and Marx, 1976, p. 387). Importantly, Marx illustrates this thesis by employing nothing but criminological statistics. He argues that law is instituted to govern the means of production and accumulation of capital, meaning that law is called in to guarantee inequality and class divisions. Law does so by securing legal rights over property relations, writes Engels, who summarizes Marx's point of view by suggesting that 'crimes against property would cease of their own accord where everyone receives what he needs to satisfy his natural and spiritual urges' (1976, p. 248). For Marx, it was clear that procedure was serving the ruling class and for that reason should be considered repressive.

The repressive character of law was further exposed by Emile Durkheim, who in *The Division of Labour in Society* (1933) distinguished between cooperative and repressive law. Providing the analogue structure for the criminal and civil law, the two kinds of law differed in terms of their execution: only the criminal law required the rule of the sovereign who could guarantee just punishment. With time, the criminal law became the first and only kind of procedural law. The rise of the civil law at the turn of the last century as an administrative alternative to the criminal law added to the procedural regime the rules of arbitration. As a mediating structure of procedure, fair arbitration came to stand for fair trial. This substitution showed the inner power of procedure. According to Durkheim, legal procedure is designed to serve the upper classes because it prescribes the division of labor: 'The real reason for the development of repressive rules [...] lies in the fact that labour is not yet divided' (1933, p. 147). One must also note that, in comparison to Marx, Durkheim was not altogether negative when addressing law; for example, he was convincing in arguing that it provides cohesion to various social structures, including that of the family. He also showed the dependence of a society on legal institutions for moral governance. Two trends in the sociological theory of Durkheim are worth mentioning at this point. One concerned the participation of the actor; the other emphasized the pull of the collective consciousness. One can say that he introduced a helpful distinction between singular and collective agency. The distinction disclosed the dependence of procedural justice on social order and at the same time, by placing a strong emphasis on the division of labor, demonstrated the role of procedure as an organic response to crime.

The same thesis was vocalized by Max Weber who was equally influenced by Marx.[6] Similarly to Durkheim, Weber problematized law as an independent institution; however, his main emphasis lay on the conditions under which law could be maintained and, co-extensively, the law's role in maintaining the capitalist order. For Weber, the notion of rational authority was even more essential than for Durkheim, for it is by rationalizing its activities that law could secure the key freedom promised by capitalism: the freedom of expression: 'The rational conception of law on the basis of strictly formal conceptions stands opposite the kind of adjudication that is primarily bound to sacred traditions' (1948, p. 216). Both kinds of law imply collective responsibility on the part of the involved actors. However, the means by which contractual obligations are secured differ. The formal law is depersonalized law. It thus secures its obligations by way of 'legal empowerment rules' (1968, p. 730). The latter provide the necessary infrastructure. In addition to procedural rules, the capitalist authority is maintained by three stalwarts: (a) professional judiciary; (b) bureaucratization of procedure; (c) codification of the rules and regulations. This three-partite structure plays directly into the kind of a social order which sits between individual freedom and collective order. As far as the bureaucratization of the procedure is concerned, the formal law requires it as an interface between an individual case and the general framework of law. With this emphasis procedure became a topic of law in itself.

Modern procedure

As a topic in itself, procedure was developed by two parallel movements that emerged in the twentieth century. Both movements contributed to law-in-action by providing a macro outlook and a micro analysis of law's certain aspects. In addition, both trends emphasized the empirical relation of theory to practice. One trend theorized practice, the other practicalized theory. The most illustrious representatives of the former, Niklas Luhmann (1989, 2006) and Jürgen Habermas (1984, 1990, 1992), may not have contributed to law-in-action directly; yet, they must be given the credit of shaping contemporary understanding of the socio-legal field overall, including the sociological emphasis on procedure. Both Luhmann and Habermas strove to create a properly sociological theory of law. At the same time, the two scholars are remarkably different in their way of theorizing law. This difference is complementary: as a humanist philosopher, Habermas continues to work in the tradition of Weber; however, his greatest interest lies in the relation between speech and freedom. His approach to law is therefore also based on the critique of capitalism and especially those capitalist institutions that restrain one's agency by colonizing the lifeworld, the immediate source of that agency. Law is identified as a means of this colonization. Relying almost exclusively on the rule (procedure), it emerges as a self-sustained system that ignores the diversity and complexity of life, seeking to reduce it to certain prescribed behaviors. According to Habermas, rational communication becomes the key means of obtaining freedom for the society at large. By adhering to the standards of rational discourse (communicative action), we can employ law toward emancipating the world. Two such principles, transparency and accountability, are already at play in the contemporary courtroom. Extending them to other institutions would bring about the sought out emancipation and set up the ground for a change toward a new concept of justice. This concept includes the notion of procedure that presupposes bridging the lifeworld and system. Once connected, the two kinds of order would liberate the procedure from an apparent one-sidedness by showing that any system draws its resources from the lifeworld and its order.

In his sociology of law, Niklas Luhmann differs from Habermas on at least two counts. First, unlike Habermas, his theory has in-built and self-imposed methodological limitations concerning speculative analysis. This feature prevents Luhmann from abstraction and idealization characteristic of the philosophical allegiances of Habermas, paving a straight path to the empirically grounded research. Law must be observed minutely and continuously, claims Luhmann (who was trained as a lawyer). As an operatively closed system, law produces its boundaries by its own operations. It thus stands out as a self-sustained system. For the key element that allows for the operative closure, Luhmann suggests normativity. If law learns, it learns only in order to enhance certain normative processes (for example, selection, attribution, identification). Change is mobilized and enacted on the strength of written codes, programs, and procedures. The procedure helps organize a legal system in terms of the center and periphery, connecting the two by an episodic structure that is reminiscent of the narrative structure that includes the beginning, the middle, and the end. The importance of Luhmann for law-in-action lies in the applicability of his notion of "legitimation by procedure" to concrete empirical research, of which this book is an example. Although we are not applying this concept, we are dependent on it in our study. In the following section we would like to consolidate Luhmann's concept of procedure to include the temporal dimension that rises from the previous conceptualization with Garfinkel and Sacks. Bringing interactivity and ethnomethods into close proximity necessitates such notions as duration, beginning and end, but also centrality; the study of ethnomethods gains from our extension toward procedure, insofar as (some) members orient themselves toward this dimension as well. In other words, we call for a multi-temporal perspective on law-in-action in order to grasp the ways and means available to defense lawyers and their clients for participating and contributing to the "here and now".

Procedure and time

> The participants [...] try regularly to attach a new past to their own case. While trying to do so, they get unexpectedly entangled with what is transformed into the procedural history and what now increasingly restricts their options in due course. Everybody, thus, who wants to develop mastery in the art of the procedure, must learn to control two pasts simultaneously.
>
> (Luhmann, 1989 [1976], p. 44)

Luhmann's account on what it means/takes to participate in procedure is instructive for our choice of procedure as it is *the* analytical frame for law-in-action research. Procedure involves participants; it alters their situations, pasts, and prospects; it is demanding; once a case is engaged, it becomes impossible to abstain from doing *procedure*. Luhmann ascribes such effects to procedure from the perspective of an integrated, dynamic, and self-referential social system. This homogeneous communicative formation contrasts with atemporal normative definitions of procedure as they are widely used in legal doctrines and political science. The latter imagine procedure as a programmed or ritualized route that inhabits interactivities. Luhmann's vision is performative insofar as activities bring about the procedure, while programs and rules provide formats and resources for these performances. By way of the participants' actual contributions, each procedural system generates meaning, as well as an individual structure of options and restrictions. The contributions of the procedural regime can be compared to a "funnel", which always brings the matters toward a completion.

Like any other communicative system, such as small talk or parliamentary debates, a procedure depends on beginning and ending and therefore duration. Procedural contributions follow certain pre-structures: formats, conventions, rituals, role-models, and so on. Different from face-to-face interactions, procedure promises more than just mutual understanding (which is, in Luhmann's view, a practical fiction). The procedure promises legitimate, socially valid decisions, meaning decisions that are (internally) accepted by the parties and (externally) respected by others. This legitimizing effect is of great value for a functionally differentiated, post-traditional society that cannot rely on shared normative beliefs or a consensus of values and convictions. Procedure merely requires the following minimal conditions: the conflict parties can freely choose what to state or claim within certain formats; all statements or claims may become relevant for the final decision; the decision is kept open or remains contingent until the very end; each party has a chance to win regardless of their social status and external roles; the decision will be binding for both parties regardless of the outcome. For Luhmann, these pre-requisites can explain both, the initial engagement and increasing involvement of the parties on the one hand and the (external) indifference of the social environment in view of the parties' choices and factual complexities deriving within the procedure on the other hand.

Luhmann's dynamic understanding of procedure as a social system collapses specificity and generality, contingency and regularity. Reasons to decide, obligations to choose, expectations about what follows – all these features are not preset by the rule but are emergent through communication. In the course of procedure, the participants take positions that become binding for future actions. These positions are themselves dynamic insofar as they reflect other positions (witness statements, judge's comments, definitions by law), procedural formats (deadlines, formal requirements, communicative slots) for bringing them forward, and pragmatic considerations of what can be lost and won under current circumstances. Luhmann's dynamic view expands to various other components: roles are taken and attributed in much more precise terms than just the obligatory defense lawyer, defendant, judge, prosecutor, witness, and so on; participants adapt their expectations to or learn from the relation of cases-in-becoming; once the procedure works on the participants, they start to negotiate facts and views that were nonnegotiable in the beginning; what seemed relevant at the outset becomes minor in due course and the other way round. The procedural dynamics narrow down what counts as factor and feature. The ongoing procedure works like a mill: it grinds contradictions, oppositions, and resistances and turns them into reasoned, accountable, negotiable, decidable positions. This is, in essence, how time is supposed to operate in procedure and how procedure operates its own time according to Luhmann. Luhmann's procedure takes time in order to make participants learn, adapt to, and accept the procedural reality. The procedural course, not the procedure as a framework, prepares everybody and everything involved for a final, increasingly likely, but still contingent verdict.

We use Luhmann's dynamic understanding of procedure as another frame for understanding what defense lawyers and their clients do and attend to. Due to this doing and this attendance, procedure unfolds as a non-repeatable chain of communicative events. It unfolds meaning move-by-move through the participants' written and/or oral contributions: whether question–answer pairs, co-narrated and re-narrated stories, or written, signed, and circulated statements. The sequence of these diverse, multi-modal contributions brings about the procedure's time-specific meaning. In light of the procedural history, an utterance can be received as repetitive, consistent, or shifting. Procedure in this perspective does more than just hosting legal rules or formalities; it sets them into motion and makes them work on various components synchronically: facts, norms, and parties. Rules – whether programs, rituals, or conventions – are necessary but not sufficient prerequisites for this procedural working. They promise equality before the law for cases like *this* in terms of reasoning, measurement, and judgment. Most of all, the procedural apparatus – consisting of steady categories, trained personnel, institutionalized arenas, cultural technologies, and so on – promises a definite decision to resolve whatever problem may arise. Every criminal matter, whether it concerns drug dealing, armed robbery, rape, or homicide, can be passed on to it.

Doing procedure explores the dynamic relationship between the black letter laws and law-in-action. Our legal ethnographies show *not only* that procedure is a meaning producing, self-referential frame, as Luhmann suggested. Our ethnographies also show *how* this frame is put into action from moment to moment by the practitioners. Their knowledge of the black letter law does not dissolve in performativity. To put it simply: they do not quote legal rules in order to "perform legal expertise"; but they do quote laws or paragraphs, because they perform certain motions or acts with these formulas. From this perspective, black letter laws should be considered in terms of world-making features which serve as indispensable ingredients of more complex moves, such as supportive authorities for strong claims, reasonable standards or measures for assessing legal validity. Putting law to work in these ways must be viewed as a skilful activity that is largely responsive to the procedural situation. From the analytical standpoint, bridging the black letter law and law-in-action on the basis of procedure means to acknowledge that the latter accommodates a wide range of unique activities that heavily rely on legal trans-procedural rules.

Luhmann's "procedural system" provides us with the frame that orients legal practitioners in their daily activities. Why is procedure of such significance? Most activities, we claim, would remain untraceable in their practical (legal) relevance without this frame. We would miss most of what the lawyers' speeches and writings do, if we referred to analytical frames such as talk, interaction, or conversation only. Claiming *that* practitioners orient toward and contribute to an ongoing procedure allows us to ask *how* they do so "here and now". There are other questions closely related to this, for example: What qualifies such contributions and how do they drive and perform a unique and integrated procedure in return? Luhmann's dynamic understanding of procedure invites such explorations into the pragmatics of doing procedure in any legal case. Participants, in order to form valid contributions, attend to the procedural past and future, that is, to the earlier contributions and to the contributions to come. This temporal extension helps us to trace utterances, statements, and cases throughout the procedural course. In other words, the members and their doings provide us with the traceability of the procedural course and its objects.

Procedure, as an analytical frame, can also be productive by providing us with some grounds to organize the comparison of our three legal fields: the US-American State Courts, the English Crown Courts, and the German County Courts. Procedure allows us to achieve some (though not full) comparability (Scheffer and Niewöhner 2010). We thus focus on certain procedural mechanisms, organized around the procedural past in the presence ("binding"), the procedural future in the presence ("positionality"), and the pure procedural presence ("failure") – the latter separated from both its assigned past and its anticipated future. Despite these temporal extensions and contractions in doing procedure, there remain countless singular features such as "instructions", "last words", or the "hearsay rule". Procedure – or shall we say, procedural regime – provides us with comparability already within each field: various procedural instances or phases show some regularity regardless of the offence, the persons involved, the evidence called, and so on. In light of these regularities, procedural systems do not just differ across the traditional divide (for example, "last words"). At times, certain regularities repeat themselves or vary in all three contexts, their adversarial or inquisitorial foundations notwithstanding. However, our comparison is less interested in these traditional units, but rather in exploring a range of procedural systems in order to gain a better understanding of *doing procedure*. Comparison helps us to move from single case analyses to regularities that delineate procedural regimes identified by certain media translations, modes of involvement, and processes of knowing.

Exploring different ways of doing procedure requires an ethnographic background. Therefore, in order to study procedure, we had to marshal a compound multi-modal field consisting of embodied speeches, face-to-face interactions, disembodied texts, and living archives. This field is not a random collection of everything "in reach" or "out there", but a discourse formation that is overlooked, ordered, and modulated by the members themselves. Hence, our empirical data derive from the members' activities in concrete and unique legal matters and cases. Thus, our socio-legal ethnography of procedure places the bits and pieces of defense casework in the order of their occurrence and in relation to the procedural situation at the point of this occurrence. In this view, the moment-by-moment analysis is complemented by the analytics of multi-modality. In other words, we do not meet on the plane of written acts or speech acts, but on the plane of mediated relations. Speech is translated into text and vice versa. What is more, certain acts link up to each other over temporal and spatial distance. The ethnomethodological innovation by Michael Lynch and David Bogen takes another turn: we divert from sequential analysis not toward an inter-textual field but toward a trans-sequential analysis that moves back and forth between processed events (such as client–lawyer interviews or court hearings) and eventful processes (such as file-work and case-formation). Just like Lynch and Bogen, we use the "here and now" as the natural ground for these practical extensions. Starting from the pressing proximities, we study doing procedure, meaning we trace how statements, facts, and cases come about and come to matter.

Ethnography of procedure

The sociological take on procedure finds much affinity with comparative ethnographic approaches to law. In this regard it might be worthwhile to recuperate some points from Clifford Geertz who, in his classical essay *Local Knowledge. Fact and Law in Comparative Perspective*, introduces the programmatic principle for the comparative ethnography of law when he suggests that 'the relationship between fact and law [. . .] *is/ought to, sein/sollen*, in other words between being and moral obligation should be examined in itself' (1983, p. 170; *emphasis in the original*). We take this statement to imply that a distinction must be made between fact and what emerges from the undifferentiated experience of action and law which exhibits the structure of moral action. According to Geertz, the need for such an examination rises from the inadequacy of anthropology to attend to law in depth. The common problem with various attempts of anthropologists to understand law lies in their tendency to view law as a transparent order built around certain universally applicable and therefore comparable mechanisms. Since in the legal context these mechanisms are assumed to govern the production of facts, the latter appears to constitute a comparable category on its own automatically. Although this appearance carries much currency in the so-called industrialized societies, those societies that do not have clearly demarcated boundaries between the legal and the everyday spheres of being produce facts in a not so straightforward fashion. There, law is not an exclusive force in determining facts, for it has to co-create facts along with other social orders locally and in a situated fashion; at the same time, not every context is explicit about this character of law, thus demanding that law be examined on the basis of participant observation.

To a participant observer, law has an ambiguous status. Its boundaries are drawn in a semi-arbitrary fashion at the intersection of locally organized communal relations. A cultural systematic of this intersection shows the possibility of unusual patterns which allow for several social orders (institutions) to claim some sort of legal authority. This does not mean, however, that we should hold "customary law" or "multi-modal law" responsible for this claim. On the contrary, states Geertz, we should investigate the most basic concepts that have informed the study of law as culture in a consistent manner. For an example, Geertz proposes the concept of custom which has been a staple tool of legal anthropological research as well as its most basic unit of analysis and comparison since the inception of the field itself. When approached unreflectively, claims Geertz, this concept reduces thought (concept) to habit and/or practice. As a result a legal anthropologist takes "custom" for the true representation of law, forgetting that law also deals with facts and that 'facts emerge from the actual human circumstances' (Geertz, 1983, p. 173). The same can be said about procedure, which can be compared to custom but cannot be reduced to it already because the circumstances of its use require an institutional context.

Therefore, a properly ethnographic study would necessarily begin, continue, and end with these circumstances. In examining these circumstances, an ethnographer should focus on the description of how 'representation is itself represented' (Geertz, 1983, p. 174). In this way, the medium (case-making) and law (for example, summons, information, and verdict) become simultaneously available for review. This connection endows the case-making medium with the power to disclose the conditions for the production of law. Thus, by way of (a) introducing the juxtaposition between law and fact; (b) problematizing this relationship through the critique of the contemporary legal research; (c) giving this relationship a new frame of interpretation; and (d) illustrating it on the basis of local concepts (for example, first appearance or plea-bargain), Geertz comes to argue that the polarization between facts and law should be considered to be central for any comparative legal ethnography.

This focus is expected to both expose the double-sidedness of procedure and serve as a methodological tool that helps the ethnographer understand law as event-full, that is driven by the urge to create cases on the basis of what first appear as events. This transformation implies the creation of an object that comes to crown case-making and which should be approached as both, a statement and a sum of the means, taken in their sequential employment and with consideration of their effects. The latter feature indicates the processual side of the procedure. In order to capture this side, the ethnographer must attend to the polarization between the how of the rules which dictate a procedural course of events and the outcome of this course, or "relay stations", or those distinct points at which a case changes its course so visibly as to presuppose a different way. Fact-finding is not archaeology, for no facts exist alone. Rather, they are meticulously and painstakingly constructed from the events in accordance with the normative imperative of a legal system.

If now we are to go ahead with the formation of the basic law-in-action theme, we will have to show a certain relevance of the procedural approach to law-in-action. This orientation towards the pre-given or pre-defined relevance is, in the course of the procedure, narrowed to a case that is available to the legal decision, and a law that is available to decide this or that specific case. This is not unlike the documentary method as it was developed by Garfinkel. Procedure is relevant because it covers successive formation of meaning that allows for the mutual specification of rule and instant, down to the facts which are ready to demonstrate guilt or innocence, while keeping in question the two initial identities, that of a unique case and that of a certain offence.

Book composition

The book is comprised of an introductory chapter, five regular chapters, and *postscriptum*. Each chapter presents an ethnographic comparative study that involves a certain comparable feature. The chapters focus on those key elements of procedure which affect the structure of the procedural mechanics. We highlight the temporal side of these effects, that is, the effects of the past, present, and future in the procedural course.

In Chapter 2, 'Field Access as an Ongoing Accomplishment', we focus on the experiences of gaining access to the procedural field. We claim that a relatively open research agenda should be a prerequisite for an ethnographic comparative study that seeks to explain procedure in terms of law-in-action. We also explain the necessity of varying the means of access to various data sources, including spatiotemporal parameters of the respective legal fields, as well as to the unanticipated interventions of local contexts. In this chapter we explore the advantages of accessing procedure through different research designs. For this study the selected design presupposes: (a) bracketing preconceived theoretical notions and academic affiliations, and (b) developing a research protocol based on the local (in situ) apprehension of emerging legal phenomena.

In the preceding chapter the authors enter the temporal perspective by showing how the procedural past is available to and comes to count for current contributions. Chapter 3, 'Procedural Past: Binding and Unbinding', explores this temporality by focusing on one core mechanism of procedure: binding. Binding relates the presence to the past by turning prior statements into norms or even templates for later statements. It thereby restricts the options of the protagonists. Binding is an effect of systematic memorizing as it connects a participant to his or her prior positions and statements. Binding, however prevalent and forceful, appears differently in different criminal procedural regimes. Different procedural regimes know varying modes and intensities of binding: for example, by creating documents, examining and cross-examining witnesses, or collecting perceptions from spectators in the courtroom. Binding renders the procedural past available for the current dealing. It also shows the procedure's selective orientation toward the past. Also, different procedural regimes, we show, protect their members differently from the past.

Chapter 4, 'Procedural Future: The Politics of Positioning', takes the reader from the procedural past toward the procedural future. Here we ask how the future is practically anticipated at different points in the present enactments of the criminal procedure. Our main interest lies in the practices that narrow down or widen the possible futures by means of an ongoing selection, strategic anticipation and/or material preparation. The concept that explicates these dynamics is positionality: the anticipated/available position(s) at various instances in the procedure hinder, prompt, and expedite various futures at different times. For example, the presented analyses showed that in the US procedural context, cases were channeled quickly toward the plea bargaining option, while in English Crown Courts or German District Courts cases were kept open for the duration of the pre-trial period up until the trial hearing when the plea bargaining option became (aka deal) unexpectedly possible.

In Chapter 5, 'Procedural Present: Trying and Failing', we access the here and now of the procedural present through the lens of case failures. Case failures are enacted at different points in the procedural course. Schematically, failures are identified as processual ruptures which take place at the stages of pre-trial, trial, or deliberation. The procedures differ insofar as they enact failures at an earlier (less damaging) or later (more damaging) stage. The possibility of failure – and the tensions connected to it – emphasizes the "here and now" together with the risks and contingencies of the procedural course. Despite the co-emerging past and future, the case can be decided at this or that very instance.

In Chapter 6, we return to the most prominent field of law-in-action research: the courtroom. In 'Courts as Ways of Knowing' we show how the courts' core efficacy – knowing and deciding – derives from the three temporal dimensions and, therefore, calls for a procedural framing for better understanding. In detail, we employ three different perspectives on comparing the English Crown Court, the German District Court, and the US-American State Court. In the first comparative round, we confront the symbolic qualities of the courtroom's architectural design. We argue that this perspective has not only been under-researched but also that it often considers the physical conditions for the production of truth as sufficient, neglecting the role of actual hearings which express truth in a different, albeit adjacent mode. In the second round, we compare interaction orders of the three respective courts. There we find a number of differences which do not, however, illuminate procedure immediately and unequivocally. Thus, instead of speculating about how different parties are positioned in the court and what socio-political implications this or that position may hold, we compare different courts which are considered as epistemic sites. Here, we describe epistemic significance of different criminal procedures by using and relating the notions of laboratory and experiment from science and technology studies. A postscript will guide the reader back to the overall aspiration of our comparative ethnography: presenting the advantages of law-in-action and ethnomethodology by introducing procedure as an additional analytical frame. In addition to postanalytical ethnomethodology, we offer trans-sequential analysis that gives focused attention to the practical orientations and methods of (professional) members in the field, thus significantly expanding the scope of observable activity.

2
Field Access as an Ongoing Accomplishment

In recent years socio-legal studies have experienced an "ethnographic turn" (Travers and Banakar, p. 215). Legal anthropologists, sociologists of law, political scientists, and critical criminologists 'left their arm-chairs' in order to conduct fieldwork in different institutions and 'laboratories of law': courts, law firms, prosecutors' offices, police stations, tribunals, and so on. In this chapter we contribute to this ethnographic endeavor by providing insights on our field-accessing and field-shaping activities. Therefore, we do not intend to present a simple programmatic success story ("We are in!"). Nor do we wish to announce a new method of accessing law. Rather, we present core pragmatics of what it means to enter a legal field, understood here as criminal casework. From this perspective, the task of the ethnographer is not to simply visit pre-given fields and get hosted by the natives but shape these fields by linking sites, persons, and materials. The ethnographer also shapes the field by integrating former and later events to processes (for example, construction of evidence or recruitment of witnesses) or activities to sequences (for example, request and response, attack and defense). In other words, we believe that our research activities in the field co-create the field of research both in spatial and in temporal terms. They do so because they respond to the demands for access; furthermore, they do so because they have to accomplish access to certain sites and types of data, otherwise their ethnographies fail.

In the following, we present three different stories about how we accomplished access, how – in the course of accessing our respective fields – we, the fieldworkers, were positioned, and how our positions shaped what became accessible and available as the field. The result-ing view of ethnographic access as an ongoing accomplishment allows us to consider other, related orientations, such as crossing over to the stranger; excesses and redundancies of novel encounters; fluidity and variability of regional and institutional fields; flexibility and reversibility of social positions. Before we proceed in that direction, we would like to introduce the first conceptualization for this study: a review of select recent legal ethnographic research. By doing so, we would like to see how previous ethnographies tackled the issue of field access. After this review, we account for the differences and similarities of the disclosed access trajectories in terms of narratives.[1] These narratives will help the reader to situate the field data that we will be employing in the subsequent four chapters in order to explore and compare doing procedure in our three ethnographic fields.

Gaining access to legal setting

Hamersley and Atkinson suggest that gaining access should not be taken as a predominantly practical issue: "Not only does its [access] achievement depend upon theoretical understanding, often disguised as 'native wit', but the discovery of obstacles to access, and perhaps of effective means of overcoming them, themselves provide insights into social organization of the setting" (1983, p. 54). In addition, they forewarn that negotiating access and collecting data should not be collapsed as the same practice. One is an interpersonal, while the other is a technical issue. Nor should the researcher equate access with his physical presence in the field. Gatekeeping should also be taken seriously. And not just in terms of overcoming it, but also in terms of it being an explication of the boundaries, fortifications, and hideouts in the field itself.

Field access is not a prominent issue in socio-legal studies. However, for law-in-action research, it seems relevant to accomplish some kind of closeness to or intimacy with the local application and workings of the law. Depending on the unit of analysis, this closeness or intimacy is part of ethnographic methods as, for instance, are open interviews, audio recordings of judicial discourses, semi-standardized observations of defined settings, or video recordings of routine legal work. Hence, field access is not just another issue for ethnographic studies, and this is hardly surprising in the case of those studies that are not based on extensive longitudinal fieldwork. Many of these studies treat field access simply as a matter of data access. For example, Rosenthal (1974) and Wheeler (1994) rely almost exclusively on interviews taken from practicing attorneys, while Carlen (1976) and McBarnet (1981) construct their theoretical accounts from observing court hearings that allow for public access. On the other hand, Bogoch and Danet (1984), Levi

and Walker (1990), Bogoch (1990), and Wolff and Müller (1997) organize their studies around analyzing recorded data in the conversation
analytic tradition some time after the data was collected.[2]

In either case, it is fair to say that the above studies do not take
access to be a problematic issue; moreover, few of them even mention
access. Although one could find problematizations of related items, for
example, the attorney–researcher relationship, or the need to maintain
neutrality in the face of some impropriety, the latter problems tend to be
thematized as a part of fieldwork rather than field access. This should not
be surprising, however, given the sources of the sought out data: interviews, judicial decisions, file contents, and courtroom performances.
Due to public accessibility, there is no expectation that accessing those
data sites should require any special consideration from the researcher.
Expectedly then, those studies that had either public access to their
fields or somehow limited their involvement in these fields did not
pose field access as an issue treacherous enough to require an explication. In contrast, for the studies that have aspired to place themselves
in the midst of legal practices beyond the publicly accessible sphere, the
problem of access is a matter of life and death, as it were.

As an example, one may consider Danet *et al.* (1980), who describe,
in their essay, the plight of the project that aspired to examine
first attorney–client conferences in civil cases. Despite continuous and
earnest efforts on the part of the researchers to access the attorney's
office, the project already failed to comply with the original research
design at the initial stage of entering the field. From a vast number
of contacted attorneys only a few were interested in participating, and
none ended up hosting the project. In the analysis of their failure, the
authors named two major hurdles on the way to the law firm: the
general tendency on the part of those US private attorneys "to avoid
responding to the needs and interests of social scientists" and "the
attorney–client privilege" (Danet *et al.*, 1980, p. 908). Although the
researchers' reflections about the failure of accessing the field stand out,
the failure itself does not: no doubt, legal ethnographies had failed to
happen before and have done so after the project by Danet and her
colleagues. The fact that little is known about these failures testifies to
both the importance of access for the entire project and its taken-for-
grantedness. In ethnographic studies, references to access as a problem
itself are as rare as they are precious.

Thus, in their examination of "law talk" Sarat and Felstiner (1990)
contrast the study of legal documents with the study of oral interactions precisely along the lines of accessing lawyer's activities that involve

conferencing with clients and colleagues. They suggest that one strategy to overcome this problem is to secure support of the judicial community, specifically those judges, who would help the researcher "convince lawyers that they were selected for some positive reason" (Sarat and Felstiner, 1990, p. 134). The judges in a position of power would then approach lawyers with their recommendations. Since the researcher him- or herself would also want to have a say in the selection of the lawyers, Sarat and Felstiner propose that a list of lawyers whose profiles fit the research design be compiled in advance. The initial number should be relatively high, for the rate of attrition is about 25 percent at the stage of actually granting access to one or more clients.

In another study, Max Travers approaches legal practice from the ethnomethodological perspective by investigating "the content of particular skills and competencies employed in different kinds of legal work with an emphasis on the technical, procedural and communicative knowledge" (Travers, 1997, p. 27). For his field-site Travers chose a small firm of criminal lawyers in Northern England. Despite a highly detailed account of the casework in the firm, Travers barely elaborates on how he actually obtained permission to "follow lawyers around the courts, sit in on lawyer–client interviews, and watch people getting through their daily paperwork" (ibid., p. ix). In his introduction he mentions, however, that getting access was his main hurdle, and that he never managed to collect all the data he had planned to. In an endnote, we discover that his semiformal position in the law firm (that of a clerk) facilitated his access to attorney–client interviews. Thus, in contrast to the previous research, it appears that assuming the insider's position prior to or in conjunction with the actual research facilitates both the entry in the field and the collection of data.

In his ethnographic study of the "mass-produced law", Jerry Hoy (1995) offers a more involved account of his entry into the law firms: "to gain access for office observations I allowed management at both firms to choose the offices to be studied. In addition, I agreed to formally limit my stay in each office to one week; to provide confidentiality for the firms, clients, attorneys, and staff; and not to interview clients about their cases or their satisfaction with the legal services provided by the firms" (ibid., p. 707). Further, Hoy describes that he met with much cooperation on the part of the attorneys and the staff and managed to secure various sources of valuable data. In his actual descriptions and analysis, however, Hoy does not return to access. It appears that once unproblematic, access becomes an irrelevant issue, and so it does not rise again for the duration of his study. In contrast, John Flood's essay about how attorneys practice law as a business provides a rich picture that describes not only the difficulties with obtaining access, as in going through an "elaborate set of negotiations between a number of law firms and myself as to how I would observe lawyers at work", but also the continuous sense of the affective character of those negotiations (Flood, 1991, p. 46). Similarly to Travers, in order to take care of the confidentiality issue, Flood entered the firm as a part-time associate, assuming a role that oscillates between the native and the ethnographer.

In contrast to the studies mentioned above, a collection of essays edited by Starr and Goodale (2002) titled *Practicing Ethnography in Law* could have become a venue for some detailed accounts of field access. Unfortunately, the majority of essays in the volume bypass access as an issue. Several studies stand out, however. For example, Susan Coutin's essay provides an extensive description of accessing Central American immigration attorneys, making valuable distinctions among accessing clients versus public attorneys and community activists. Presenting access as a painful political issue, Coutin is meticulous in supporting her claims with actual or reported data. She also brings cultural differences to the fore of her descriptions: "arranging interviews with Salvadorans and Guatemalans who were seeking legal status was more difficult" (Coutin, 2002, p. 115). As the three authors discovered, nationality and the position of the client due to his or her political status present a serious problem to access informants. So also does the researcher's position, which according to Coutin connotes class, thus paving the way to the inevitable reality of having to define access and the fieldwork in political terms.

Robert Kidder's description of ethnographic work in the contexts of Amish and Japanese legal communities counts as yet another way of pursuing access. His comparison seeks "to find out how people who shun legal institutions arrange their affairs so that they can appear recognizably Amish or Japanese in the face of conflict" (Kidder, 2002, p. 90). Kidder positions his method as explicitly ethnographic: "observe and participate in conversations and actions on legal themes" (ibid., p. 91). Similarly to Coutin, Kidder dedicates much time to explaining how he actually managed to access these sites. In both cases, he accessed the field through an insider, who also happened to be a scholar. Being a cultural outsider turned out to be a benefit. At the same time, in the case of a Japanese law firm, Kidder was asked "to submit a full description of the research objectives and plans" (ibid., p. 102). Only after a general board meeting was his research approved and access granted.

Finally, in his research, Herbert Kritzer problematizes a wide variety of ethnographic issues, including field access. For example, he states that participant observations "can be relatively unproductive given that it is not possible to restrict the observation to activities or events relevant to the research, and that much of the observation may involve extremely repetitive activities" (Kritzer, 2002, p. 143). This approach points to the need for the researcher to enjoy a greater control over the place and the time of his or her involvement. In turn, the best way to obtain this kind of freedom is to strike a personal connection with the informants. In an early footnote, he elaborates on how he met his "hosts" (for example, personally, in the local bar, during the preliminary stage of research). The personal way of accessing the site allowed the researcher to "be literally sitting in his office watching them work regardless of whether that work involved interviewing the client, talking on the telephone, reading documents, writing a brief" (ibid., p. 20). Kritzer has achieved his position through informal personal contact and faces extreme cooperation as a result. In exchange, the firm expects him to assume the position of a neutral observer.

Summarizing this brief review in relation to the question posed by this chapter, we come to the following conclusions: (a) field access for the researcher is but a practical issue; (b) it ceases to be a problem once initial entry is granted; (c) access is considered to be successful only if and when it secures data collection. What the reviewed studies do not show, but still allow us to intuit, is that access bears upon the fieldwork the kind of complexity that cannot and perhaps should not be resolved on the pragmatic level. Crossing some kind of border does not automatically result in access to data. Nor is the fact of entry sufficient for positioning the researcher in the field. Some transformations occur at the point of crossing to both the fieldworker and the field. The researcher and data form a productive union. In other words: the sense-making researcher is placed as an "epistemic subject" (Knorr, 1999) in the midst of "where the action is" (Goffman, 1967). As an epistemic subject the researcher does not just access the field, but also creates versions of what the field is. From this perspective, all the studies that we have mentioned above take the field or its existence for granted.

Accessing multi-sited fields

The research questions raised for our comparative project led to a particular research design (see Scheffer, 2005) that sought the kind of access that would not only embrace various legal venues but also allow the researcher to observe the relational structure of the various activities encountered at different legal sites. Thus, from the very beginning, it became clear that, due to different artifacts (for example, archives, files, documents, notes) produced and utilized by different legal discourses, the methods to be used in the three different settings would also differ. This is to say that, depending on a specific legal context, for the defense, preparation materializes differently, appears at different points in the procedure, and creates different pre-trial and trial relations. In view of these anticipated differences, the project's open research design allowed for a great degree of adaptability during the field research. Instead of using streamlined approaches to standard data, the field researchers were meant to hinge on the data fabricated and utilized by the members themselves. That is, the three fieldworkers were virtually free to make use of whatever techniques, tools, and methods there were available that would fit the observational tasks at hand.

Given that the project's overall objective was to study events and processes toward disclosing systematic connections between investments at the pre-trial stage and their dividends at the trial stage, the project's research was defined as basic rather than applied. Thus, it shuns making macro assumptions about fairness of one legal system versus another; by the same token, it is not concerned with evaluating legal normativity, institutional performativity, or professional competence. It rather explores minor differences – for example, where, when, and how participants contribute to the procedure as well as their intrinsic efficacy in terms of the resulting cases. At the same time, for an international project, the comparative component must remain essential. So, an apparent contradiction emerges. On the one hand, the openness of accessing and dwelling in the field lets the researcher focus on the difference in the name of difference. On the other hand, a comparative project requires if not an object or way of comparison, then at least shared systematics (Kozin, 2010; Hannken-Illjes, 2010). In this view, the minor differences are added up to structured aggregates or even real types.

For the present chapter, we have chosen narratives as the shared platform to explicate our analogous and diverse trajectories and tactics of field access. We narrate our winded paths into the legal sphere of doing procedure. The importance of narrative knowing for human sciences has been emphasized by many a theorist.[3] Explicating this significance in greater detail defies the purpose of this study. Our appreciation of narrative theory is linked to perspectives about something (epistemology) and experience of something (ontology); hence, the generality of our understanding of narration being "a special form of discourse for comprehending and explaining human actions, a discourse appropriate for the human sciences in their study of human experience and behaviour" (Polkinghorne, 1988, p. 71). Narrative meaning gives form to the understanding of one's purpose in life, his or her actions, but also various social structures with their uniquely shaped activities and events. Narrative understanding allows us to both construct and give sequence to personal and cultural histories. One may say that narrative integrates temporally different events into a single whole (Danto, 1985). Narrative explains by clarifying the significance of events that have occurred on the basis of the outcome that has followed. It always includes a complex of events expressed as a whole that includes points of transitions, lines of development, emergent and ongoing crises. Accessing the field without losing the sense of access, that is, reflecting on it, grasping the transition as an ongoing achievement, and telling about it are necessary conditions for our ethnographic and Comparative production of meaning.

Narratives about field access

Lining up the three narratives about access already implies the possibility of comparing the facets of our law-in-action research. The fields rise and fall, transform and disappear, contract and expand, all the time giving more of each. The three narratives below attempt to capture this more in unique voices and from unique points of view. This position might explain the diversity of narrative formats, styles, and perspectives. We see this diversity as an advantage: it is by not forcing the narratives into a comparison frame that we prepare the ground for comparison. In the final section of this chapter we translate the three thematic outlooks into some lessons and recommendations.

The English case study: Exploring proceedings

It seems that studies of criminal proceedings 'naturally' begin and take place in the courtroom. The same holds true for my first steps in the English criminal legal process. The courtroom appeared to me as a 'natural' starting point for my inquiries into criminal cases: the site where defense and prosecution confront their cases in front of the judge and the jury in the open court.

In the criminal court

In light of the issue of access, the courtroom seems an unproblematic site since the "open court" is considered as a basic condition for a fair trial.[4] Correspondingly, I arrived and stayed in that court just as any other member of the public. There is no need, I thought, to identify myself as researcher, while speculating about the backgrounds of the others in the public gallery (they were friends and relatives of defendants or victims). In addition, some people had to wait outside to be called in: witnesses waiting to be called to give evidence; barristers welcoming them and exchanging niceties. Although just 'being a part of the public', I apparently did make myself noticeable as somebody who seems generally interested. Only few (elderly) citizens turned up for different hearings in a row: trial watchers by conviction or habit.

Being a member of the public

The open court appeared as an observation-friendly site at least compared to 'far away' encounters referred to during the course of the trial (such as the police interview, the solicitor–client conference, the jury sitting, the plea bargaining). This impression was fostered by the initial visits only. First restrictions became apparent at the security check designed to keep out certain items and to exclude certain practices.[5] Once in the public gallery, I chose the upper benches to obtain a good view of the overall scene. Later I moved down to watch the actors more closely. What a performance! From the gallery, the court hearing resembled a role play including props, costumes, speeches, characters, and so on.

Profiting from the hearing's recipient-design

At first, up there, I appreciated a 'perfect position'. I was an undisturbed and not disturbing observer. I could overlook the scene. Even conceptually my position made very much sense. Everything relevant had to pass by and to be expressed right there in front of the jury. Wasn't this 'bird's eye' perspective facilitating the collection of rich data on "what is going on"? Everything seemed nicely explicated for the general public, the common sense, for all these lay people. Did I not profit from the involvement between and among all these different roles: the lawyers being the translators of legal concepts and technicalities, the jurors being the ambassadors of the world out there? I reached this kind of optimism when I started taking notes of well summarized matters, repeated lines of argumentation, plain explications, captivating stories, and so on. I found that the criminal legal machinery was introduced to everybody in a nutshell, including me. This was where things started to somehow get complicated.

Taking notes in court

The notepad has to be blamed for the first complication. I was about to leave after a good deal of rather confusingly rapid pre-directions hearings, when the usher came over. She was the first human being in this setting to address me. "You cannot take notes just like that", she protested. Suddenly exposed, I was struggling for words. "You could at least ask the clerk for permission!" she went on. She walked out and apparently expected me to follow. "Yes, the clerk", I rushed after her with an apologetic introduction: "I am German researcher, new in town, sociologist". But the usher just carried on walking, unimpressed by my plea. She crossed the corridor and turned downstairs toward the clerk's little office. The clerk was chatting with some colleagues and took this affair rather nonchalantly. He gave me permission to take notes: "No problem, but not up there..."

Gaining a special status, taking a specific position

Instead he suggested I sit on the "press bench", which he considered to be a perfect position for a researcher like me. I sat on the right hand side of the recorder,[6] opposite the witness stand and with the jury box right behind me. This placement became a standard solution for my extra role: here I could make notes without confusing the court's spatial division of activities. Guests took me as a journalist, while the staff soon began to refer to me as the "researcher from Germany". Indeed, at first, my outfit resembled that of a typical journalist.[7] From the press bench, matters looked different. From a distance, people were not just a group of talking heads: they were whispering and sweating; they exchanged notes, read books, browsed through magazines, and so on. Then there were others who carried files, delivered messages, and distributed copies. From down here, I could see how court staff and parties were constantly in motion. With time, the staff got used to me. They included me in their small talk during breaks, when the legal machinery stood still.[8]

A failed attempt to change position

New boundaries surfaced when I asked to move to a different place in the courtroom. My motivation was simple: I could not see the jury from the press bench, which seemed unfortunate with regard to my 'research field' (witnessing in criminal courts) at the time. The clerk claimed: "The jurors don't do anything special. They are simply sitting there watch-ing." No need to move, he insisted. "Like puppets", I teased, which provoked an uneasy comment by the recording secretary: "The court deserves our respect!" My request failed. There was no bench or seat available for me. Everything seemed reserved either for the defense or the prosecution. At least, that was what the clerk told me. I could obtain a view of the jury-in-action only if I returned to the public gallery as a non-writing observer.[9]

How to follow paper trails

It is hard to say when or why exactly I became unsatisfied with my press bench in court. It was probably due to the amount of paper that was carried in and out the hearings. Each case necessitated files, briefs, and notes, somehow routinely distributed amongst lawyers and assis-tants. Or perhaps it was because participants frequently expressed what "the file says" or what one "finds in the written statement". Another general impression made me rethink my position: the dominant mode of talk in court. By this I mean the 'artificial' questioning of the wit-nesses, their stilted 'learnt by heart answers', the recurrent permission (especially for police officers) to "refresh the memory" by help of their notes, and so on. Things seemed to be always already written down to some extent. I hoped that the writing activities on the back stages of the trial could explain how these 'documented' trials are rendered possible. What I became interested in was the scriptural configuration of these oral hearings.

Accessing preparation

At this point, I won't be able to draw on all the repositioning that occurred during my passage through the field. I would only like to refer to two major shifts: me accessing a small law firm and, later, a barristers' chamber. Generally speaking, I moved on to the workbenches, the text-production units, of the inter-textual and multi-local projects of representation. I accessed the offices where cases were put together for the approaching court hearing.

Finding a law firm

I found my law firm less through a methodical search and more by way of a coincidence. It was a colleague of mine at the local sociol-ogy department who, together with her husband, a "partner" in a local firm, introduced me. It took several pints of beer and personal encour-agement to persuade George to invite me "to carry out my studies". He felt obliged to aid this German fellow. We quickly agreed on a number of issues, including the "dress code" and "confidentiality". He dictated a short contract, specifying my duties and obligations. I signed. Moreover, I promised to report my results before they were submitted to journals. What can be learnt for field access here? I suppose the fact that I was conceived to be an outsider and a harmless academic helped a lot to disperse doubts and fears about my participation from the onset. This German guy would not disturb much, seemed the general consensus on my request.

Getting my personal scout

The "partner" then formally invited me to come over and use his firm for my inquiries. Once in the firm, I was introduced to two criminal lawyers: one working on Crown Courts cases and the other in charge of the lower Magistrates Court. I offered my assurance again: "I don't wish to evaluate your work. I am simply interested in how, here in the UK, cases are prepared." I shared an office with the Crown Court solicitor and happened to spend entire days just sitting in with him (interrupted only by coffee-cigarette-football-chat-breaks). We became friends in some way: nobody else gained that much insight into what he actually did. He was too self-confident to hide his own 'achievements'. He just took me everywhere and allowed me to read through everything I found to be of 'sociological' interest.

Negotiating the mode of data-access/collection

After another week, I asked him if copying documents, such as police protocols, defense statements, long letters of correspondence, barrister's briefs, and so on, would be a problem. He asked me to blacken names and addresses, but apart from this, he could not see any difficulty. In fact, the change in data recording was a huge step in terms of field access. It opened up chains of representation that would have otherwise remained hidden for the sheer reading/noting-experience. My justification for this access was as follows: casework is by and large paper work: "I need the papers to get a complete picture."

New personnel in the second fieldwork phase

It was a year later when I came back to the firm for the "second phase of fieldwork". In the meantime, a lot had changed. My gate-keeping solicitor had gone; his role had been taken over by his female colleague. These personal discontinuities forced me to renegotiate data access and to explain to her again my data needs in light of research purposes.

I carefully referred back to the old agreement. I used the original research results to demonstrate how harmless my use of this data actually is. The lawyer presented herself as careful and protective when it came to file-access or to client–lawyer conferences.

Access to special meetings

At this point, the issue of field access was not entirely settled. There were more zones and areas of casework that required negotiation of access. Special occasions, for instance, turned into an ongoing concern for both the caseworker and the fieldworker. From time to time, my solicitor-informant denied me access to her meetings with clients or to her barrister conferences. She gave straightforward reasons for this occasional exclusion: the respective client would not agree to have anybody other than her sit in ("I know him!"); the issues to be discussed during this meeting would be too sensitive ("Next time, ok?"), or the client was described as being very anxious at that time ("We had better not ask her!"). Surprisingly, all these exceptions and special situations disappeared after a while. She began to include me naturally, often without even asking the client. In passing, she would introduce me as *her* German researcher, *her* shadow: "He is just interested in me (...) well [with a grin], in my work anyway."

Following the chain of casework

It was on one of these special occasions when I met the next gatekeeper and field scout: a young Barrister (aged 32 or 33) with impressive job experience (12 years). The first introduction and joint meeting made it easier to ask him to "have me for a week or so". I explained that I would like to know what actually happened to all these instructions written by my solicitor. The requested week turned into a whole month and then, after several months, into the third phase of fieldwork. Through this barrister I got to know new aspects of the legal process: prehearing conferences, plea bargaining sessions, library work at the Chambers, court days, and so on. This new field access imposed new negotiations on access: for example, the barrister vetoed my request to copy the list of work hours attached to completed cases. To my surprise, he simply preferred making the copies himself. At times he did not want me to accompany him to the cells under the courtroom, due to "time pressure" and "the narrow room down there". Through him I got to know a certain barristers' culture of hospitality. We went out for meals to discuss the general picture of 'law and society' or to celebrate that "This case is done!" I experienced the same with his colleague, who later took over this informant role whenever my main host was absent.[10]

Retrospectively, field access appears as an ongoing activity closely linked to the analytical re-framing of the research itself. The quest of field access interacted with attempts to systematically place defense work in a field of meaning production: legal procedure. Field access, therefore, was not a point in time, but a process that included different places and closures, different activities on the forefront and in the back, different professional cultures with their no go areas. In due course, the field both expanded and narrowed. It comprised not just immediate situations, but past and present ones, co-present and absent contributors, oral, written, and filed contributions. My experiences from the pilot study enforced minimal requirements concerning fieldwork: (a) access criminal cases through the professional caseworkers; (b) select a small law firm to gain insights into all parts of this work; (c) include all the resources and materials that are used by caseworkers; (d) follow all stages of the resulting criminal procedure.

The German case study: Accessing case files

Coming from the disciplines of rhetoric and argumentation studies that have quite a close relationship to law and jurisprudence theoretically, I was new to the practice of criminal law. To me criminal proceedings used to be dramas in which the hero, most likely an innocent defendant, overcomes all obstacles and finally succeeds. In order to get an introduction into the field's systematics, I started my inquiry by meeting Lisa, an acquaintance who had just started her own practice as a lawyer, hoping that she could introduce me not only to the German criminal procedure but also to the field itself. I learned that, in Germany, lawyers rarely contact witnesses before the trial, lay judges have no access to the files, and one can do magic in court. In addition to this introduction she named three lawyers who could be worth contacting. This conversation transformed a rather uncoordinated bundle of ideas, anxieties, and expectations about the field into a clearer picture of who lawyers are and what criminal trials are about, and forced me to readjust my wording and conception of the project.

Getting in touch with potential hosts

Equipped with this information, I took two different routes, both of them being rather informal. The first one was Lisa's idea: I went to see trial hearings at the "Amtsgericht" (lower court) in order to establish contact with lawyers and also to see how the preparation of criminal trials aims toward the main hearing.[11] Unfortunately, in most hearings the defendants did not have a lawyer.[12] The few lawyers I had met made me hesitate because of their routine ways of handling cases and clients. Then, the lawyers whom I actually did talk to were mainly concerned with civil cases. Despite these setbacks, I found myself placed inside the field. While sitting in on numerous criminal cases, "the trial" was starting to come into focus. The proceedings appeared more and more to be routine processes. If a criminal trial was a drama, I concluded, it would rather be an endless replay rather than a premiere. Parallel to the courtroom observations, I carried on contacting informants and collecting contacts.

My first contact

The contact that ultimately led to success initiated a rather complex reference chain. Two civil lawyers, whom I have known in a different context for several years, were interested in the research and gave me several names, stressing two of them: Lisa and a "very good" lawyer in Weggingen. I called the latter and e-mailed him the project's description. He replied two weeks later: unfortunately he could not provide access to his firm as any form of "walking around" with him and his colleagues "would have to be seen as a distraction" – they were very busy at that time. However, he forwarded his e-mail to some colleagues and asked them to consider supporting the project by hosting me. I did not really expect any outcome from this exchange but I appreciated the gesture. Below I would like to briefly follow the chain of professional contacts because it seems to capture unavoidable involvements.

Accessing a small law firm

Mr. Gabriel's name was among those Lisa gave me, and he had been mentioned by many people I'd talked to. I contacted him via e-mail, but did not receive a response. When I spoke to him on the phone a little later, he did not remember my e-mail, but he had received one from the attorney in Weggingen. Mr. Gabriel seemed a little hesitant that somebody wanted to come and "look through his files", as he put it, but agreed to a meeting one week later. I prepared for this meeting thoroughly, setting out all possible arguments for and against me accessing his law firm. After our phone conversation I was not too optimistic about my chances. This is why the first thing he said at the meeting took me completely by surprise: "Well, I could imagine taking part in something like that." Our talk lasted for 20 minutes during which he asked about the project and outlined some of his concerns: the time frame (interesting cases are rarely done within three months), my having no legal background (but yes, it could be interesting for an outsider to look at narratives and counter-narratives), and confidentiality (I should sign a waiver to keep all confidential information in check). After four weeks I had accomplished what I had imagined to be the main obstacle for our project: accessing a law firm.

Trust and distrust

On my first day, I entered the law firm rather nervously. Mr. Gabriel gave me the file of a case he considered would be interesting to me and I was assigned to the meeting room. He also introduced me briefly to his partner, Mr. Schwarz. Before leaving me to my file, he noted, in a half joking tone, that my door should stay open so that people could see if I was sneaking files into my pocket. I was taken aback by such an explicit demonstration of distrust. But then again: they did not really know who I was, and still I was allowed to look through the files of current cases without any benefit for them; this exhibited trust already. At that point, both the lawyer and I seemed to be struggling with how to define our relationship and the degree of my "inclusion".

Accessing cases – reading files

As it turned out, I had entered the firm but did not enter criminal casework. My first entry point to this casework was through the file and Mr. Gabriel's brief introduction of it. Thus, I found out that in the German context there are basically two different types of files: "Ermittlungsakte" (discovery file), containing an entire set of inquiries undertaken by the police and prosecution, and "Handakte" (lawyer's file), consisting of communications with the defendant, court, prosecution, as well as various "formalities" like the sheet for "Wiedervorlage" (new motion), and the notes. Mr. Gabriel took it upon himself to select cases for my research by placing a file right in front of me ("I have something for you"). His way of picking cases seemed to be basically driven by two considerations: first, he chose only those cases that had an interesting twist to them and, second, the selected cases were supposed to cover as many different offences as possible. Although I was not interested in diverse offences or appeals, he stuck to these criteria, thereby following the practice commonly applied to interns.

Through the discovery file I accessed the development of a case from the perspective of the prosecution. This kind of file contained testimonies, informal notes by prosecutor and police, pictures by the pathology, and so on. Working through these materials allowed me to gain a kind of insight that I had not previously taken into account. My first case was an instance of infanticide. A young woman had given birth to a child and then left the baby to die in the backyard. The stories and pictures from this case haunted me for days. Just after I had readjusted my conception of the field from the fictional to the realistic, there it was: a drama, and bigger than I had bargained for.

In comparison, the lawyer's file opened my view on the development of a case from the perspective of the defense. This kind of file usually started with the name and address of the client and with information on relatives who could or should be contacted. It also contained correspondence between the lawyer and the client. However, an access to these files was restricted to some cases – with Mr. Gabriel's cases some lawyer's files were outside my reach. Once we talked about preparation, and Mr. Gabriel stated that in criminal law as little should be put down in writing as possible. His preparation indeed left only few traces in his file. This attitude toward defense work seems not to be unusual for the German system: "Let them [the prosecution KHI] make a case and defend it, then we'll see". And "then" could very well be no earlier than in the courtroom.

Attending lawyer–client conferences

The next obstacle on the way to field access was the lawyer–client conference. Mr. Gabriel agreed in general to let me sit in on meetings, but we never found an appropriate occasion. I did not push the issue too much, merely addressed it twice. The reasons for my lack of persistence were twofold: First, I negotiated access to the law firm by stressing that any access they could provide would be sufficient. I had, however, hoped that it would be easier to renegotiate access, especially once a greater degree of familiarity had been established. Second, those cases and clients that Mr. Gabriel worked with involved highly sensitive crimes: murder, rape, manslaughter. From this perspective, his reluctance seemed reasonable. Only later, with Mr. Schwarz, did I have a chance to observe lawyer–client conferences. Mr. Schwarz encouraged me to ask questions and engage in the conversation with the client. He also took me to informal chats in front of the court, which turned out to be more influential than the conferences themselves.

Visiting court hearings

In German courts accessing main hearings is unproblematic, with the exception of juvenile courts. Problems arose once I started to take notes (just like in the English context). Most of the judges did not mind, while others insisted on being asked in advance. The latter wanted to assure that I was not providing witnesses with information on the ongoing trial. One judge only let the press take notes. He could not see any necessity for a researcher to do so. However, once I began to appear in the company of an attorney, my position in the main hearings changed considerably. I was "with them" and thereby acquired the role of someone involved in the trial. I was even able to sit in on two non-public hearings in juvenile cases. In both cases the lawyer introduced me as a researcher who conducted research in the firm. One time I was permitted to sit in on a "tatsächliche Verständigung" (deal), something that, as stressed by my lawyer, even "Rechtsreferendare"[13] were usually not allowed to do. Again informality proved to be the key: Mr. Schwarz muttered something like "I am sure you don't mind her staying". Nobody really cared enough to debate this issue. There were cases, however, when the victims regarded me with suspicion. One defendant even referred to me during one of his long diatribes in court.

There is much more to tell about entering the field, the law firm, and casework. The hosting law firm often did not provide the kind of access I had hoped. More importantly, I could not establish a relationship of trust and respect beyond a certain point. As the lawyers and I had agreed only on one phase of fieldwork, I began to look for a new firm for the second phase. I ended up in Lisa's new little firm, finding it to provide a very open and friendly environment. She did not have many cases, but I was able to join her in almost all her casework activities. She only restricted the access to lawyer–client conferences when she expected the client to be affected too much by my presence (fall silent altogether or, in contrast, start to perform for me). To me, access turned out to be an affair that depended largely on the local and inter-personal dynamics.

The US case study: Too much field access

As with the rest of the group, my field-site was not predetermined. Nor did I have a detailed plan of my prospective fieldwork before leaving for my site. This was my first full ethnographic immersion, and I didn't want to be deprived of precious virginal impressions. This is not to say that I was going into the field unprepared: various ethnographic literature accompanied me on this journey.[14] Armed with practical advice, it was easier for me to imagine how I was going to get to the law firm, meet my informants, and how soon, very soon, I would enter the place where all things legal resided. There, I expected to find a vantage point from which, by sitting in, observing, and recording legal practices, I could successfully hunt for legal data. I thus pictured myself as an adventurer on his or her way to some hidden legal treasures of sorts; the more data I could grab the better my research was going to be in the end. The only problem was where to find such an inexhaustible source.

Divergent expectations

My first attempts to find a site, any site, in the United States were less than rewarding. A friend of a friend who happened to be an attorney in a big law firm in New York City managed to put me in touch with "an intellectually minded" colleague at his firm, but our subsequent exchanges revealed that the latter's expectations of me boiled down to assisting him with some low-key legal work. Excited at first, I soon found out what he meant by "legal work": copying, filing, and hand delivering important documents. That picture promised little ethnography; the prospect of becoming a delivery person was unappealing and counterproductive. I withdrew my request. My next contact from Boston was more upfront about my presence in his firm. Unequivocally and from the outset, he stated that "having an outsider witness all the dirty laundry that our clients haul over here can be detrimental for both the firm's image and the attorney–client relationship. If you would like to, you can go to court with us and do your research there." The offer sounded half-hearted: I knew that I did not need an attorney to observe court proceedings. I did not follow this contact any further. From these, and some other similarly problematic encounters, I inferred that semi-formal negotiations with a large metropolitan law firm do not automatically secure a rich site of data. And so it seemed to be common sense to take an informal route: I began e-mailing and calling around those friends of mine who had some, no matter how remote, relation to law.

Family links to the field

It was then that my friend Julia suggested that she put me in touch with her brother Jack, a private attorney, who lived and practiced in Mound City, NW. She told me that he was a successful and ambitious attorney with a massive and diverse caseload. "He runs more cases at one time than any other lawyer in town", she wrote in her e-mail. She mentioned several disadvantages: Jack's firm was small (in addition to himself, he had only two partners in the firm), so I couldn't follow several attorneys at once; the other obstacle seemed to be Jack's specialization, that is, family law; my interest on the other hand was in criminal cases. These problems appeared to be more like inconveniences to me. From Julia's description, Jack struck me as an important, enigmatic, and, at the same time, accessible figure. His profile indeed promised the very wealth of data that I was so anxious to harvest. When Julia introduced the project to her brother, he expressed tentative interest at first, but, in the course of our e-mail exchange, I managed to gain his approval of my research plans followed by an invitation to come over whenever I wished. A postscript at the end of his last message did away with my last worry: in exchange for his hospitality, Jack expected nothing from me, not even a confidentiality waiver. A small but busy practice, an ambitious but friendly attorney, the conditions seemed ideal. I came to believe that, for all practical purposes, I was in and that data would start falling into my hands as soon as I arrived. With this expectation, I left for Mound City.

First encounters

Two days later I met Jack and realized immediately that my access to data had not even begun. My second realization was that my relationship with Jack and his family would influence my fieldwork to an extent that I could not predict. Jack's personality, his communication style, social standing, and circle of friends, all appeared to be alien and, at first sight, incompatible with my personal interests, preferences, and beliefs. He turned out to be that very inaccessible alien I feared most. More importantly, I felt that my research was of little interest to Jack. Our first conversation was distressing: there was little continuity, very few questions were asked about the project and my prospective fieldwork, while my questions about Jack's practice were either dodged or answered in the ironic register. Even more alarming was the resistance of the legal setting to my probing that had already begun at the time of the first meeting. Having come with only a remote idea of how law follows legal rules and procedures, I found myself at a loss in the face of an entirely unfamiliar context. In the beginning, I tried to account for these difficulties as being typical for an initial encounter with a complete stranger; yet, I couldn't help but feel that it was me who was an absolute outsider, and that it was my 'home', so to speak, that stood as the biggest hurdle on the way to a successful passing. I also realized that, in contrast to my ideal expectations, the actual access to the site would have to be earned in a journey different from the trip itself. The two days of driving westward was not the journey; that was simply transporting myself to the location. But, what was the threshold that I needed to cross? The answer to that question seemed obvious: I needed to become an insider.

Being introduced as the other

As I have already mentioned, I entered the firm as a protégé of a family member. It was in that role I presented myself and would be most often presented by Jack to his friends and colleagues: "This is Alex, a friend to my sister, who came here to study the US legal system." The formulation gave a clear designation of my relation to Jack: quasi-family. My research business was mentioned but it always came second, a necessary indicator that I might perform some activities outside of the familial, and familiar, realm. With time, after several weeks, the introduction had changed. From justifying my presence through the interpersonal connection, Jack switched to: "This is Alex, a researcher from Berlin who is here to study the US criminal system." The reference to the outside origin of mine was not prompted by me; however, it benefited me indirectly, as it legitimized my involvement across different legal contexts and figures. It also brought relief: playing into the image of a quasi-family member made me feel like an impostor. So, somehow, at some point, both Jack and I figured that my position in the firm had changed. Later, in retrospect, Jack provided his rationale for the reformulation: "People ask me a lot about what you do. I tell them that you are from Berlin and that you do legal research. Is that right? Tell me more about it because they ask." Thus, having obtained my story, Jack could relate to me in a way that was formerly unavailable to him, as a colleague of sorts. In addition, this change allowed him to identify with me formally in the present rather than informally, through the quasi kinship, in the pseudo historical past.

Insider and outsider

Simultaneously with identifying me as a business associate of sorts, Jack stressed my outsider position: "A researcher from Berlin ... who is here on business." I liked the introduction: it had an audible ring of privilege to it. It sounded as if now I was both the insider and the outsider. The insider/outsider duality got solidified in the next alteration: "This is Alex, he is a researcher from Berlin, he shadows me." With this formulation, Jack helped me with the final rite of passage: I became the outsider, whose business became that of the insider; a shadow of the insider, to be exact. The last formulation bore an even greater privilege: in addition to the business connection, I became connected interpersonally, albeit by implication only. With Jack's reformulations, I underwent a series of transformations: from the illegitimate insider to the legitimate outsider.

It was at that point that data began to flow in. There were no restrictions on Jack's part. The clients' permissions provided, I could sit in on his conferences, look through his files, and accompany him to the court, jail, and prison. I made notes, copies, and recordings. I found my data treasure, I accessed it, and was filling up my bags. It was then that I sensed a change, a loss that, upon reflection, pointed to the 'other': Jack and his legal practice. In a paradoxical reversal of my intentions, I lost the very thing I had nearly acquired: the encounter with the alien, whether the alien is law or the attorney or both.[15] At the same time, I lost the feeling of my own home and therefore my own perspective of the encounter with the other. And yet, I did not feel as if I had acquired anything instead. I fell under the illusion of crossing some threshold and it was that illusion that had prompted me to cross it in the first place. Now, I understand that the encounter with the other is not owned by the researcher, that there is no threshold to cross, no continent to conquer, no goodies to collect. At the time, I could only sense that access was a phenomenon that stood at the limit of experience. It was at the limit that it was given to me, during the very first encounter with the other, my first meeting with Jack. As my familiarity with him, his firm, and his work grew, accessibility also expanded until it completely faded in the dark. To put it differently, I managed to accomplish access but only to see it escape my grasp.

Conclusion

In this chapter, we have presented three narratives about accessing three respective legal fields, hoping that the narrative form would allow access to first appear in a new light, as a phenomenon of significant complexity and depth, and second, let it find its proper place amidst other pressing ethnographic issues. While rendering our experiences in the narrative form, we have tried to be mindful of the pragmatic objectives that brought us to the field in the first place, namely, law-in-action research. The three voices, three perspectives, are intended to appear unique in their tenor and import. It is in this sense that the narratives both respond to the general theme of this chapter and speak for themselves. However, some final comments might be beneficial for reading our subsequent chapters and to foster future legal ethnographies.

On-going-ness

Indeed, at first sight, our thematizations of access have appeared somehow similar to the themes brought about by our predecessors: like them, all three of us had to negotiate our access in advance; like them, we found it easier to enter the field through personal channels; we also had to face difficult choices of selecting the right site; and we had to deal with various gatekeepers on the way to data. At the same time, by reflecting on access as a continuous and changeable phenomenon of its own, we have collected a number of insights that have taken us beyond traditional views of access as a onetime event bound to the initial phase of fieldwork or a technical problem that gets resolved as soon as the ethnographer obtains a permission to join a law firm. Thus, all three of us learnt the need to maintain a distance, and not just an abstract kind of distance or physical distance but a finely tuned relational distance that is locally and meticulously negotiated on a day-to-day basis.

In some cases, the distance appeared to be so large that the site was barely observable. The German researcher had particular difficulties in that regard. Too close was not good either, and the US researcher also testified to this predicament in his narrative. At the same time, distance turned out to be less essential for access than a particular perspective. Thus, the English case study showed that even in a public forum, such as a courthouse, the point of physical presence gives different outcomes, different data, and establishes different relations with the informants. The effects of positioning are only enhanced in the close environment of a law firm. There, the researcher goes through continuous self- and other-redefinitions. One day he is treated as an insider, the other as an outsider, the rite of passage turns out to be a swinging pendulum that poses on the upswing but only for a moment before it falls down and away again. The latter theme became particularly important for it brought to the fore the very aspect of access that has been traditionally ignored: continuity. In all our narratives we emphasized the ongoing and changeable nature of access, something that cannot be overcome by a point of arrival.

Access does not equate data collection

The distinction between access and data collection was another theme that provoked an unexpected variety of observations. With the notable exception of the researcher in the US, who, by virtue of his training, chose to focus on audio recording of the natives' activities and comments, the other two members of the group came to their sites espousing merely text-related methods of collecting data, such as taking field notes, replicating oral comments or written paragraphs, and copying documents. Altogether, we anticipated that access to legal settings and materials would be contingent on the researchers' co-presence. In other words, it turned out that data collection depended largely on access and positioning; both activities resulted in more or less close and persistent associations with individual legal practitioners. The ongoing negotiation of the 'ins' and 'outs' of these researcher–native associations led to generating some "insights into social organization of the setting" (Hamersley and Atkinson, 1983, p. 54). For example, in the German case, copying files was problematic from the outset. It constituted *the* barrier that provided an intriguing insight into the constraints of the German procedural regime. Similar effects of self exposure were noted by the US researcher: unable to record in the court and at attorney–client conferences, he placed a strong emphasis on carrying out continuous audio-recordings outside of formal settings and ended up with a rich collection of impromptu interviews. A similar strategy became available in the English case study. Here, the focus on the live discourse of the court hearings and the corresponding speech activities was relativized by the concentration on the seemingly lifeless and only preliminary bureaucratic paper trails.

Ethics and interpersonal dynamics

A further comment concerns the ethics of accessing the legal field. Like ethnographic fieldwork, ethnographic ethics spelled out ongoing implications for both access and fieldwork. Entering and maintaining the relationship with the other cannot help but carry the burden of making certain choices that reach above and beyond the immediate objectives and far-reaching goals of a research project. Most simply, accessing the field requires giving and fulfilling some kind of promise. No wonder, then, that the issue of trust resounded most strongly in all three narratives. In addition to keeping the promise, the researcher brings and upholds personal responsibility before the informant, self, and his or her colleagues. For some of us, this responsibility was defined in terms of hospitality, for others in terms of reciprocity and collaboration. In either case, it is the ethical side of field-working that has led us to face the greatest risks and also enjoy the biggest rewards, leading to the most unexpected results. Moreover, it is the commitment to the people whose work we have studied that keeps access afloat, so that even now, after our field-working is long over, we are still accessing our fields and we are still keeping our promises by talking and writing about them.

Shaping the field

Field access shaped those fields that are not categorically defined in a certain analytical manner. Criminal procedure appeared as the seesaw of staging and preparation (the English case), as a strategizing game (the US case), and as a prolonged court hearing (the German case). Apart from this initial characterization, one can identify a range of analytical frames that unfolded in the course of accessing and positioning: The field turned out to be more than the sum of social situations, more than divergent or convergent arrays of interpersonal encounters, and more than paper trails. The field became available as a nexus of diachronic and synchronic events, linked by circulating objects and accessible by reformulations and documentations. In other words, the ethnographic field has emerged as work processes that surpass various sites and locales. Fieldwork, therefore, was demanding insofar as we had to change our positions, get in contact with various participants, and trace work products over time and space. This made the field appear multi-sited, but also multi-temporal, multi-modal, and overtly complex. These qualities triggered our shared experience of *partial access* and *ongoing accessing*. From the point of view of the ethnographer, there were always some components missing, some documents inaccessible, or some conversations unavailable.

The irritation of partial access could have been circumvented by framing the field in a traditional fashion: as the organization (law firm), as one series of rituals (the court hearing), or as a selection of conventional situations (first interview, plea bargaining, client–lawyer conference). Such reductionism, however, would have placed the need for clear-cut boundaries leading to the challenge of having to actually understand how "doing procedure" is being done, meaning how criminal procedure is co-enacted by different means, in various modes, at different sites, and by various actors. This does not mean that we accessed legal procedure directly. All three of us experienced "what is going on" through defense lawyers' activities. We followed the lawyers and denoted the methods by which they rendered cases accessible, observable, and approachable for all practical purposes. In this way, we owe much gratitude to their know-how, confidence, and patience with us, outsiders.[16] Today, our research still lives in the traces of the lawyers' casework left in our field notes, in audio and video records, in documents and files. Again, there are good reasons to account for the employment of these sources as ongoing field access insofar as the field or the cases expand in time and space.

In conclusion, we would like to present our experiences in the format of advisory rules, some of which may be conceived as rather counter-intuitive. The rules may help following socio-legal ethnographers to preserve openness and curiosity for the local and socio-material dynamics of law and for its surprising extensions and faces: (a) define what the field actually is, but do so only provisionally; (b) treat data as the field's means of reproduction; (c) explicate what you would like to know now; (d) demonstrate limited understanding; (e) celebrate failures of access; (f) move on to another site once you feel at home in the previous one; (g) demonstrate results to the informants no matter whether they are interesting or not; (h) mark your personal involvement as a core constituent for the research, not as bias or distortion; (i) cultivate contacts within the field after the fieldwork is over. These rules may help, but won't suffice, to create the curiosity and respect necessary to carry out ethnographic explorations into the situated as well as multi-sited workings of the law.

3
Procedural Past: Binding and Unbinding

In the previous chapter we introduced the reader to our ethnographic enterprise and the access gained through ethnographic fieldwork. It is now time to move closer to the actual subject of our study, namely the forms of "doing procedure" in our different procedural regimes. In the following three chapters, we are going to study procedure in the light of doing the procedural past, the procedural present, and the procedural future. Tracing these temporal orientations requires a good deal of natural data, such as records and protocols, plus some insider's knowledge on how to use these materials and how to attend them in the procedural course.

In this chapter, we start with the procedural past and its influence on the current dealings. The conceptual term to introduce the past in the present is binding. Somebody is bound now to what happened earlier in the past. In this manner, we focus on binding statements and how they put pressure on current contributions, especially those given in court. Binding statements extend the present dealings into the procedural past. They push members to turn back and account for earlier responses, versions, and accounts. Binding imposes a conservative orientation on the current dealings and the parties. What is more, binding does not appear as an even force that smoothly covers all the procedural moments. Binding differs in the procedural course, between cases, and, what is more, between our different procedural regimes.

How can we explore the *binding forces* that emerge in our different procedural regimes? We do so by studying in detail how defendants are bound to their initial defenses. In addition, we ask whether the binding effect shows similarities or differences in the three procedural environments. The analytical concepts of "procedural history" and "discourse formation" as presented by Niklas Luhmann and Michel Foucault, respectively, provide an analytic frame for this endeavor. Both theories describe past statements as "virulent" in present stages: participants have to take their own histories into account when engaging in their current dealings; in addition, these current statements must confront past statements, generating inconsistency and contradiction. We use this perspective in order to compare systematic variations of binding in light of eight case-narratives observed during fieldwork in the United States, the United Kingdom, and Germany. These micro-histories trace the binding effects of early defenses through pre-trial and trial. Our observations lead us to conclude that the binding mechanism appears less determinative in practice than in the claims of theory. Alongside the several effects of binding, we identify a variety of protections, interruptions, and even unbinding effects.

Binding effects and the procedural past

PC: What's happened last night?

Steve Striker: Well I was out with my brother and his mate in a night-club. Just coming back from the toilet, this guy bumped into me, so I turned round and said, "Sorry," and he just pushed me...then I started calling him...I don't know exactly what I was calling him, "dickhead;"..."faggot."

PC: He was calling you?

Steve Striker: No, I was calling him that...cos I thought there was no need for pushing me...cos I apologized...and then he came up to me, punched me, I fell on the floor, and then him and this other lad started stamping on me. I had me drink in me hand, so when I got up it was empty, so I just hit him with it. I got the chance to get up and then I just hit him with it.

Steve Striker provides here what can be called an early defense. His defense is stipulated by the police officer's question, "what happened last night?" At least this is how the interview protocol makes Striker's version available for later stages of the procedure. His defense, then, is, first, a response to the police's allegations of "assault" and second, it emerges without a lawyer instructing him. Our concern in this chapter is not how such responses emerge during the course of the police interview; rather, we are interested in how it matters for what may follow: the client–lawyer meetings, the pre-trial sessions, the plea-bargaining, or the trial hearing. To what extent does the early defense bind its instigator? How does it allow or disallow modification?

"I didn't do it!" "He started it!" "No comment!" The variety of early defenses is extensive, both in style and content. Commonly, legal scholars discuss early defenses in two ways: how a "no defense" strategy should be available for the trial hearing (the right to silence)[1] and how professional legal advice should safeguard all relevant appearances (the right to legal representation).[2] Both, we believe, are facets of a bigger theme that remains widely unaddressed: the binding or committing character of early defenses. By *binding* we refer to the procedural mechanisms that impose some requirements and sanctions on the statements to come. The binding mechanism places any new statement in a series or tradition, which norms of repetition and consistency do not allow much modification of let alone a fresh start. Concretely, our goal is to determine how defendants are bound to their earlier defenses and how this binding works in different criminal procedures.

First, however, we must explain our use of *binding* as a category of inquiry for socio-legal studies. What is it that we will be inspecting when we examine the phenomenon of binding in our comparative exploration? Defendants, we argue, are bound to their early defenses by means of an organized or procedural memory. And they are bound in different ways, depending on the criminal procedure dealing with their individual case. Binding, thus, is inspected as a phenomenon generated amidst the sequence of statements that create the discourse of a particular legal proceeding. Obviously, this understanding is quite different from the classic notion of binding, which focuses upon the relational bonds that pertain between society and individual.[3] The member is bound to the collective by means of conventions, norms, laws, contracts, beliefs, and so on.

What approaches deal with binding as a procedural effect? Where can we find studies on binding effects that work directly on statements and only indirectly on the individuals held accountable for them? Socio-legal scholars interested in this mechanism are well-advised to depart from grand theory and turn toward meso-theories on the legal process. Niklas Luhmann introduces the concept of binding alongside the concept of "procedural past" (Luhmann, 1989, pp. 43ff., 93ff.). For Luhmann, binding attains the temporal integration of legal processes. Binding reduces options, alters expectations, and disciplines the contestants. For Luhmann, binding effects are necessary to understand what drives legal procedures. He names textual and archival memory as their vital and often underrated gears.

In his inquiry, Luhmann makes extensive use of the notion of the "procedural past" in order to emphasize the transformation of statements into (binding) "norms that are contestable only on special grounds" (Luhmann, 1989, p. 93 (our translation)). This transformation explains the frequent triumph of procedures over the contestants. To put it simply, "legitimization by procedure" works as follows: Something is – carefully or carelessly – uttered at an early stage. The participant is identified with this statement and tends to adjust his or her following contributions in relation to it.[4] The procedure, thus, creates a past that reaches out into the present.

In legal procedures, according to Luhmann, "every communication, even the unintended presentation that contributes to the proceeding, counts as information that opens, thickens and excludes opportunities that define the acting persons and their relevant history and reduces their options to decide. Every contribution enters the case and can be reinterpreted but not neglected" (Luhmann, 1989, p. 44 (our translation)). Luhmann names a number of preconditions that are needed for this forceful mechanism to work: the contributor can decide freely between several options; he or she is accountable for the decisions taken; the outcome of the contest remains undecided until the very end. "Legitimization by procedure" means that the contestants can hardly gather solidarity against a verdict that derives from their own voluntary contributions.

Binding does not resemble determination, pure obedience, or even physical force. It emerges as a growing limitation by involvement. Binding materializes by providing robust criteria for assessing what is said here and now.[5] Early accounts are available to receive and probe current testimonies. The procedural past matters as a valuable (internal) contrast that discriminates consistent from inconsistent, likely from unlikely, and reliable from unreliable versions. These norms, guidance, and selections are not necessarily backed by external proof. They primarily derive from inside the legal discourse itself.

We can now summarize Luhmann's idea of binding procedures in a rule: a contestant gets ever more entangled in the unfolding discourse. Every contribution made reduces the range of options left. The contestant is bound not by external coercion, but by the ways of self-involvement and the traces it leaves in the procedural past. The one who is accountable for these discursive facts cannot get rid off them easily. As a result, binding institutes norms about what should or should not be said "from now on".

Our micro-histories subject this rule to an empirical test. They enable us to uncover variation in binding mechanisms across different cases and procedures. The existence of variation in turn leads us to reconsider the sufficiency of binding as a category and to develop alongside it a counter category: unbinding.

Unbinding may be characterized most clearly in accordance with a principle of orality. Documents, files, and the archive are banned from the "just" oral exchange in court. But unbinding can cover more phenomena. It may already occur during pre-trial. It may forcefully interrupt paper trails and their effects on the collection, selection, and memorization of evidence. Unbinding can "cut off" an event from the past. Unbinding can induce a fresh start. Unbinding separates statements from their foregoing formation.

In short, we claim, in contrast to Luhmann, that criminal procedures utilize both mechanisms: binding *and* unbinding. They do so in various ways and to different degrees. We believe our empirical inquiry bears this out.

The eight micro-histories and our interpretation of them reflect shared analytical grounds. The shared reference points are statements on their way to employment in court or in alternative settings such as plea-bargaining.[6] This focus reappears in our comparative work on binding. The comparison starts out with early defenses, and derives from here to the binding mechanism with reference to subsequent contributions.

The eight micro-histories focus on procedures, in correspondence with our desire to examine Luhmann's model in action. Our objective is twofold: we gather the varying components by which procedures generate binding effects, and we offer a re-specification of Luhmann's model in light of the variations found. Procedures, we state, differ in the ways they relate the procedural past and the presence. These differences transpire when including *unbinding* effects that free defendants from their early defenses and interrupt the forensic rationale of repetition and difference.

Case Study 1. Early accounts in English criminal cases

The Crown Court procedure is characterized by an extended pre-trial that invites independent inquiries into the matter by prosecution and defense.[7] Both parties interview witnesses, visit the crime scene, or employ experts. These inquiries amass two files, not without linking their documentary content. During the pre-trial, the prosecution has to disclose the evidence (for example, protocols of police interviews such as the one presented in the beginning of this chapter) gathered against the defendant. Moreover, the prosecution discloses the "list of unused items" that may be relevant in light of the defense case. By this "secondary disclosure", the prosecution responds to the "defense statement" that announces the outline of the counter-case compiled by the defense.

The court hearing takes place as a preconfigured event. The exchange of materials,[8] interpretations, and positions encourages pre-trial resolutions. The parties separate settled issues from debated issues. They reduce the scope of the trial. The process works as a "funnel" (Luhmann, 1989). Moreover, in order to ease the court's management burden, the parties announce the design of the trial: the number of witnesses and the estimated number of court days. The court is booked, and sometimes overbooked, in light of the scripted cases and the contestants' agreements.

Crown Court cases are heard by judge and jury. The jurors are called the "judges of facts", while the judge decides on the law. He referees the contest in open court. The cases are to be presented by barristers, which introduces a peculiar division of labor within the legal profession. Barristers cannot be hired directly by clients. They are hired by solicitors and work either for the defense or the prosecution. Barristers are in-court lawyers who act according to the solicitor's instructions. The solicitor, in contrast, does paper work, administers case files, and initiates inquiries into the matter. Solicitors put together pre-trial correspondence and "instructions to counsel". They serve relevant forms and materials and gather disclosed materials. The defense solicitor reminds the Crown Prosecution Service (CPS) of outstanding evidence. In other words, solicitors consult their barristers in a wide range of legal and court-related issues.

How do first defenses occur in Crown Court cases? The three defenses presented in the next section were instigated by the police. They were gathered and recorded by police officers in the course of a police interview. The accused was questioned in light of allegations about 'what really happened'. The police interview itself was not yet part of the procedure. What is at issue is the decision by the CPS on whether there is a triable case. In the following cases, the police interviewed the full cast of the alleged incident: the alleged victim, perpetrator, and eyewitness.

The interview protocols provided the only evidence on which to make a decision about the cases.

Sticking to the first version

We can now return to the interview with which we began, involving Steve Striker and the fight in a night club. Steve was arrested on the spot. He was drunk and, as reported later, resisted the arresting officers. The police interview takes place the morning after. The *recorded* account lines up one detail after the other: what he had in his fist; where he hit the victim; what happened afterwards; whether he regretted it; and so on. His presence at the scene was not contested. Neither was the fact that a fight took place. The interview became *the* reference point of the proceeding.

The interview protocol is made available first to the CPS and later to the defense. The written protocol serves as the core object for creating binding effects. In order to demonstrate its binding force, we can jump right to the final stage: the trial hearing in the Crown Court. The statement reached the defense barrister as a part of his brief. During the day in court, he used the document for various purposes: to take instructions, to exchange views with his colleague, to formulate questions during the witness examination, or to detect inconsistencies in the answers.[9]

How is the early defense binding at this final stage? How does Striker's testimony in court refer back to his defense in the police-interview? Does he stick to it despite the largely altered situation?[10] The data shows a remarkable resemblance between the early and the late account:

Q.: And how long were you on the floor for, could you say?
A.: About a minute.
Q.: And who was involved in the stamping and kicking?
A.: Jonathan Victim and his friend, the blond one.
Q.: What happened then?
A.: Well then, after they had been stamping on me, I stood up and I had the glass in my hand and I spun round and just – just went for him.
Q.: Right. Well, did you have any difficulty getting up?
A.: Yes.
Q.: Why did you have difficulty getting up?
A.: Because they were still stamping on me. I just managed to get up somehow.

Q.: And at what point did you start to swing the glass?

A.: Well, as I got my feet on the floor I just spun round and lashed out as I was standing up – at the same time as I was just standing up. I was like crouched down.

The testimony in court seems to re-enact the first defense in detail: "the glass", the "blond guy", the exchange prior to the confrontation, the single blow, and so on. The duet of defense barrister and defendant creates a reiteration of these details.[11] This, however, can only be observed by weighing the oral testimony against the *original* protocol. In court, this contrast is only available to the barristers. The defendant, as witness, is not allowed to use the original protocol. The jury is not allowed to employ it either, which is officially explained as the primacy of oral statement. The principle of orality is protected against the 'mundane' authority of the written document.[12] Neither the judge nor the jury is, what one could call, a binding other, since they do not bear any procedural memory exceeding the trial hearing.

Does this case show any binding effect of the early defense? It does so in a rather self-explanatory way. All reiterated details work in favor of the defendant. Obviously, the defendant repeats a beneficial defense strategy. This can be extended to include the repetition of harmful points as well, as it happened at the end of the defendant's friendly examination. The defense barrister brings up a problematic part of the police interview in order to neutralize it:

Q.: And then you were asked, "Did you feel remorse for what you had done, or anything?," and you say, "No, I wasn't finished." What did you mean by that?

A.: I don't know. I was still very angry. I just – I don't know.

Q.: And, when you struck with the glass, what did you intend to do?

A.: I don't know.

Q.: Did you think about the fact that you had the glass in your hand?

A.: No.

Q.: Did you want to cause him really serious injury?

A.: Not really serious injury, no.

By reading out this protocol section,[13] the defense barrister forestalls the likely cross-examination and gives the defendant an opportunity to repair his procedural past in front of the judge and jury. By doing so, the defense barrister knew that his counterpart would dispose of the police protocol. He knew that the prosecuting barrister was eager to call the documented 'lapse'[14] as evidence in order to challenge the defendant in the witness stand.

The first defense can be shortened

Binding does not necessarily trigger reiteration. Under certain conditions, a defendant can eliminate the harmful aspects of an early defense. This is what happens in our second micro-history, an indecent assault case. Despite the corrections, the case remains an impressive illustration of binding effects. It demonstrates how difficult it is to erase harmful points from the procedural memory.

In this case, again, the suspect did not exercise his "right to silence".[15] Tim Blue collaborated with the interviewing police officers. His responses reappear months later in court during the sentencing hearing. Defense and prosecution agreed on the 'basis of the plea'. The two barristers agreed to cut short the defense as it was recorded in the police protocol. The final version – up to "page five" (out of eight pages) – reads like this:

> BLUE: ... just snogged with her, just played with her breasts, as far as I know that's all I did, then I got up and she said you had better go and I just apologized, I just said sorry, I said you won't say a word to Jane will you?
> DC: So you'd started kissing with her, did she resist that?
> BLUE: She did at first and then she just relaxed afterwards.
> DC: Is that because you told her to relax?
> BLUE: No I didn't say, can't remember saying that.
> DC: Right so you've been kissing with her and she's told you to go and you've carried on kissing with her, was that with consent or without?
> BLUE: Without I should think – all I can do is remember just cuddling up to her and just touching her breasts.
> DC: Is this outside her clothing or inside her pajamas?
> BLUE: Inside I think.
> DC: And what was she saying while you were doing this?
> BLUE: She just said you had better go.

Blue was bound to the first five pages of the interview protocol. He was unbound from the remaining three pages. Binding appears here as a measurement of achievement. The qualified binding prompts questions of cost and benefit, of win and loss.[16] Or, to put it differently: what price does each side pay for this "bargaining of the facts"? The barristers had to answer similar questions – of the client, of the victim – in order to get permission for the deal. They compared the final agreed version with the first defense.

During the police interview, Tim Blue was confronted with the allegations put forward weeks prior by the complainant. The complainant reported, in her interview, that Blue had entered her bedroom, started kissing and stroking her, and that he went even further and made her "do things". The interviewing police officers raised these details in order to confront the suspect with 'what really happened':

DC: ...She then says that you undid your trouser zip and your belt?

BLUE: No – I can't remember doing that.

DC: And that you then took hold of her left wrist and pulled her hand and put it down your trousers and inside your underpants and made her touch your erect penis?

BLUE: No – I can't remember doing that.

DC: And you then put your hand down her shorts and began to touch her vaginal area, do you remember that?

BLUE: No, no, but I can't remember that bit. I can remember going out the door but I can't remember taking my glass back.

Instead of offering an alternative version, Blue responded by creating blanks. His responses left room for imagination. The allegations filled these gaps. They provided – without being countered – the hegemonic account.

The attempt to be noncommittal failed. The gaps triggered binding effects, since they were taken as approval. The defense fought the binding by repetitively stating that 'he did not go that far!' Simultaneously, however, something else happens. The defense version is stealthily adjusted to create the hegemonic account. The array of defense accounts indicates this binding effect: that presented in the solicitor–client meeting, those deriving from the drafting, that used to instruct the barrister, or that used to advise the plea. From one version to another, the defense admits more breaches and rejects fewer allegations. The plea-bargaining finalizes this adjustment by defining up to which page number ("5 out of 8") Blue's statement is binding for both parties.

The barristers put their deal in writing, signed it, and handed it over to the judge.

The first defense is too ambitious

In our third micro-history, the first defense is more promising. Linda Fury presents an alibi. She does so during the police interview in the presence of her solicitor.[17] The interview protocol including Linda's first defense was only served months later. The solicitor used her own notes instead. According to her report, the police officer accused her client of having punched a man in front of his house, thrown stones at him, and even attacked him with a knife. Just before this interview, the complainant had selected Linda Fury (out of nine) in an identification parade. The police had good reason to hold Linda as the prime suspect.

According to the solicitor's notes, the police officer opened the interrogation by asking the following question: "Is there anything that you would now like to tell us following that identification parade and following that identification?" The solicitor reports the following responses by his client:

6. I think it was Kim's sister, who wanted some cigarettes and so we went to get some. I remember that we went back across the wooden gate it was on our way back to her mum's home that we passed a woman and a lad. Kim told me that the woman was called Lucy and that she was having problems with her.

7. I thought that the lad with Lucy was her boyfriend. He was carrying some shopping.

8. Next to the wooden gate, I remember that there is a sort of stony road. I don't know where it leads, as I didn't go up it.

9. Kim, me and the other girl, who was about 8 stood at the end of the stony road whilst Lucy and the lad were a bit further up it.

10. Kim and Lucy started to argue. The lad, who I heard was called Andy, dropped his shopping. He seemed to be aggressive. I did not join in the argument. But stood close to Kim.

11. I noticed that whilst the argument was going on, a police van was stopped at the end of the lane...

12. I can't really recall how long the argument lasted. I did not join in and I did not in any way threaten Andy or Mandy, or use any form of violence against them.

13. Following the argument, we went straight back to Kim's mother's home...

(pp. 25–26/21.1.1)

The defense was started from this basis and the solicitor made the alibi the heart of the case. In order to do so, the defense had to put together an official "notice of alibi". The notice establishes those details of the alibi that the defense is willing to state in court. The notice allows the prosecution to prepare for counter-arguments. Moreover, it initiates what is called "secondary disclosure": the obligation for the CPS to make available all materials that refer to the case of the defense.

Approaching the deadline for the "notice of alibi", the solicitor intensified her written exchanges with the instructed barrister. She posted a bundle of documents comprising the drafted alibi-story, the official indictment, and her summary of the police interview. In her instructions, the solicitor promoted Linda's early account as being the core of the case:

> She was interviewed at X-village Police Station in the presence of X from instructing Solicitors. She confirmed that she had been in X-village and met her friend Kim and that they had been to Kim's house and they then went out with her little sister to buy some cigarettes. She stated that they came across a male and female and an argument ensued between that male and female and Kim and her sister. She stated that the male involved took an aggressive stance. She denied that there had been any violence whatsoever between her and the male. She believed the male to be called Andy and Counsel will have noted the aggrieved in this allegation is Andy Collin who on November 10 was staying with his sister who lives at 13 Kings Street, X-village. That is on the main Counsel housing estate in X-village and our client has indicated she would not go onto that estate willingly because she has an ex-boyfriend who lives on the estate and would not wish to bump into him.

(28.3.1)

What happened here? The aim of the letter to the barrister was not just the delivery of necessary information. It, additionally, took the chance to test the story in a protected and friendly environment. Consequently, the solicitor highlights functions and relevancies of the account. For instance, he points out that the aggressive guy ("Andy") in Linda's version is identical with the aggrieved ("Andy Collin").

Through the instructed account, solicitor and barrister have managed to synchronize their views. The instructions allowed the lawyers to agree on a (defense) case. In this protected sphere, solicitor and barrister discussed strategic (story and case) as well as tactical questions (support for the story). Given the current state of their case, the lawyers did not opt for the story without reservations[18] because there was still a need for an alibi witness.

Three months later, and without any such witness, the account is presented to the CPS by the official "notice of alibi". This pre-trial document provides the basis for the secondary disclosure, meaning the disclosure of materials that the CPS did not use.

> The defendant states that this would be about fifteen minutes after they had left the house to buy the cigarettes. They came across these people having just crossed a wooden gate on the way back to X-Street. The defendant did not know the other two people until Kim informed her that the woman was called Lucy.
>
> The defendant thought Lucy was with her boyfriend, but now believes the other male present to have been the complainant. An argument ensued between Kim and Lucy, and the male adopted an aggressive stance. She believed the male to be called Andy. The defendant did not take part in the argument, but stood close by…
>
> (p. 50/13.4.1)

Binding does not only emerge because the early defense circulates through both camps. It also emerges within the defense ensemble. Client, solicitor, and barrister must agree on a mutual version. They choose and mobilize this version for trial. These investments do not allow indefinite changes of strategy. On top of this, the defense is pressured to give a binding announcement. The "notice of alibi" marks a point of no return.

Once announced as an alibi, the account demanded backing by "Kim, her friend", who had supposedly accompanied Linda that day. The disclosure of so far "unused materials" released surprising news: this "friend" had previously been interviewed as the prime suspect, before Linda. During this interview, Kim incriminated Linda as the one who had in fact carried out these attacks. The defense was trapped in the binding mechanism: it stuck with the original claim ("alibi") that 'on stage' lacked any substantiation ("alibi witness") – and coherence. At least, Kim's incriminating statement was not admissible since it had derived from allegations made against her.

Summary for the English cases: Conditional binding

The three micro-histories resonate well for our conceptual focus. The early defenses were echoed in the late stages of the proceedings. They reappeared even in those aspects that were not entirely beneficial to their authors. In this regard, we can demonstrate that binding effects were at work.

We are able to identify a number of regimented sources that triggered binding effects. The division of labor between solicitor and barrister forces the defense to explicate the case prior to the actual hearing. There is the need to define a position and to invest in this position during the course of the pre-trial and trial. These investments, together with the need to agree on a defense strategy, trigger some binding effects within the ensemble even before the prosecution is informed.

The Crown Court procedure organizes the availability of early responses by the means of (formatted) documentation and (rules of) disclosure. This availability shifts the inner binding toward an external binding. The procedure urges the defense to publicly announce the main arguments of its case in the "defense statement" prior to the hearing. This announcement opens up pre-trial settlements and discourages so called "surprise attacks".

The available memory exceeds these rather general pre-trial announcements. The binding past is more detailed than this. It embraces the disclosed statements of the witnesses who are due to be called in court. For the defense, this includes the police interviews taken from its witnesses, including the defendant. No matter whether the latter testifies or not, his former statement is likely to play a role in court: as evidence, or as binding source. The documentary memory forces the defense to relate to the early defense during the trial examinations. It allows the contestant and the court to draw conclusions from present responses and past silences.

Binding nonetheless remains an incongruous mechanism. The early defenses are not, per se, available to the judge and jury. The court is not provided with a binding other outside the opposed camps. Certain early defenses are, furthermore, protected by lawyer–client discretion. Nobody outside the defense ensemble will be provided with or informed about the internal pre-tests, adjustments, and improvements. All of this remains unavailable for the court procedure unless it brings about "promising" points that are announced and disclosed to the contestant. Besides, even a whole range of documented and disclosed "slips" is rendered inadmissible (and not binding). To some considerable degree, the

Crown Court procedure seems to shield the defendants from their procedural pasts. The binding and its restrictions deserve further inquiry.

Case Study 2. Early accounts in US cases

In this section, we examine the emergence of binding effects in minor criminal cases in one of the Western states of the United States. The US legal system is commonly defined as adversarial; that is, it identifies 'what really happened' through the course of argumentation by prosecuting and defending attorneys. In the lower courts, this contest is placed before a group of lay jurors who decide upon the truthful conditions of the criminal event in question. The judge then pronounces sentence based on the jurors' verdict.

The cases at issue are 'driving under the influence' (DUI). Most cases falling into this category are considered to be a minor violation or 'misdemeanor'. A misdemeanor is a crime punishable by less than one year of incarceration. In contrast, a felony is a crime punishable by death or at least one year in a State or Federal penitentiary. However, a repeated misdemeanor may become a felony. In this case, it travels to the higher court. Dependant on the criminal law of a particular state, the DUI exhibits a gradual build-up: it stays a minor offense when prosecuted for the first time; the second conviction leads to a loss of the driver's license, a steep fine in lieu of jail time, and extensive alcohol dependence evaluation; the third conviction brings about incarceration.

The two cases that we present for analysis here are similar in that both were plea-bargained and both attempted partial alibi as the defense; however, they differ in the way plea-bargaining was carried out. In one case the plea-bargain route was chosen right away; the other remained much contested for a long time. The differences between the two cases present defense casework in its self-modifying capacity. We begin the analyses with a state case.

The first defense is reiterated

In this case, the defendant, Thomas H., was arrested for DUI. He and his partner and co-defendant, Teddy, were arguing at the time when their vehicle pulled over into a private driveway. The suspect attempted to leave the scene, but was located by a back-up police unit and taken back to the scene for investigation. As a result of the investigation the suspect was arrested, booked in the local jail, and then released on his own recognizance until further notice. In addition to DUI, the defendant was charged with reckless driving, simple assault, resisting arrest, and domestic violence. Shortly after, the defendant hired a private attorney, who designed a defense strategy that lead to a guilty plea and conviction. We begin our analysis with the first document on the case, a police report, where a defense was attempted for the first time. The first defense statement to enter the procedural history was made by the defendant himself: "Officer Conduit had now returned with Thomas in his patrol car. We performed the tests together. As we were doing so, Thomas kept on saying: I was not in operation of the vehicle" (Incident Report: 4/17/2004).

The location of the statement is essential for its force in the subsequent defense. Made to the police officer, the statement ends up in the police report, which is designed to both collect evidence and to account for the manner of its collection. The rules that specify both activities give the officer's accounts the appearance of fact. In contrast, the defendant's statement appears as a lone-standing denial of the officer's formulaic account. For the prosecuting attorney, it means little: under US procedural rules, the not-guilty plea is a structural necessity; it is entered at the stage of first appearance automatically.

The matter is different from the defense perspective. If, during an arrest, the defendant produces a plausibly distinct account of the events that could have led to the defendant's release (for example, alibi), but it is ignored by the police officer, the defense attorney may cite impropriety and ask the judge to dismiss the case on a technicality. In order to confirm or disconfirm this possibility, the defense must obtain the discovery materials from the prosecution. For this, the court requires an official request from the defense attorney. While waiting for the evidence, the defense designs a provisional defense strategy based on the defendant's own account.

The account is collected during the attorney–client conference. In this case, the client did not offer a new defense to the attorney, but chose to reiterate his denial: "I wasn't in the car behind the wheel...I wasn't driving when he arrested me." The formulation of this statement is worth examining. In its emphasis, it matches the statement in the police report ("I was not in operation of the vehicle") by bringing to the fore the denial of the potential charge rather than the defendant's guilt. The defendant does not claim that he was not drunk, nor does he claim that he behaved as a model citizen. Instead, to support his counter-claim, he proffers a legal reason: "I was not in operation of the vehicle." However, since his plea failed, it is the defense attorney who is now in a position to bring this up with the prosecuting attorney. The object of the discussion would then be the rules of investigation and arrest and their possible violation. This is how the attorney transforms the defendant's denial.

In his letter to the client, the attorney goes straight to a possible cause of disputation, the officer's assertions:

> ...As you are aware, the main thing that we want to show on that tape is that the arresting officer's recollection is inaccurate and untrue....
>
> (Correspondence: 4/27/2004)

Since the only evidence in this case is that collected and documented by the officer, it is to that evidence that the defendant's denial gets attached: the evidence may be incorrect because the police officer failed to follow the rules of evidence and thus produced a faulty account. The statement forms a provisional strategy: "Therefore our entire drive has to be to convince the State Attorney first, the jury second, that they have made a big mistake in this matter...". There is a complication, however: the defendant has prior convictions. For the defense, these convictions, including the previous DUI, brings the triability of the case into question.

In the subsequent letter to the prosecuting attorney, the plea-bargain option is tested, but on evidentiary grounds. On the strength of the defendant's story, the attorney deploys a fishing device:

> Jack, I have a fairly credible witness (mentioned by the defendant) who will contradict Officer C.'s assertion that he saw Mr. H. get out of the vehicle.
>
> (Correspondence: 4/27/2004)

The attorney's claim can be considered a reformulation of the defendant's original statement. The claim accounts for the defendant's denial by creating an alibi. The defense–prosecution exchange points to the interactive character of the plea-bargain stage. Once plea-bargain is identified as a preference, it is common, and encouraged, for the adversarial parties to communicate their views on the case and evidence so that there is no delay in resolving the case quickly. This does not mean, however, that the defense's offer is accepted to his advantage, if at all. Still much depends on discovery.

As soon as the defense attorney receives the prosecution evidence, he sends a letter to the co-defendant with an evaluation of the evidence in terms of its usefulness to the chosen strategy:

As you have seen, it is paramount that Tom gets a witness to testify that he was not in the vehicle when the officer saw him. There is also an additional report put together by the cops. It contradicts our previous assertions.

(Correspondence: 4/30/2004)

From the letter, it is not clear whether the evidence received from the other side undermines the defense strategy completely. It is clear, however, that the prosecution decided "to play hardball", in the words of the attorney. It conducted an additional investigation and produced new and beneficial accounts. For the defense, the prosecutor's response meant availability of a credible eyewitness. This fact points to an uphill struggle: not only must the defense ensemble overcome the fact that the officer's word would typically be taken over the word of the ex-convict, but, by now, the defense's anonymous phantom witness faces concrete witnesses on the side of the prosecution. The alibi defense no longer looks promising. No eyewitness has volunteered to step in to support the defense by the time of the preliminary hearing.

Shortly thereafter the defense attorney receives an e-mail from the prosecutor:

> In reviewing the reports for the Prelims this afternoon, I have decided I would offer a plea agreement wherein the defendant pleads guilty to the DUI as a 2d offence. I will dismiss the balance of the charges.
>
> (Correspondence: 5/13/2004)

The prosecutor's message is laconic and virtually account-free. For his counter-offer, the prosecuting attorney selects the balance of the charges (assault, battery, reckless driving, and so on). It is at this stage that the negotiations between the defense attorney and the prosecuting attorney broker an agreement in the adversarial form. The defense ensemble, therefore, fails to engage the defendant's statement to its benefit: the evidence offered by the prosecution stands strong, while no evidence has been generated to support a defense by alibi.

Nice guy but needs to lay off the sauce

Our second US micro-history file is another DUI case, which was handed over to us by the attorney with this short synopsis:

> Robert Delonie, second time offender. Nice guy but needs to lay off the sauce. Last Saturday, he went to a local pub, got wasted, closed

the bar, drove home, then, on the way, picked up a couple of under-age girls, and then damaged someone's car, but not too badly. There was a cop who saw him, as he was driving away. When the cop pulled him over, Robert was drunk, the minors were drinking, and, to add insult to injury, the cop found a gun underneath the seat of the vehicle. Lo and behold, Robert got arrested. Now he faces his first DUI, Contributing, Possession, and other charges. May lose his license, get some jail time.

The outlined case went to plea-bargain without much hesitation on the part of the attorney. However, in contrast to the first case, it had a different venue as it was adjudicated in a tribal court. Tribal court is a hybrid between the State and Magistrate's Court specific to the legal environment on Indian reservations in the United States. Several jurisdictional exceptions apply. For example, certain crimes that fall into the category "serious" are investigated by Federal agents. Moreover, if an impropriety is suspected, the FBI may investigate any crime on the "Indian Territory". In comparison to the State and Federal court, the tribal court means a much more relaxed approach to both process and procedure. This is manifested expressly in unexpected omissions in the documentary field: for instance, in this case no arrest report was filed with the defense. This is an interesting variation on the previous case. From the letter to the client:

> I will see you at the Lower Brule Courthouse at about 3:30 to 4:00 on Monday, October 6. If you can get the arrest reports on this case by then, I will bring those with me, however, it has been my experience that I will have very little chance for having that done.
>
> (LC: 10/3/2003)

The attorney explained: "The tribe never sends anything on time; plus it's all here, anyway." The procedural stage of the public hearing that brought the defense and the prosecution together apparently allows for this gap: the matters of evidence were discussed face-to-face.

In the meantime, as in the first case, the defense requests, and obtains, the defendant's story. In contrast to the first case, the defendant does not narrate his story as a defense during the arrest. The absence of a documented statement means that the defense attorney is free to design a new account. This difference specified the objectives of information-gathering during the attorney–client conference: in the first case, the attorney sought ways to support the defendant's statement. In this case, the attorney accounted for "what happened" in terms of "what should have happened" rather than "what really happened". In his letter to the client he outlines the defense strategy for each separate charge:

> Relative to 6 charges against you in the...Court for Reckless Driving, DUI; Leaving the Scene of the Accident, Felon in Possession, Contributing to the Delinquency of...(name), and Contributing to the Delinquency of...(name) (Correspondence: 11/5/2003).

> (Felon in Possession): As I understand it, last year your father bought you a black powder rifle because you have a previous conviction for receiving stolen firearms in federal court in 1995. As a result, you are unable to own or possess firearms. However, your father, being an ex-police officer, is aware of the fact that you could probably have a black powder gun. In my opinion, you don't have the problem there.[19]

The first charge mentioned in the letter is not the first one stated in the information. Its appearance is not haphazard, however. On the one hand, "Felon in Possession" is the most problematic charge. However, according to the attorney, the defendant has "no problem" with it. When evaluated on legal grounds, the problematic nature of the charge is circumscribed. The ease with which the problem is resolved should not lessen its importance for the procedural history: as we have mentioned, prior convictions establish the relation to the procedural history retroactively. For the defendant, this relation is a mixed bag. As the attorney explained it to the client, "they know you are a trouble-maker". This statement shows how a procedural history is never a one-time but rather a cumulative record. The other possible reason for the appearance of this charge at the beginning of the letter lies in the attorney's follow-up: "this is really something we can work with." The reference is to plea-bargain:

> II. (Reckless Driving, Leaving the Scene of the Accident, DUI): I understand that this entire thing occurred as a result of you nudging (name of the plaintiff) car in (place name) at (date). However, it is going to be very difficult to prove that...I understand that you had a second individual in your car (name...) but that is really not going to work as alibi, because the girls who were with you as well will undoubtedly say that you were drinking and driving. At this point in the game, we need to make sure that the Feds stay off your back, and we

need to look at the arrest report to try to strike the best plea bargain agreement that we can.

As this extract shows, the attorney continues his assessment of the charges in the order of their diminishing problematic nature. This time, the charge of "Leaving the Scene" gets evaluated as "difficult to prove". The second charge is not problematic either, or, shall I say, it is the most problematic for the defendant but not for the defense. In the plea-bargain context, DUI is the central charge. The system demands its acceptance. This might explain the haste with which, during the attorney–client conference, the attorney dismisses the defendant's suggestion to name the second person as the driver. The problem with this scenario is the witnesses ("the girls") who are liable in criminal court themselves (underage drinking is a criminal offense) and thus susceptible to the pressure of the prosecution. With the dismissal of the last opportunity to generate new evidence, the case is moved forward along the plea-bargain route. Procedurally, the case may still be halted: "we need to look at the arrest report to try to strike the best plea-bargain agreement that we can"; however, there seems to be no need for discovery materials:

> III. (Contributing to the Delinquency): Lastly, you need to have both of the girls present at the courthouse...to see what they are willing to say about you providing them with alcohol. We need to have them testify that they had already been drinking before they got into your car. With any luck, the prosecutor will probably gladly let you plead guilty to a DUI and drop the rest of the charges.

In this paragraph, the attorney qualifies the previously mentioned police report. Important as it is, the report is not useful for the defense. From the previous descriptions one can see how, in the best case scenario, the advantageous plea may as well proceed without it. It is also expected that if a difficulty arises it will be raised by the prosecution. As it stands, the plea-bargain seeks to dismiss virtually all the extraneous charges in exchange for the guilty plea on the DUI. If the drinking minors absolve the defendant from his involvement in their delinquency, and that means if the defense attorney gets to them first, Robert faces a smooth ride. At the preliminary meeting, the prosecutor dismissed the Felon in Possession charge while the Reckless Driving and the Contributing charges were downplayed on account of reluctant witnesses. Finally, although the police report was provided, the tape from the police cruiser was missing. All these circumstances lead to the closure of the case in accordance with the defense strategy and to the defendant's advantage. As the attorney concluded in his last letter to the client:

> As you are aware, you were charged with (list of charges...). The plea bargain resulted in one plea of DUI, which resulted in a $60.00 fine.... This went really well. You suffered virtually no costs and this matter is behind you.
>
> (Correspondence: 11/4/2003)

Summary for the US cases: Bound bargaining

Several specificities characterize the two cases. First, as an arrest crime, DUI tends to generate hard evidence: video and audio recording, as well as observational and scientific testimonials. This basis produces silence rather than competing (and later binding) accounts on the side of the defense. Second, the solid evidence collected for DUI cases renders plea-bargain to be a preferential route for DUI cases. The plea-bargain option interrupts the process by waiving the trial in favor of a guilty plea with subsequent sentence reduction. In this option, binding arises within pre-trial activities. Finally, the DUI cases are characterized by an early option to exit. The attorney tries to avoid any definite – and binding – defense in order to keep his negotiating position flexible.

In the second case this is achieved by creating a new defense strategy without generating much binding. The defense capitalizes on legal errors allowed by the prosecution. It successfully argues for the dismissal of all extraneous charges and negotiates a good deal for the defendant. In the first case, the attorney has to deal with a first defense: a minimalist alibi. He tries to strengthen the case within the binding limits by introducing an anonymous alibi witness. The race for forensic support ends with only the prosecuting attorney generating a substantial account. As a result, the plea-bargain option is enacted at a disadvantage to the defense. There is no further mention of the alibi witness.

The difference between the two cases underlines the importance of the binding mechanism. In the plea-bargain configuration, the early defense, at least in part, needs to be dismissed. A binding defense complicates the plea-bargain negotiations. The first case showed these complications as the new additions to the case proved to be detrimental to the procedural past. In contrast, in the second case, the focus on undermining the allegations created the procedural "fit", thus immediately demonstrating conditions for either success or failure.

Case Study 3. Early accounts in German criminal cases

Considering the common distinction between the adversarial and inquisitorial systems of criminal procedures and their criteria, one would expect that cases tried in the German system would exhibit the strong binding force of the proceeding's history on the trial. Some comparativists state that in the inquisitorial system, the trial basically performs a pre-established text. This text is held in the shared file, available to all participants. For the Netherlands they state that "the most salient feature of the pre-trial process [...] is probably the degree to which all parties cooperate in arriving at a pre-prepared version of it that is subsequently recorded in a case file or dossier as the basis for the coming trial" (Jörg *et al.*, 1995, p. 47). Hence, we would expect a strong determinative power of the proceeding's history for the trial.

The three cases presented and discussed in this section were tried at different courts. The first two started out at the *Amtsgericht* (the lowest court) and ended up at the *Landgericht* as appellate court. The third case was tried at the *Landgericht*[20] in the first instance. In general, the *Amtsgericht* tries cases in which sentences of two years jail time or less are expected, with single judges. Cases in which sentences of up to four years are expected are tried with one professional and two lay judges. The *Landgericht* is responsible for cases with an expected outcome of more than four years.[21] As the lawyer informant assured, the *Landgericht* will not convict as easily as the *Amtsgericht*. Once the *Landgericht* convicts, however, the sentence is likely to be harsher.

Trials at the *Landgericht* are likely to take more than a day, sometimes even up to several years. The trials at the *Amtsgericht* are rather brief, which explains the huge caseload. The length of the trial has profound effects on preparation. At the *Landgericht*, the lawyer will have plenty of time during the proceedings to design or rearrange the defense in light of the ongoing trial. This is different for cases that are tried in one day. Although a lawyer may ask for a break, the greater part of preparation needs to be completed prior to the trial.

In the German criminal procedure, the defense lawyer accesses the so-called "inquiry file". This file provides the ground for the "court file", a shared file for all participants. Demanding access is usually the first action for a defense lawyer to take. Not to do so is considered bad professional practice. During the inquiry, the lawyer learns not only substantially what the prosecution knows, but also procedurally what routes the prosecution took and where those routes led. The lawyer can learn about the prosecution's failed inquiries as well as their successes.

At the stage of inquiry, the rules of documentation are formally equal between the two courts. The practice of documentation, however, exhibits strong differences, especially with respect to the protocols of the police interviews with the accused. The protocols are very diverse in format. Most of the time, they are just summaries of what was said. This ex post style gives the impression that the accused entered his or her account freely and fluently without having been asked or prompted much. As one judge said, "You read the witness' statement in the file and think she talked the police officer's head off. Then you sit across from her in the court and you have to worm the statement out of her."

Another issue that has a strong impact on the lawyers' and the defendants' preparation of the case is the judge themselves. At the *Amtsgericht*, cases are assigned to judges by initials of the defendant's last name. Hence, a defendant who has repeated encounters with the criminal court will have a good chance of sitting in front of the same judge. In these cases the defendant's criminal record enters the proceedings not only by the reading of the defendant's prior convictions, but also through the interpersonal relationship that has been established in earlier trials. Hence, not only the history of the case but also the defendant's criminal history influence the trial.

Focusing on the binding forces that develop during the proceeding, one may wonder where and how a criminal case is actually instigated. For the lawyer, a case often starts with a client calling and saying "I have a problem." At this stage, the defendant's case has already developed up to a certain point – the police already have a file, and inquiries are under way. Often clients have already been interviewed by the police prior to seeing their lawyer. Some, especially those who have been in contact with criminal investigations before, will not show up for the interview or remain silent. Others will give a first account at this stage of the investigation, producing a protocol to be filed by the prosecution. The following three cases will illustrate what it means to talk early, to remain silent, or to maneuver in between.

Digging yourself a hole with words

In the rather complicated case that comprises our first German microhistory, the defendant talked to the police at a very early stage without consulting a lawyer.[22] Mr. Becker was charged with leaving the scene of an accident where three pedestrians had been hit by his car and were severely injured. One day after the accident Becker[23] is interviewed by the police as a suspect.[24] He states that it was not him driving his car, but a friend of his by the name of Frauke Schumann.

> Client: I waited for her yesterday at 6 p.m. I started worrying when she was not there by 8 p.m. However, I could not call her, because my phone card was empty. Then the police called. I told them that I lent the car to an acquaintance. I gave them her name, Frauke Schumann. Her nickname is "Schumi".
>
> Police: Has Mrs. Schumann contacted you?
>
> Client: No
>
> Police: There actually is no Frauke Schumann, is there? Whom did you actually give your car?
>
> Client: I only know this Frauke Schumann. I do have her phone number...

In the three police interviews that followed over the next four weeks, Mr. Becker repeats the story that Frauke Schumann was driving his car. During these interviews, he refines the picture of the acquaintance. Upon request, he tells the police where he met her, where she is from, that she has a boyfriend, and so on. He seems very cooperative. He even gives them "Frauke Schumann's" phone number. He adds details and accounts for gaps: "I did not try to call her because I did not mean to disturb the ongoing investigation." Becker thereby attempts to render the story more coherent and plausible.

One month later, Becker consults his lawyer for the first time. He offers her the same version that he presented during the police interviews. The lawyer prepares a (first) file note on what the client told her: "The client states that he lent his car to an acquaintance. The client states her name as Frauke Schumann."

The first meeting precedes the lawyer's access to the files. Thus, she neither knows what Becker, her client, already said during the police interviews, nor how the police have evaluated his story. The lawyer's work is further complicated by the fact that access to the files is delayed. The prosecution office states that it cannot send the file yet due to ongoing investigations. Later, the lawyer receives only an extract of the file in which the testimony of the key witness is missing. The lawyer has to trust the client with his version of the case. Her file note shows that she is cautious to do so.

In the meantime the police locate the actual driver (Schobanowski) and passenger (Vogel). Both are friends of Becker. In another interview by the prosecution, Becker is confronted with this new development and the disintegration of his story. According to the lawyer, the prose-cutor yelled at Becker saying that a warrant of arrest would be issued if he did not immediately tell the truth. None of this was recorded in the inquiry file. Just a tiny file note marks this meeting as important for the proceeding: "The client wants to sleep on it." Becker retreats from his story a day later in a written statement that his lawyer sends to the pros-ecution. "With respect to the day of the accident, I would like to correct my prior statements: I did not lend the vehicle to Frauke Schumann but to Regina Vogel."

By making this statement, Becker inadvertently admits to a felony – he attempted to mislead the investigations and thus committed an obstruction of justice.[25]

The story of Frauke Schumann never makes it to trial, but it is under-mined and then retracted during the process of investigation. The process of developing, strengthening, and then retracting the story is placed in the realm of a procedural public that comprises only the prose-cution and police on one side and the defense on the other. The account never makes it to open court. In the trial, Becker makes use of his right to silence.

Leaving a blank

The second German micro-history describes what happens when the respondent stays silent from the start. Kai Kuhnau was charged with driving a motor scooter without obtaining liability insurance for the vehicle.[26] Two police officers allegedly caught him in the act when he was standing on his scooter, heading home. This was his second charge with respect to the scooter. Kuhnau followed the summons but he remained silent throughout the police interview. He had remained silent from the moment he was stopped with his scooter by the police and confronted with the charges.

During the trial, Kuhnau introduces his account of what happened for the first time. He does so while one of the police officers is questioned as a witness. One of the police officers is asked, as a witness, whether the engine of the scooter was running. He replies, "I do not know if the engine was running or if the defendant pushed the scooter himself. We did not check whether the engine actually would have worked."[27] Right after this statement Kuhnau states, "The engine did not work at that time. That's why I pushed the scooter myself. The engine had gone wet and was not working properly." When the witness, a police officer, was asked about this version, he stated that Kuhnau never said that before "although he had the opportunity to do so." The police officer thereby marks his silence as a blank or a missing response that can be interpreted as a decision. A decision then allows inferences about intentions and involvement.

This notion of a blank becomes even more pronounced in the subsequent appeal hearing. Kuhnau had been sentenced to jail without probation. He appealed against the verdict.[28] In the appeal hearing the same witnesses were questioned, among them the same police officer:

Judge: Did he say that the engine was not working?
Witness: No, he started saying that at the *Amtsgericht*. Otherwise we would have tested it right on the spot.

Here, the police officer marks Kuhnau's initial silence as strategic. The silence, the officer stated, was meant to outmaneuver the treacherous situation when he was caught *in flagranti*. No matter what Kuhnau had said on the spot, it would have resulted in a resolution of the matter. Either the police would have found that the engine did not work so there would be no case at all, or they would have found the engine functioning, thereby strengthening the allegations.

Kuhnau was acquitted after the appeal hearing because his version could not be refuted beyond reasonable doubt. The judge said, seconded by the prosecutor, "There is a small possibility that everything happened the way you described it. And in that case: *in dubio pro reo*."

Hence, leaving a blank did not work entirely against the defendant. In some respect, it enabled him to formulate a beneficial counter-narrative without being bound to a first defense. However, as the lawyer added, with a different judge the outcome could have been different. Perhaps another judge would have dismissed the "excuse" as barely credible because it had not been documented. Another judge might have rejected the statement because it was staged in the appeal hearing without being bound to and hardened by an earlier and similar version.

Confronted with the past

The final German micro-history is that of Henning, a young drug addict. The case is available due to the ethnographer's field notes. Full access to the file was denied. He is charged with robbery in six cases. More precisely, Henning and his friend are accused of robbing six elderly ladies of their handbags and causing severe injuries to some of them. The accusations rest on the testimony of a third suspect. The case is tried at the juvenile court of the *Landgericht.*

Without his lawyer being present, Henning is arrested and interviewed twice by the police. In the first interview he denies any form of involvement. He even gives an alibi for one of the robberies, stating that he was in a video store at that point in time. However, he did "hear" of such robberies and also found two of the stolen handbags by accident. He openly accuses his friend (and later co-defendant) of the robberies. Finally, he offers an unspecified alibi – "I sleep in very late." The robberies were committed in the morning.

In the second interview, four weeks later, and again without a lawyer, Henning once more denies any involvement in the robberies. He stresses that he committed shoplifting in the past only because he needed money for drugs. The police officer asks him several times how he could know about the robberies at all. Henning opts for an unbinding maneuver: "Because they (the police) wanted me to say something, I was afraid during the interview." As another general alibi, he then states that he still lives with his grandma and hence would never do "something like this."

How do these two police interviews affect the trial? At the beginning of the trial, the lawyer introduces two lines of defense that were already documented in the shared dossier. Henning is asked by the presiding judge if he would like to say anything with respect to the accusations. Again, Henning claims innocence. He gets up late, and therefore he could not be involved in the robberies. His lawyer asks him where he lives. At his grandma's, Henning says. The early defenses are reiterated.

Later on in the trial, after several witnesses have been heard, none of whom can identify either of the defendants, the presiding judge (PJ) introduces the two protocols of the police interviews.[29]

PJ: In order to proceed quickly I will introduce the police interviews of Henning X. (After he read out parts of the interview) Did you tell the truth or did you lie?

Henning: I lied. I had stomach cramps, so I just admitted everything.

PJ: Everything was just a big fat lie – just the way you do it at the police station.[30]

Henning: Yes (after his lawyer whispered in his ear) No, some things have been correct. I could reconstruct a lot due to the statements I was reproached with by the police officer.

PJ: That doesn't work. Either you had stomach cramps or you could concentrate on the statements.

Henning: First, I said that I have nothing to do with it. But then I felt worse (physically).

PJ: Well, I don't let you take me for a ride.

Henning: I just admitted to what I was reproached with. The police destroyed my first interview saying we cannot give this to the judge.

PJ: If that should be wrong you will be facing charges of wrong allegations. (*The grilling continues.*)

At the end of the trial, Henning and the other defendant are acquitted because the main witness retracts his statement.

Although Henning is protected from the full impact of his statements, they are not "disposed of once and for all." They are not dropped from the procedure, but they change their status and thus their relevance. They can no longer be ascribed to the defendant without difficulty as he rejects ownership. Still, they can count as a "minor piece of evidence", as one lawyer put it.

Summary for the German cases: Protected from the procedural past

The presented cases show that early defenses encompass various consequences in criminal proceedings, depending on when statements enter the procedure, how they are processed, and by whom they are received. In the above cases, the procedure protects the defendant during the trial, to a great extent, from the procedural history. Interestingly, the form of protection differs during the criminal legal process. In court, the defendant is confronted with weak points or conflicting versions. Prior statements are treated as stable, reliable entities. The binding does not, however, determine what is actually testified to and what is rendered relevant in court.

The formal protections from the procedural history are juxtaposed to everyday reasoning. If, for instance, somebody said something in the past, why doesn't he or she stick to it now? If somebody had good reasons prior, why didn't he or she give them right away? If somebody gives a motive for his or her actions, how is it that the actions do not seem to fit this motive? These unwritten rules are virtually infinite in number, impossible to ban by means of legal ruling.

The same is true with regards to the principle of orality. As Seibert (2004, p. 182) stresses, the spoken word in open court has to prevail, counter-procedurally, so to speak, over the content of the file. But orality in court does not mean that one is entitled to a fresh start. The early defense is still available by means of documents that were collected in the shared dossier. This written mode prevails throughout the pre-trial, while what is introduced orally in the trial is received with distrust. The staged testimony is decisive on one hand, but variously bound to written documents on the other hand.

The court's distrust or "competent skepticism" (Wolff and Müller, 1997) overhangs what is said and the unsaid. Early defenses influence the trial hearing, no matter whether they provided answers or not. The silence is rendered meaningful because it occurred at points where feasible responses were requested. A blank or gap left by the accused demands rationalization. One way not to leave a treacherous blank is, at least from the viewpoint of the accused, is not to follow the prosecution's summons in the first place. This physical absence, however, is also interpreted as meaningful silence. Systematically speaking, it obviously stands out as a decision not to produce binding effects. In this line, the formal and "unbinding" right to silence is easily undermined by shared and mundane theories of how to spot inventions.

Conclusion: Binding and unbinding

Our small collection of micro-histories supports Luhmann's model of the binding history. We encountered statements and decisions that were bound to the corresponding early defenses. The latter generated some binding (selective, formatting, reductive) force in the procedural course: during the plea-bargaining, the staging in court, or the appeal. On top of this, the eight micro-histories called for some indispensable specifications of the binding mechanisms – not everything uttered enters the procedural past; not everything that entered the past would be available later on; not everything available in the future triggers binding effects. Binding appears as a gradation rather than as a twofold structure. Defenses are more or less binding, more or less available, more or less integrated in the proceedings.

Here, we would like first to summarize the specifications for each group of micro-histories. Second, we will list those features that actually organize binding *and* unbinding. We start with brief summaries:

1. In the three English Crown Court cases, the accused entered defenses during police interviews. All the accused did so without having received prior legal advice. The Crown Court pre-trial regulated binding by means of horizontal and vertical circulations of the first defense. Its carrier, the protocol of the police interview, circulated within the

prosecution according to its division of labor from police to the CPS. The protocol circulated across the camps from CPS/Police to the defense solicitor (primary disclosure). Similar circulations were instigated on the defense site: the solicitor discloses the defense statement to the CPS (secondary disclosure). Inside the defense division of labor, the solicitor provided case materials with instructions to the defense counsel. Already during the pre-trial, the competing cases turned into shared objects that could be negotiated and contested (embracing trump cards and blanks). The circulating police protocols did not prompt binding only. They integrated the adversarial camps, which strongly built on the separation of public front regions and protected back regions, of internal and external communication. As a result, unbeneficial parts were exchanged outside of the reach of the binding mechanism. Binding, here, was conditional.

2. The two cases from South Dakota showed some resemblances to the English and German procedures. The cases did not begin with accounts from the accused but with robust evidence against him. The defense work was confronted with police reports that recorded the on-site and in-jail tests and observations of the police officers. On top of this, we find an adversarial emphasis on defense-steered inquiries. Accounts were selected and mobilized internally before they could be used publicly. Compared to the other procedures, the DUI cases comprised intense and informal pre-trial exchanges between the adversarial lawyers. The attorneys used (modified) early accounts to impress the opposing colleagues. The pre-trial exchanges refer to accounts as the means and ends of the respective deals. Utilized accounts are binding not so much for the unlikely court hearing but for the ongoing bargaining inside the lawyers' "contact system" (Luhmann, 1989). Contact systems could sustain a number of cases. The lawyers here dealt with the current matter in light of past and future negotiations.

3. The vertical (within the ensemble) and horizontal (between the ensembles) circulation of pre-trial documents appeared differently in the German cases. The differences seemed to be linked to the features that are commonly assigned to inquisitorial systems, namely, the central role of the judge, the state monopoly, and the continual nature of inquiries. Often judges remained the same at both the pre-trial and trial stages. Thus, they turned into the embodied procedural past themselves and, therefore, into concrete (not generalized) binding of others. The shared dossier binds by its omnipresence. There were, conversely, some unbinding mechanisms at work, namely, the right to silence and the principle of orality. In the German cases, interviewees at the police

station remained silent. Only in one case did the interviewee run into trouble by trying to account for the accusation. In the "no answer cases", the defense were able to develop a supportive account shielded from the procedural public. The defendants' accounts entered the court by surprise. This surprise went along with the strong notion of "orality" in German trials. The staging in court allowed for new versions that departed from the dossier or filled its blanks. The open employment of (partial, incomplete) documents triggered the unbinding effects.

Our elaboration of these micro-histories informed Luhmann's model of binding by showing various horizontal and vertical boundaries that disintegrate the procedural realm. The procedures operate within these boundaries and procedurally available front stages and unavailable back stages. They demarcate the ways in which stories and arguments are permitted, and how they are trimmed to traverse the procedural territory to best advantage. To put it differently, the proceedings are fragmented due to a range of disruptions: front and back regions, formal and informal negotiations, disclosed and undisclosed documents, admissible and inadmissible information. These disruptions obstruct a determinist and accumulative procedural past. The procedural course, thus, is far from linear. Rather, it meanders through a number of temporal relations, among which binding covers only one kind.

Unbinding is another such relation. A range of regulations works as protection against the binding past. Defendants are protected against their own words. They are protected against being trapped by good investigators at the preliminary stages. They are protected by the right to legal representation and the right to silence. The procedures include mechanisms to reopen the "funnel" (Luhmann) and to unbind the author from his or her past. To put it more generally, various procedural rules appear as steering devices that trigger, condition, postpone, or even forbid binding.

Some major components demonstrate this conclusion. The ensemble's *division of labor*, for instance, binds the client with regard to his or her representatives. This binding transpires during the professional efforts to establish an accountable and coherent case for all practical purposes. The *organized memory* is an essential precondition of binding. The cases rest on documents, files, and archives, which somehow follow the client through the procedure. Memory, however, always embraces a hidden opposite: the forgetting of what remained unrecorded, of what was not filed, or what did find its way into the archive. *Availability* introduces another procedural condition of binding – not everything documented and archived is made available at the later stages. Procedures obtain rules for how documents can be used or even cited in court. Binding is, furthermore, regulated on the basis of *passage points* that force the parties (with or without the judge) to disclose relevant details before any public contest. Through these exchanges, the parties jointly settle on how to proceed. These passage points are systematically arrayed and often scheduled and, thus, placed under time pressure. The pressure culminates in the finale *staging* of the cases vis-à-vis a more or less pre-informed audience. All these components can be turned into judicial steering devices, identifying when, by whom, to whom, and how early accounts dictate the current dealings. Overall, the binding mechanisms appear as functions of a private–public gradation with a range of internal, adversarial, or general public.

In a broader sense, the diverse features of procedure (division of labor, memory, availability, passage points, staging) point toward systematic differences. On a subsequent stage one may opt for discourse analytical notions such as "regime", "dispositive", or "apparatus" to identify procedural workings. These abstractions would indeed integrate the diverse features of binding and unbinding in single discourse productivities. The binding force fits (and re-specifies) these abstract categories, insofar as it produces regular effects no matter what the statements bound. It fits these categories insofar as it becomes an object of legal regulation and reform. However, our ethnographically noted and officially documented case episodes could show that the binding forces do not adhere to a single logic.

What is more, the binding forces meet unbinding counter forces. The two do not integrate in a dialectical or balanced system. The unbinding components resemble rights and protections; others, however, derive from suspicions vis-à-vis the lay judges, especially the jury; other unbinding simply accounts for something like the human factor and imperfection. The study of unbinding shows that the procedural frame is more heterogeneous than the system metaphor implies. This is the case because there is not just one overseeing audience involved, but various – present and absent – authoritative ones.

4
Procedural Future: The Politics of Positioning

In the first chapter, we compared the ways in which the participating members are able to realize the procedural past with the help of various means of preparation: stories, documents, files, testimonies, motions, and correspondences. As can be seen from the past, "doing procedure" takes place whenever members quote from the protocol, repeat a story, or ask questions about the facts that have already been introduced. Doing procedure takes place whenever members realize the procedural past for all practical purposes. From this perspective, it seems that the procedural course is prepared by the various members who make a contribution to it. But we need to ask: is the stage of preparation and trial a right, a systemic necessity, or a most relevant concept? Can it indeed explain why and how casework is carried out?

Our comparison of cases in various procedural regimes demonstrates that preparation means many different things. Moreover, there are cases which do not take place at all. In comparison, other cases remain postponed until the last stage of criminal proceedings, the trial. In other cases, preparation forestalls the very case components that are intended to travel as statements all the way to the trial hearing. Overall, the aim of preparing in advance is to account for various (un)certainties about the challenges that are expected and how one ensures they are met. As for our studies of "doing procedure" what one would refer to as preparation or preparing a case does not offer itself as a concept to compare doing procedure in different procedural regimes. It does not function as a *tertium comparationis*. It is not a constant task, not even a general phase of casework.

Doing procedure is backward-oriented because it refers to certain adapted or referenced materials, and therefore to a procedural past. Current moves are attached to case materials and gain certain relevance in light of that past. Doing procedure is also forward-oriented. It is contingent on anticipations of a procedural future. Without this future orientation, certain activities would make no sense whatsoever, since they do not pay out for the current procedural stage. This chapter will specify the orientation forward or ahead which is implied in the ongoing casework. The authors tackle this component by introducing various ways by which members realize positionality that can materialize fully only in the procedural future. By positionality, therefore, we refer to the set up – both enabling and disabling – of certain positions in the procedural future. Therefore, positionality comes about as being inclusive of both static social positions that come with the job, so to speak. The judge who walks into the courtroom from his or her chambers is going to preside over the proceedings in the pre-assigned position as a judge. This means that he or she is going to rely on a particular social identity. There exists a substantial literature on social identity as a position. Beginning with Goffman's famous examination of "keeping a line", the history of positionality has been very much a history of achieving a behavioral status in a community, lay or professional, vis-à-vis the members of this community (Harre and Moghaddam, 2003).

Some socio-legal research has concerned itself with the notions of positioning and positions (Haldar, 1994; Silbey and Ewick, 2003). Largely descriptive, this kind of research seeks to reveal the constraints that delimit participant positions at each stage of the criminal process, beginning with an arrest and ending with either a newly acquired freedom or, on the contrary, incarceration. In addition to the focused studies of role positions, positionality is examined in comprehensive studies of legal proceedings (Carlen, 1976; Colbert *et al.*, 2002). This strand of research emphasizes the symbolic implications of positioning the defendant in the legal process. For example, Carlen (1976) concedes that "the placing of people on public occasions such as court proceedings is strategic" (p. 21). From that perspective, specific spatial arrangements of the criminal courts inevitably produce dominance of the court over the defendant.

Preceding the spatiotemporal positions in which the defendant is physically placed by various figures of the legal process are the corresponding rules of the court, or any other legal setting. Empirically, these rules are accessible in the discursive mode. It may appear that the physical ways of placing the defendant before the law should take priority over a much less tangible activity of communication, regardless of whether this communication is conducted in private, for example, the attorney's office, or in public, for example, the court of law. In fact, standing at the heart of any court proceeding, positioning and discourse connect legal rules and institutional practices to a degree that defines the very foundations of case-making. The actors know what to do by following the prescribed paths of action. This particular perspective has been at the forefront of the legal research agenda since the inception of the studies themselves (Rüschemeyer, 1973; Cain, 1983; Philips, 1987; Conley and O'Barr, 1990; Drew, 1992; Komter, 2003).

For example, Conley and O'Barr (1990) discovered that judges of the lower courts position the defendants as "regular people" and therefore explain matters to them in terms of common sense. Komter (1998), who examines the turn-by-turn talk as it unfolds in the course of the interaction in the courtroom, demonstrates consequentionality of interactive positionality (for example, fact finding, accusations, and defenses) by ascribing to it the defendant's inability, in the end, to distinguish "between genuine and non genuine expressions of morality" (p. 97). In addition to the courtroom investigations, legal scholars dedicate much attention to the ways in which the client is positioned during the interaction with the attorney (Hosticka, 1979; Lynch, 1982; Bogoch and Danet, 1984; Yngvesson, 1988; Flood, 1991; Cain, 1994; Sarat and Felstiner, 1995). A common outcome of examining attorney–client communication has manifested itself in such issues as expertise and professional ethics. From this perspective, in addition to the judge, who "moves" the defendant by way of pronouncement, the attorney "moves" the client by way of reformulating the ordinary discourse into the legal discourse.

If we combine the static definition of role position with positioning as a way of placing a person for some practical task, we are going to arrive at the notion of positionality. Positionality originally resounded as a phenomenological concept in the work of Helmuth Plessner (1961), who, with Marjorie Green (1968), conceived of it as "the way in which an organism takes place in the environment" (p. 75). To translate this definition into legal terms means to extend the concept of the ecological body, which defines our knowledge about our own body in terms of space and time, and, at the same time, its own awareness of that knowledge, thus allowing for it to be constituted as a social body, into the symbolic body that dwells in the broader social environment. Positionality is, thus, as much an individual activity as it is an epistemic product, a particular kind of knowledge that allows the involved parties to anticipate particular outcomes of their shared activities *before* these activities are completed. It is from this perspective that positionality is always a "social positionality" (Butler, 1997, p. 36). Social positionality is observable in social rules and cultural values as well as individual actions that produce distributive effects from a specific task but being directed at the whole matter under constitution. In the legal sphere, this matter is the legal case.

The significance of procedure, from this perspective, lies in the fact that it provides a whole set of activities that allow for the positioning of the case toward some anticipated future. Opening a procedure or a case is the basic motion in this regard. By opening a case, a full range of positions – from being punished as an offender or being acquitted and normalized again – is moved to the horizon of current activities. Once a procedure is opened, a decision *must* be made about the person's guilt or innocence, regardless of what happens in its individual procedural course. In the procedural course, the realization of possible (and impossible) futures takes place to varying degrees of temporality (for example, near future, far future), varying degrees of specificity (as defendant of a specific crime; as defendant with a specific defense, and so on), and to varying degrees of selectivity (as somebody who will be no longer permitted to give evidence, or as somebody who can still enter all kinds of defenses). Again, doing procedure – or here, the procedural future – follows certain prescribed regularities, while it takes place always only in a certain case with its individual past and future. The relation of rule and case transpires in the practical dimension as well. Law-of-the-books analyses of procedure would identify a series of legally defined positions and connect them to increasing or decreasing rights and obligations. Our analysis of doing procedure does account for a series of positions, the way they are enacted in situ with certain effects for the procedural future. The procedural future is always realized in a dual sense: as legally possible and as previously accomplished. The procedural future arises from the situated activities that apply certain rules but are not determined by them.

Narrow or wide, selective or open, available or unavailable – the procedural future, understood from the moments of its doing, can take different shapes and carry various practical implications. Below we would like to compare our three procedural regimes with the focus on showing how the future evolves and what kind of future it is that is evolving. The procedural mechanism, meaning the procedural drive toward a decision, would be impossible without this future-making right from the start. We will return to this issue in the conclusion, after discussing various ways by which positionality is accomplished in the US context, the German context, and the English context. We start with the US-American State court procedure which emphasizes positioning toward the future, meaning that the participating members achieve their positionality within a specific procedural course.

Positionality in the US context

For the defendant in the context of the US criminal system, the first position is achieved with arrest and booking. It is then that an individual's ordinary standing outside of law gets disrupted for the first time, by someone's (for example, a police officer's) judgment that gives the person the ex-centric sense of not belonging. In accomplishing the first position, the US criminal procedure delimits the defendant to certain context-specific rights such as the right to silence (governed by the rule of communication); the right to a counselor (rule of representation); and the right to a trial (rule of procedure). The discursive vehicle for these rights is the Miranda rule.[1] The most tangible outcome of the arrest is the constraint of the defendant's body: no longer free to move at will, it loses full possession of itself. This loss is defined in pragmatic terms as a matter of relevance; the everyday identity is no longer definitional in the court of law. A suitable procedural identity must be constructed first. This identity is constructed in accordance with certain distinctly shaped and sequentially organized activities.

For example, the arrest must be preceded by an investigation, which, in practice, already subjects the arrestee to various discursive procedures (for example, "being held for questioning"). The person who is set to undergo these motions is categorized as the "suspect". Regardless of whether the charges hold the suspect in jail or let him or her avoid incarceration, unless they are dismissed by the prosecution as unsubstantiated, the suspect's next position is in court at the stage of First Appearance. It is at that stage that the client will hear another kind of dividing judgment, this time from the highest authority in the court of law, the judge, who, by announcing the charge or charges against them, positions the defendant before the law as the "defendant". To consolidate this position, the court offers the defendant the services of an attorney. The latter can be hired earlier, in anticipation of the subpoena, but typically, the first-time client tends to wait until the judge forwards the charge.

From that point onwards, the position of the defendant changes again. Together with the attorney, the client will form a defense ensemble. According to Komter, the first task for the attorney is to turn the first-hand knowledge of the case which is "owned" by the defendant into usable second-hand knowledge (1998, p. 12). A typical venue for the transfer is the first attorney–client conference (Sherr, 1986). The criteria for the attorney's evaluation vary widely; some are presented as objective: those dependant on the rules pertaining to adjudicating a certain level and type of crime; others are shown to be subjective and depend on the patterns established in regards to processing certain cases by the local courts and their executors. Still, somewhere in between there lie specific circumstances of the case which will be determined at a later date, after the evidentiary disclosure. In the context of the US criminal justice system, the disclosure of evidence is a crucial point for determining the defendant's positionality. It is at this point that the defense ensemble makes the decision concerning a choice between two procedural trajectories: plea-bargain or trial.

As a speedy and economical alternative to trial, in the course of the last 20 years plea-bargain has become a way of doing justice in its own right. This means that plea-bargain exhibits a distinct structure with clearly delineated activities (for example, offering a deal, establishing negotiable points, offering a counter-proposal, conducting a preliminary negotiation, and so on) (Maynard, 1984; Lynch, 1994). The choice of one or the other route is typically made right before or right after the preliminary hearing. The strength and scope of the prosecution's evidence may indeed be sufficient to persuade the defense that plea-bargaining is the only way to mitigate the inevitable defeat. Likewise, for certain crimes, such as DWUI, for example, the charges are not worth fighting for. As the US informant intimated, "you spend thousands of dollars on the dog and pony show that has only a two percent chance to exonerate you, and then you begin to think that maybe three hundred dollars in fines and a misdemeanor on your record is not that bad of a thing, especially so if you lose."

For the constitution of the defendant's identity, the crossroads between the two options spells out two possible ways of approaching the final stage of the criminal process, the sentencing. In relation to the sentencing, plea-bargain defines the defendant as "guilty by own admittance", while the trial route leaves the defendant with the original plea of "not guilty" (automatically written during the first appearance). In the first case, the defendant finds him- or herself in the position of waiting for the sentencing; in the second case, the defendant awaits the trial. The two kinds of procedure differ so much so as to allow us to suggest that they produce different procedural identities. Below we present several brief analyses of the ethnographic data collected at the US site. In our analyses we focus on the plea-bargained cases. This choice is stipulated by the suggestion that for certain kinds of crimes plea-bargain should be considered a systemic preference. The crime in focus here is DUI (driving under the influence).

First position: Arrest

For illustration of the position that emerges at the site of the arrest, we present an excerpt taken from the transcript of the police videotape that was turned in by the prosecuting attorney to the defense attorney as evidence. The videotape was made by the camera installed in the police cruiser. It was handed over to the defense attorney by the State attorney as "discovery". The presented episode features the first five minutes of the arrest. It takes place in the summer season on a Friday night at the time when local bars close their business and their patrons return home, very often, under the influence of alcohol. The local police are aware of this phenomenon and make it their business to investigate it. There is often a police cruiser sitting at the junction of the main street and the "strip", or on a short stretch of the local road along the river that houses eight bars, restaurants, and a gentleman's club. The local lore stresses the allegedly predatory behavior of the local police who, on a regular basis at the weekends, "stalk the unfortunate and the stupid", as the US informant put it. The case that began with the video footage testifies to the outcome of that practice. The actors include: two male police officers (designated as PO1 and PO2), two citizens, a man (K) and a woman (L), and the radio dispatcher (R).[2]

Mound City, Central State, 5 June 2004
3:14:42 AM

001 PO2: He's slowing down (10) now we're at the far end of the ...
002 PO2: (2-second pause) Seems like stoppin' for a yellow light
003 PO2: Now he <u>did</u> stop for a yellow light.
004 PO2 (on the radio): 3-60-5 (2.5) 10-44
005 R: [unintelligible]
006 PO2 (on the radio): 10-44-36-Victor-0-3-2, 36-Victor-0-3-2 (.)
007 PO2: We are on the [the] junction of Marian and Illinois.
008 R: Clear for 10-21.
The suspect's car stops. The police cruiser stops.
PO1 gets out of the police car approaches the suspect's car from the left.
009 PO1: Open the window (3) [to the other police officer]. Can't get the window open. He's still trying (4) Still can't get the window open ... (6)
The driver opens the door.

010   PO1: How are you, sir?
011   K: Hi (2) Ah good.
012   PO1: Driver's license with you?
013   K: Yo.
       PO1 is inspecting the suspect's driver's license.
014   PO1: (15) Mr. Tooth? Do you know why I stopped you?
015   K: I was going too fast?
016   PO1: No, as you were coming down the road there you stopped
       for a yellow light. (2.5) Is there any reason why?
017   K: I don't know.
018   PO1: Hm. Smelling- you're smelling a little bit like alcohol,
       have you been drinking tonight?
019   K: Yes, <u>sir</u>.
       PO2 approaches the car from the right.
020   PO1: (2) Do you have proof of insurance for the car? Is this her
       car or your car?
021   K: Hers.
022   PO1: Where do you live at? (5) Where do you <u>live</u>?
       [unintelligible]
023   PO1: (15) OK, I want you come with me please.
       K gets out of the car and shuts the door. Both officers and the suspect
       move towards the police car.
023   PO1: Have a seat. Did you drink tonight quite a bit?
024   K: Yeah. To tell you the truth, yeah.
025   PO1: All right. Will you take some sobriety tests for me?
026   K: (2.5) Oh man. Jeez. I guess.
027   PO1: Okay. What I want you to do is come and shift on your
       seat so that you kinda face me a little bit. Can you do that? I'm
       gonna turn the camera around a little bit for us all right?

From this instance it becomes clear how the rules of criminal procedure
orchestrate the actions of the police officer and the emergent interactional pattern. The "probable cause" that implies "suspicious activity"
transforms observing as an activity of patrolling the area into identifying a "suspicious vehicle" (line 001–007), checking and confirming
the suspicion with the dispatcher (line 006), and establishing the spatiotemporal coordinates for the event under investigation (line 007).
Next comes the question–answer session (lines 10–22), which ends with
the police officer requesting an explanation. The right of the police officer to ask questions and expect answers is embodied in the role of the
police officer who enacts this role vis-à-vis the role of the suspect. It is

within the general role of law enforcement then that the police officers in the above excerpt elect to exercise their interactional statuses.

Specifically, in line 014, the police officer poses an open question that contains the officer's reference to his own actions ("Mr. Tooth? Do you know why I stopped you?"). The account given by Mr. Tooth (line 015: "I was going too fast?") deviates from the police officer's observation (line 003: "Now he <u>did</u> stop for a yellow light"), causing further "fishing". The following exchange that occurs in lines 016–019 creates a context-specific interactional pattern: (a) statement from the police officer (" ...you stopped for a yellow light... "); (b) request for an account from the citizen ("Is there any reason why?"); (c) inability of the citizen to produce an account to the officer's satisfaction ("I don't know"); (d) a hybrid observation/request for account ("Hm. Smelling- you're smelling a little bit like alcohol, have you been drinking tonight?"); and, finally, (e) the citizen's admission of the probable violation ("Yes, <u>sir</u>"), which becomes the act of agreeing with the police officer. Next, after some formalities concerning the car's insurance, the citizen is asked to follow the police officer for further questioning. The pivotal point which separates one activity (questioning–answering) from another (requesting–fulfilling) arrives at lines 023 and 024, when the police officer asks the citizen if he has been drinking. Not a crime in itself, drinking becomes such only after the suspect has been tested for the permissible amount of alcohol in their blood.

Therefore, it is paramount for the police officer to obtain the person's permission to conduct the tests. Their results will constitute the bulk of the prosecutorial evidence. The laboratory testing is usually carried out on the premises (for example, jail or hospital); it is preceded by a PBT and a number of on-site alertness and concentration tests. In line 027, the officer begins to prepare the suspect for these tests. The suspect has the right to refuse them; however, the emphasis on cooperation, on the one hand, and for those better informed, the knowledge of the DoMV's rule about the automatic suspension of the driving license for a year, often prevent the suspect from refusing to fulfill the requests made by the police officer.[3] The need for the officer to support his preliminary observations with situational evidence of criminal liability requires a particular interactional status as "collector of facts" or "evidence-maker". Most importantly, the recording of the performed tests does not just "contain" the evidence but also provides justification for its collection. The physical removal of the defendant's body from the social environment at large and the placement of this body into an environment (police cruiser), where it is going to be manipulated and those manipulations are going to be recorded as the facts of the matter, turn the probable suspect into a would-be defendant, the first position-identity.

Second position: Attorney–client conference

In order for the first position to hold, so to speak, it must be further proceduralized, this time in accordance with the rules of the court. Implicitly, these rules have already been in play during the arrest. As the previous section has shown, the police do not just collect evidence; they construct it on the basis of the rules of discovery. The construction continues when the defendant meets his attorney for the first time. During the first consultation, the defendant will be given an evaluation of the case in terms of its outcome. The assessment will allow the defendant to assume a specific procedural position. Depending on the choice of the strategy (plea-bargain or trial), the defendant will be introduced to the strategy-relevant rules of the court, and the accompanying rules of communication. Below we would like to show how in one instance of the DWUI the defendant receives a case assessment from his attorney. The exemplar consists of an excerpt from a recorded attorney–client conversation. The conversation took place in the law firm. In the excerpted case, the defendant is designated as R. The attorney is designated as A:

260	A:	Alright anyway on your deal here (.) what we're gonna
261		do is when we get the uh arrest reports (.) we're
262		going to go ahead and look 'em over to see what they
263		say and uh you go to court on uh Monday at one
264		o'clock plead not guilty uh and uh (1.8) and
265		normally what they're gonna do is they're gonna set
266		you up for a ↑jury trial↓ or a trial court trial
267		bench trial and u:h uh just say well (.) I
268		understand that I'm gonna appear back here on the
269		nineteenth now (.) what that's gonna do is giving me
270		three weeks basically to ↑go through↓ and to discuss
271		it with Richard and make some decisions about wha-
272		which way we're gonna go (.) ↑I would estimate that
273		(.) >it's up to you< but uh the only way you're going
274		to u-↑walk↓ out of that court room is by trying the
275		case and have the jury acquit you (.) but again (.)
276		you know (.) justice costs <u>money</u> and and I don't
277		think you wanna spend four or five thousand ↑<u>Dollars</u>

278		to uh beat some charges that are really only gonna
279		cost you two or three hundred dollars of ↓fines (.)
280		but what I'm my job is going to be is to try and get
281		the absolute best deal I ca:n an now=
282	R:	= yeah

Before approaching this episode, we must note that in the interaction preceding this excerpt, the attorney collected all the preliminary facts: name, place, charge, and a summary of the pertinent circumstances (for example, "what happened"). During the first conference, textualization takes place by way of the attorney's notes. The notes will be filed together with various legal documents (for example, letters to the client, prosecuting attorney, clerk of courts, or potential witnesses). Textualization serves several purposes: most mundanely, it is a mnemonic device; on the other hand, as an officer of the court, the attorney must leave a record of exchanges. Here, textualization affects the client's identity in the same manner that a personal identification does: it verifies certain basic facts, leaving other matters on the periphery of the case as pre-facts. Since the defense file is composed by the attorney, it is technically speaking "owned" by him. The file provides the common epistemological ground for both the attorney and his or her client. It also provides a frame of reference for the discussion.

For example, in the excerpt above, the attorney refers to the documented evidence (lines 261–263: "when we get the uh arrest reports (.) we're going to go ahead and look'm over to see what they say") in order to outline the preliminary strategy (plea-bargain instead of trial) and then contextualizes this strategy in terms of the upcoming procedural stage (line 263–264: "go to court on uh Monday at one o'clock plead not guilty"). The three "items" are bound together by the attorney's reasons for the plea-bargain agreement; in this excerpt, they are mostly financial (line 276: "justice costs money"). However, there is an important omission which, for the sake of the case, needs to be reconstructed from ethnographic observations. It is the procedural nature of the crime that has been omitted here. In the USA, DWUI is a crime adjudicated on two levels: administratively, by the Department of Motor Vehicles, and, criminally, in the court of the lower instance. The administrative punishment (loss of the operator's license) is often more severe than the criminal one (small fine and a misdemeanor on the record). One cannot claim that DWUI is specific to the US criminal code; yet, its administration is (cf. Schumann, 1977, pp. 73–84).

According to my informant, DWUI is "a very difficult crime to defend." Indeed, prosecuting DWUI is a relatively straightforward job due to a strong evidentiary base: police procedure requires that video-taping should begin from the moment of the pull-over. The videotape made at the time of the arrest, plus the on-the-spot sobriety tests, and finally the blood test, all this evidence contributes to a DWUI case. From that perspective, unless the probable cause or a specific procedure violated during the collection of evidence is in question, the defense rarely has a good DWUI case/defense. The collected evidence is tested for usability on several occasions and by several parties: first after it is passed on in the documentary form (Police Report and test results) to the prosecuting attorney by the police, then at the preliminary hear-ing in a discursive mode deployed as a pre-contest to the main event of the trial. The specificity of this position manifests itself not only in the US-systematic rules of evidence, or the specificity of the crime, but also the direct connection of what counts as evidence.

Third position: Discovery

The disclosure of evidence (discovery) is a decisive moment for the def-endant's positionality. Executed under the Rule of Disclosure, the trans-fer of evidence takes place within a certain period of time. For the preliminary evaluation of the evidence, the attorney does not need to meet with the client. My ethnographic experience shows that in over 80 percent of the observed cases, the attorney prefers to write a letter to the client, where the meaning of the evidence can be explained with an eye on the upcoming strategy and the discussion of other options can be minimized. The law of evidence is epistemological: it imposes on witness' accounts the law's views on what constitutes a fact and what sources of information can be considered as veritable. However, lay peo-ple come to court with their own epistemological assumptions; hence a conflict between the official discourse and "folk narrations". The attor-ney mitigates this conflict by writing a regular update letter to the client. One may call the written mode of information exchange a form of con-trol; however, it also must be noted that, as an officer of the court and a member of the bar, the attorney is "recommended" to keep a record of his or her advice. In turn, we suggest that writing helps proceduralize the case and, thus, constitute the client as the client by describing his or her problem as requiring a stepwise solution. For example:

> Find enclosed paperwork on your case, including the arrest reports, the complaint, and the other related information. Please review it

carefully. The most important thing is the arrest report. As you can see, the arresting officer was Officer Pollman of the PPD. The police received a report that your Explorer was seen leaving the Chuck Wagon after a fight. Furthermore, the taxi service also called in as you were driving across the bridge, and advised them that you were having a problem driving straight. The cops then caught up with you, and made the same observation. By the time you ran over the traffic cones, they had already decided to stop you. You refused to do the alphabet and counting test, but you did try to do the finger to thumb dexterity test. He also said that you failed in the horizontal gaze test, and you blew a .202 on the PBT. You were then arrested for DUI and transported to jail. It is good that you did not answer any of the questions or gave blood. The PBT, although outrageously high, is not admissible in Court. Therefore, we can probably do o.k. The State's Attorney is never going to give you a reduction given the PBT. Please get back to me. As you are aware, we have a preliminary hearing on Feb.18, 2004.

(Letter to the Client, 06/02/2004)

This correspondence shows how the defendant moves along the procedural belt that schedules his arrival at the Preliminary Hearing less than two weeks after this letter. At the preliminary hearing the attorney will question the evidence, and, regularly, will keep the not guilty plea. The preliminary hearing is significant, for it is at this point that the client appears before the court for the first time with his attorney. As a defendant, he will be sitting next to his attorney. Apart from the general information provided prior to the hearing by way of introducing himself, his participation will be limited to brief conferences with his attorney, who, at all times, will carry out the questioning of witnesses and the discussing of evidence. This passive position makes the client a witness to his own re-enacted crime. Before the hearing, the attorney will prepare the client for witnessing the discussion of the matters "about" him. In this position, the identity of the client bifurcates into that of the subject of and the object in the proceedings. As a subject, the defendant is subjected to the course of the proceedings. As an object, he embodies the purpose and the content of the proceedings. This "reflexive" position is based on the presumption of accessibility, except that by having been positioned for access, the client could no longer be flexible as to his own perspective, for, by now, it will have coincided with the position of the argument. Of course, the defendant can take a more proactive stance, if requested; however, an opportunity to testify will most likely not be taken unless his attorney is assured that this will be likely to lead to the dismissal of the charge(s).

Shortly after the preliminary hearing the attorney brings the defendant into another position: presenting the balance of the case from the position of the judge, by way of an anticipatory judgment. If the preliminary hearing is waived, this final estimate is given in lieu of the preliminary hearing. Skipping a venue does not connote a defeat, especially if it is an unnecessary step in the process, where the degree of ambiguity should remain high due to the object under discussion, the evidence. The defense attorney would want to keep this ambiguity, for it helps him or her maneuver for increasingly more advantageous positioning (Shuy, 2001). The rule of the court that allows this jumping of a procedural stage takes into account the possibility that the other side could approach the prosecution for plea-bargain negotiations, while, at the same time, still in action, the rules of evidence create possibilities for accepting and rejecting old and/or generating new evidentiary items (claims). The connection between the rules of evidence (rules of procedure) and the rules of the court (rules of proceedings) fixes the client's position as an attendant, that is, someone in attendance for the duration of the coming matters. In the DWUI case excerpted below, the client's position gets reinforced as the matters come to an end at the preliminary hearing stage, after the attorney concedes that the prosecution case is as strong as was originally expected. For the client, the attorney's concession means that they agree to the plea of guilty and are scheduled to face the judge one last time during the sentencing. The end result of sentencing is the attorney's letter to the client summarizing the case in terms of its outcome:

> This letter confirms my appearance with you on [Date, Place]. As you are aware, you were charged with felony possession, DUI, Reckless Driving, Contributing to the Delinquency of a Minor (2), and Intentional Damage. The plea bargain resulted in one plea of DUI, which resulted in a $60.00 fine. You also have to take an alcohol evaluation and successfully complete the recommendations. You are supposed to have the evaluation done within thirty days, but if you have to go and fight fires, they will give you an extension. This went really well. You suffered virtually no costs and this matter is behind you.
>
> (Letter to the Client, 08/03/2004)

One may say that after the sentencing, the defendant's procedural identity has been accomplished. No longer a defendant he becomes a criminal, who is archived, and if archive is to be understood dynamically, the legal trail will continue to position the subject for various enactments, whether in subsequent evaluations or further brushes with the law. In the excerpt above the attorney sounds reassuring: "This went really well." His perspective is understandable: the final stage in the criminal process was accomplished, and the case is no longer active. Yet, for the defendant, the meaning of this position goes far beyond the judge's pronouncement. This is where the difference between the probationary conviction and the conviction with incarceration seems to be especially significant. In the first case, the legal system builds the criminal's identity on the anticipation that it could be finalized. A person on probation is not quite a criminal. In the second case, the fact of imprisonment coincides with the definitional status for one's identity. At the same time, regardless of outcome, whether he is put on probation or sentenced, the subject does not return to the ordinary world from the same place that he began his defense. There are new and odd senses of the self that have been incorporated into the living presence of the person, who has been positioned and re-positioned in the sphere that until recently was outside of his reach. After the sentencing, it has become a legitimate constitutive terrain for his identity.

Positionality in the English context

In the English criminal process, the client is also given a wide choice of positions; at the same time, his or her journey toward the crossroads that separate the trial from the voluntary plea is rather different. There are a number of categories used in the English legal process that signal procedural positions (for example, suspect, client, defendant). Significant is their successive order: the participant has to assume one position in order to reach the next one. Before we present positionality in action, we would like to give an overview of those role-positions which are accomplished by way of adhering to the successive order of the English Crown Court. The starting point for an individual to become an object of the legal process is *suspect*. Similarly to the US case, this position-identity is called in to assist in police investigations. It is therefore closely linked to the "police powers", for example, search warrants (Police and Criminal Evidence Act 1984, pp. 15, 16), entry of premises (ibid., p. 17), seizure of evidence (p. 19), or arrest (ibid., p. 24). The police powers enable the police to gather evidence to support or rebuff the suspicion. The suspect, in return, is granted various means of protection, such as the right to remain silent, or the right to legal representation.

The latter provides the immediate grounds for the next position-identity – *client*. The English system offers a general financial scheme to cover the costs of legal representation. The legal aid scheme finances "all such assistance as is usually given by a solicitor or counsel in the steps preliminary or incidental to any proceedings", plus "advice and assistance to any appeal" (Blackstone's 1998: D 27.6, p. 1662). The law distinguishes between compulsory legal aid (for appeal cases or serious charges such as murder) and discretionary legal aid. The latter is decided in the light of the likely sentence, the legal properties of the case, and the "nature of the defence" (ibid., p. 1663). Becoming a client requires a completed and signed contract ("Form B"). In line with the category of suspect is that of the *defendant*. After the Crown or Prosecution (CPS), the defendant is named as the "second party of criminal proceedings" (Blackstone's 1998: D 2.37, p. 1032). The identity of the defendant is performed by way of an official indictment: a formal speech act declared by the CPS. In itself, the defendant category is neutral: unless the person under criminal charges is found guilty, he or she is considered to be innocent. Similarly to the US case, the prosecution carries the burden of showing "guilt beyond reasonable doubt". The defendant can be freed from the official accusations in various ways. The prosecution can rest the case, the judge can instruct that there is no case to prosecute, or the jury can decide the verdict of "not guilty".

Differently to the inquisitorial rationale, which prohibits the defendant to speak on his or her behalf, in the English context the defendant can be a *witness* for the defense. The defendant's testimony, although given in self-defense, shall be treated equally to any other testimony. The right to testify cannot be turned into an obligation; the defendant cannot be questioned against his or her will. Once willing to testify, the defendant must also be available for cross-examination. Being a witness turns the defendant into an epistemic subject for the court's truth-finding mechanics. The defendant's positioning in court is therefore split into an obligatory part (no trial without the defendant being present) and a strategic part (testifying or not). Once the defendant is found guilty, the potentiality of this position is turned into an actuality. For the study of positionality, another aspect is vital: the convict cannot be questioned by the sentencing judge in the light of the jury's guilty verdict. Matters such as regret or remorse are left to the lawyer's mitigation or outsourced to psychiatrists, forensic psychologists, and probation officers.

Taking position in the defense ensemble

The emergence of the central position in the English context can be easily overlooked. The transcripts and field notes are used to inform about the client–lawyer relationship, the use of control, power, expertise, and so on, as if the relationship was always already in place. Our question is: *how is the client actually placed next to a lawyer?* We suggest that positioning here is a double movement for both, the 'client' and 'the representative'. There are actually three paths that organize the 'coming together' or 'sitting next to each other': The usual way to get next to a (new) client is to be called by him or her from the police station. This first meeting on foreign ground is highly problematic since the lawyer is supposed to act for the client who is in fact not yet his or her client. In other words, the representational position is not yet in place. Positionality here means: the 'client' is acted for and positioned in prospect of his likely future status. At this point, the lawyer is confronted with some ambiguity; he or she needs to act on very general grounds of fairness and rights. The lawyer does not know the case yet and, thus, how to intervene in the client's name. Comparable instances for a first get-together are preliminary hearings. All criminal charges arrive at the lowest court first. The Magistrates' Court hearings place 'clients' and 'solicitors' right next to each other. Limited and enabled by the public defender scheme, the solicitor needs to gather sufficient information in the minimum of time prior to the hearing (Scheffer *et al.*, 2007).

To position client and lawyer next to each other for an expected Crown Court matter is more complex due to the professional division of labor at this level of jurisdiction. In England, solicitors are not accredited to represent clients in this court setting. They require the in-court representation of a barrister, who would then be briefed and instructed by the solicitor to speak for the case in the Crown Court. In this line, the client needs to be motivated to attend scheduled meetings and talks. Conferences with the counsel are arranged prior to the trial hearing and form an integrated defense ensemble. It is an act of team-building, so to speak. Often these conferences take place right before the hearing. This dual representation gives way for a peculiar division of labor between the solicitor as caseworker and the barrister as the case's voice in court. There are two major channels for integrating these triads. Introductory and sensitive issues are dealt with during face-to-face conferences. Motivating and routine issues are dealt with through a rhythmical flow of letters. However, all the meetings and correspondence are placed in the charge of the solicitor. In turn, it is the barrister who instructs the solicitor. By means of correspondence, the solicitor does not just circulate case information and communicate requests, but positions the client within the defense ensemble and the criminal proceeding. The shared dates, ideas, information, and legal motions link up firstly the solicitor and his client, and secondly these two with the barrister. The emergent defense ensemble thereby constitutes the defendant's identity as a partial identity that is restricted by the hierarchy and division of labor.

Professional positioning of the 'absent' client

The solicitor's letters organize the defense ensemble as the professional site. They establish a defense case as a strategic-practical entity on the grounds of the "client's instructions". The letters are discursive acts kept out of reach for the procedural public. They circulate internally. At the outset, they remain unavailable for the adversary party, the prosecution. The letters fulfill various purposes in the developing case. They perform the client's positionality in the procedural course. For instance, in a case of burglary the solicitor in charge of the Magistrates' Court formulates a letter in order to instruct her colleague. The letter anticipates the course of law, here the passing on of the matter from the Magistrates' Court to the Crown Court and the likelihood of a trial. The letter performs the client's positionality as a defendant to be represented in a Crown Court trial. The solicitor transfers the case to her colleague in charge of Crown Court matters:

> Please find herewith this file as this matter has now been committed to the Crown Court. Plea and Directions hearing is to take place on 8 June 2001 at Midtown Crown Court (. . .)

> You will note from Client's statement, that he denies the offence of burglary. However, he would plead guilty to an offence of receiving stolen goods. I have already written to CPS offering this, see my letter to them . . . , but at that time they were not willing to consider this offer. The only evidence to suggest that Client was involved in the burglary is the statement of PC Andrew Catch who attended the property the subject of the burglary in a police van. He says he saw Miller at the right hand side of the property which is an end terrace. He says he heard Miller shout 'Police, Police' and he was shouting towards the house. (. . .)

> You will see from the statement that Jack denies shouting anything. He says he was sat on a wall at the back of the alleyway which is

down the side of the property and that he simply turned round when he saw the Police Officer and jumped off the wall so that the Police Officer could have only seen his back after officially spotting him. There is a possibility that the two boys in the property saw the Police and it was one of them who shouted 'Police, Police' before they ran out of the house...

The information served here exposes the client to possible future positions: (1) as the represented (but absent) *defendant* in the plea-bargaining negotiations. This position is envisaged by comparing the strength of the case ("The only evidence is..."). It suggests a strong negotiation position. It announces future statements (He "will state that..."); (2) it envisions the client as a *witness* for the defence that counters the allegations ("Jack will say that the two co-defendants were responsible for the burglary") and that is cross-examined in the light of the police officers allegations; (3) additionally, the communication contains further information on the mitigating factors deduced from the client's "character". The solicitor adds "a report from one of Jack's former teachers", some insights on him being "expelled from School", or that Jack "suffers from ADHD and is prescribed Ritalin." This information anticipates the logic of mitigation performed in a common sentencing hearing. The served material also helps calculate and communicate the likely sentence in the case of a conviction. The three positions are not just imagined or anticipated, but actively kept in play. They are cared for as options for all procedural and practical purposes.

The solicitor–solicitor communication is only one step in the professional case-making. The exchange between the solicitor and barrister is the next step. This time positioning takes place without the client. In the "instructions to counsel" the solicitor repeats the threefold positionality. The client is placed in front of the barrister as a capable and useful witness, an agreeable and firm principal of plea-bargaining negotiations, and a concerned subject of the sentencing calculations. Three core phrases introduce the case to the barrister in its current state:

Jack will plead not guilty and defence statement has been filed.

Jack would plead guilty to receiving stolen tobacco.

Jack will say that the two co-defendants were responsible for the burglary.... Counsel will see that Jack only has one previous caution for shop lifting.

The three phrases cover the three optional positions vis-à-vis the law: the client as a witness (next to others), as the only principal to the plea-bargaining, and as one measure (amongst others) for the sentencing. In Jack's case, the preferred choice of legal action is finally signaled in a letter to the barrister. The solicitor does not discuss (and reject) the "Police, Police" claim any longer, but presents a useful collection of mitigating factors that will later be used in the sentencing hearing:

> The solicitor's list of mitigating factors entails "the value of the stolen tobacco was minimal; the offence could not be classed as sophisticated; Jack's admitted involvement in the whole incident was extremely limited; he had no idea of the ultimate destination of the goods and whether the burglars themselves were expecting any profit; he played no part in the burglary and had no idea it was to be committed until it was, as it were, well under way."

Is this a hint that the professional team is heading toward a plea-bargain? Do they finalize the case in this direction? These questions have an immediate pertinence for the defendant who has so far been largely absent from any decision-making that could define his position.

Taking the statement

Taking a statement is central for solidifying the procedural identity in the English context. The statement serves as a key instrument which is used to keep the various procedural positions open. I claim that this openness by case-making is kept until shortly before a (jointly with the CPS) scheduled trial hearing. Its role can be observed in the initial letters to the client. After the solicitor reminds Jack that the "Form B" needs to be completed and signed, she invites him and his parents to attend the law firm:

> In view of the further information which has now been served on ourselves, I would suggest that an appointment is made for Jack and Mrs Miller to attend at this office to go through matters. A Barrister will be introduced in due course to represent Jack in the Plea and Directions Hearing. However, I do need to take a full statement form of what he recalls of the incident on the 7th June 2002. I do have access to his taped interview and I also have a copy of the statement which he provided to the Police when he made the formal complaint against the Aggrieved in these proceedings. Which will help.
>
> (June 12, 2002)

Taking a statement does not mean that the lawyer conducts an open interview. It rather means that she asks the client about the "taped interview" containing his version of 'what really happened'. Taking a statement, moreover, is not at all a completed task once the guided interview is finished. Taking a statement rather resembles an ongoing writing process, moving from the first draft, to the second and third, and so on. The drafts display the complex composition of the client's positionality. The drafts provide excellent data to study how the client is placed on the legal conveyor. The completed statement is used in various contexts inside the defense ensemble; it is also directed toward the adversary. The written statement serves as the instructions for the solicitor; it is distributed within the defense ensemble; it provides the basis for the official "defense statement"; it gives associative space for the assessment of the competing case; and it serves as the instructions for the barrister. To conclude, the statement orchestrates the defense ensemble according to a *single* case. Inside this ensemble, some crucial positioning takes place.

The following series of statement drafts shows a drive toward the 'best possible case' (for the defense). It mobilizes the case and the client as if it/he would have to stand trial. The drafting provides grounds for a beneficial testimony vis-à-vis the judge and jury in the open court *and* for a successful bargaining for the truth of the matter in a deal with the prosecuting counsel. It represents the routine appropriation of defense cases by Crown Court solicitors. Below you find quotes from Jack's statement in its two versions. The selected episode tells us about what happened when the Police officer entered the scene:

> I carried on waiting for them on the wall but then I saw a police van pull up. It pulled into the alley way and a police man saw me. I thought to myself 'I'm off'. I turned and jumped down behind the wall and ran towards the cul-de-sac. As I was running off I heard a lot of banging. I am not sure whether that was the van door or someone coming out of the house. I could not tell as I was facing the opposite direction making my getaway. I did not shout anything when I saw the police. I just wanted to get out of the way. I still had the tobacco in my pocket.
>
> (May 10, 2001)

> I carried on waiting for them on the wall but more or less immediately after I assumed they had gone back into the house for a second time I saw a police van pull up. But this time I had put the tobacco

into the pocket of my trainer top. It pulled into the alley way and a police man saw me. I thought to myself 'I'm off'. As I was running off I heard a lot of banging. I am not sure whether that was the van door or someone coming out of the house. I could not tell as I was facing the opposite direction making my getaway. I did not shout anything when I saw the police. I just wanted to get out of the way. I still had the tobacco in my pocket.

(June 5, 2001)

Comparing these two versions, it becomes clear that the changes are of minor relevance. The 'witness' still claims that he did not shout "Police, Police". He still sat on the wall waiting. He still had tobacco in his pocket. However, a number of clues signal the aims of positioning: not directly for a plea-bargaining route but for a mitigating session. The positionality embedded in the changes points toward the client in the position of a witness and toward the possible usage of his testimony against the main witness for the CPS: the arresting police officer. The second draft specifies the first version by adding "a second time" and "the pocket of my trainer top". Additionally, the phrase "I turned and jumped ... " is deleted. To put it briefly, the three changes offer one direction to cross-examine the arresting police officer 'just in case'. As a counter witness, Jack would specify his appearance and that of the two others at the scene. This could, in contrast to the police version, suggest that the officer could not identify the one who was actually shouting "Police, Police".

In sum, statements are not prepared for obtaining a singular position. A strong claim of innocence keeps several options open: a "not guilty plea" plus the adversarial contest in open court (including the defendant as a witness for the defense), a "fact bargain" that seeks to lower the involvement of the defendant, or a plea-bargaining (in order to grant at least some discount for the plea).

Client and barrister in court

How can the lawyer keep on positioning the client? How is it possible to change the direction of the case in the course of the proceeding, and, here, even at the very last stages? These flexibilities, I argue, refer to stabilities in the staging of the claims and cases. The open, un-decided positionality is possible, because it can affect standardized procedural stages. The Crown Court is such a set of standards that allow the anticipation of various positions in the course of a trial hearing or a sentencing hearing. The fixed positioning in court – in terms of temporal/sequential and spatial order – allows for the anticipation of cases, both as performances in front of the judges ("judge of the law" and "judges of the facts (jurors)") and as measurements to contrast the strengths and weaknesses of prosecution and defense cases (Scheffer, 2005). But the Crown Court does not only provide stable horizons for 'last notice' anticipations. It also requires some prior consultations in order to fit together the sequential and spatial arrangements. In terms of the defense case in general, it needs to be outlined generally prior to the hearing. The same is true for the appearance of the ensemble in court because the defendant is, in contrast to the US court or the German court, detached from the barrister. He or she cannot instruct Counsel in the course of the proceeding, or during the ongoing examination of witnesses. He or she cannot whisper ideas, doubts, or impressions. The detachment is only partially overcome by using the solicitor as a medium. In the Crown Court, there are two different speech positions generally destined for the defendant. Firstly, the defendant's bench: it is placed opposite the judge and is distanced from the lawyer. From here, the defendant is talked about. Differently to the German court, the defendant is not allowed to speak back or give comments. It is the lawyer who answers any questions that are asked about the defendant. The only exception is the first question of the plea: guilty or not guilty?

Another position is constructed at the witness stand. From here, the defendant can testify to the jury as *witness*. The defendant-witness, like any other witness, is only allowed to answer questions. The willingness to testify is encouraged by the relative "impression control" during the friendly examination. The counsel is, differently to inquisitorial, judge-centered examinations, able to introduce 'his witness' with "friendly questions". Here positionality is facilitated by means of interactional standards and (discursive) "conditions of possibility." Pre-trial preparation anticipates this platform for self-presentation. In other words, the witness statement is prefigured by means of drafting a statement, by rehearsing and contrasting it. The option to speak out as a witness remains an unpredictable risk due to the cross-examination. Similarly to the judge's questions in an inquisitorial context, the cross-examination creates a moment of contingency. This does not mean that the client as witness is at the mercy of the cross-examining barrister. There are ways to estimate and prepare the likely lines of questioning. There are tests to confront the 'witness-client' with critical questions prior to the hearing. Defense barristers anticipate hostile questions on the grounds of the indictment, the disclosed evidence, and (generally) by knowing the counterpart from the Chambers or previous trials.

In the English context, the defendant's positionality is finalized only on the last day in court. Before that the case is prepared in consideration with the possible range of positions: as a defendant and witness in a jury trial, or as the (absent) instructing figure for the plea-bargaining. Additionally, information concretizes the prospective conviction. In these ways, the course of the case remains somewhat open. This undetermined positionality is flanked by disclosure and simulations. Pre-trial defense work aims to reduce the risk of "bad performance" (self-reference; removed for blind review), of blocked options, and of surprise attacks. Positionality dissolves only right before the hearing. Only then, the barristers decide for one course to take: plea or trial. The legal norms support the wait-and-see attitude of the defense ensemble: the decision to appear as a witness can be made at the very last moment. Given this situation, the implications for the criminal identity are as follows: although there is always a possibility of defeat for the defense, the actual act of criminalizing the defendant comes as the last stage of the process and, procedurally, becomes distinguishable only at the trial stage.

The German case study

Positioning the client in the German context is a multi-layered and multi-directional activity, combining and integrating systemic, symbolic, and discursive components. The rules of procedure (*Strafprozessordnung*) position the person, who (for the defense attorney) will always be only the client, by labeling him or her differently at the stages of the procedure. In the German criminal procedure, the client is moved through three formal positions: *Beschuldigte*, *Angeschuldigte*, and *Angeklagte*, which refer to three activities of being charged, with the implications of the charges becoming stronger. Prior to the formal stage, as *Beschuldigte* the client is a suspect to the inquiring agencies (that is the prosecution and police); however, this label has no equivalent in the rules of procedure. If a suspect is questioned prior to becoming a *Beschuldigter*, his position counts as that of a witness. The three labels correspond to the three procedural stages of inquiry (*Ermittlungsverfahren*), intermediary procedure (*Zwischenverfahren*), and main procedure (*Hauptverfahren*) with the trial. In theory, the aim of a defense attorney is always to interrupt the labeling: a *Beschuldigte* should not become an *Angeschuldigte*, an *Angeschuldigte* not an *Angeklagte*. In practice, many clients do not contact a lawyer before they are already indicted, hence being an *Angeschuldigte* already. The data collected at the German site, does not show a single case in which the trajectory anticipated by the rules of procedure could be interjected by the defense. Hence, the questions for this section: How does the preparation by the defense make possible the spatial positioning in the court room of the defendant? Through which activities does the defense aim for this anticipated position? How does the defense respond to the defendant's positionality?

In German criminal trials, several spatial positions are available for the defendant, depending on the charges and whether or not he or she has a defense lawyer. However, the defendant will have only one assigned position: they will not move to the witness stand as they cannot testify but can only make an *Einlassung*. This kind of statement is not a testimony, it is not given under oath and explicitly does not need to be true. In trials with just one defendant, he or she will usually sit alone or, in some courts, next to his or her lawyer behind a table. This table is, as is the prosecution's table, situated vertically to the judge's bench, so that the three different tables and benches form a U-shape. The U is closed by the table for the witnesses who sit across the judge's bench. When the trial involves co-defendants, they and their lawyers will sit next to each other.

Positioning the client next to the lawyer

Taking up a mandate to defend means to position the client for the proceeding and that implies the position in general for the trial. In order to do that, the lawyer needs to 'deliver' the client for the proceeding that is to announce her representation. For this she needs the *Vollmachtsformulare* (power of attorney) signed by the client. Requests by the lawyer to do so are a part of every examined file. This is also often the case when the lawyer needs the client's cooperation and support. It is often featured in the correspondences where the lawyer either asks to return the signed form or reminds the client to do so. In one case the lawyer wrote the following formal letter:

> Dear Ms. Müller, may I remind you, with respect to the above named case, to return the signed forms . . .

Two weeks later she sends the client an informal handwritten note via fax:

> Please do not forget to send the power of attorney in its original!

Signing the power of attorney marks the shift of the defendant's position from the single to the joined, as the representation by a lawyer creates a team with the client. The shift occurs automatically. There is little that the client knows in advance about the inner structure of this team (who is in charge, who may speak, and so on). Through the power of attorney the lawyer positions herself in the immediate proximity to the client: whether it is going to be next to the client or in front of her will be negotiated. However, the way in which this request has been answered hints at the possible resistances on the part of the client.

A second activity that is not demanded but remains an essential part of good defense practice is requesting *"Akteneinsicht"* (access to files) from the prosecution. This action is also essential for the lawyer in order to define the client-identity properly. In the German criminal system, the defendant's file is shared by the prosecution and the defense. This means that, although the file is initiated by the prosecution, it exchanges hands as the two sides engage in preparing for the inevitable trial. Through accessing the file both sides receive the other's perspective. Before the attorney receives the file, all she has to go by is the defendant's story, which provides a preliminary position for the lawyer herself:

> In a case of leaving the scene of an accident, the accused, Mr. Becker, tells the police that although his car was involved in the accident, he was not the driver. He claims to have lent the car to a friend named Frauke. The police are suspicious of this claim, suspecting that Frauke does not exist. Mr. Becker is asked several times in interrogations by the police if this Frauke really exists; a phone number of Frauke proves to be phony and nobody in Becker's proximity has ever heard of this woman. Mr. Becker tells his lawyer the same story as the police. As the lawyer get access to the file relatively late, in the beginning she has to follow his story. Only when she finally receives the file, can she start to prepare for what the case really is.

In order to adjust the client for the proceeding the lawyer needs to know what the prosecution has. By accessing the file, the lawyer comes into possession of two positions about the case. The rules of procedure put the lawyer in front of and ahead of the defendant. Not only does she have all the information, she also knows how to read a file.

Although the lawyers encountered in the German context would discuss the file with their client, one should not view this as necessarily cooperative: examining the file is not about sharing but rather about clearing up uncertain points. This becomes clear when taking into account the positions that the lawyer and the defendant tend to assume during the lawyer–client meeting. The lawyer would in most cases sit behind his or her desk, with the file in front of them, while the defendant would sit across from the lawyer and hence would not be able to read in the file. The lawyer would go through certain passages, ask for clarifications, but would rarely show pieces of the file to the client. By having not only the general access to the file but also the actual material file in front of them, the lawyer clearly becomes the leading figure in the defense ensemble. This is to say that by demanding access to the file the lawyer fills a position that the defendant could not have occupied on their own. The lawyer thereby strengthens the defense, but at the same time he or she moves the client to the periphery of the defense ensemble. How far the client is going to be moved differs depending on their willingness and ascribed ability "to stay in the right position", in the words of the German vis-à-vis.

Promises

The client is kept in the allocated position by means of promises, threats, and prognoses. To promise a good outcome for a trial can serve to motivate the client to collaborate. On the other hand, the file serves the attorney's argument. As a defense lawyer in an interview put it:

> One thing is clear. The lawyer, who tells his client, all those people will have to apologize to you that they, yeah, even started this investigation . . . has much higher reputation with his client than the lawyer who says, look, you might not have such a strong case.

Other forms of prognoses are directed at the client's expectations. If anything, the client must not to get his or her hopes too high up. These kinds of anticipations are visible in the lawyer–client correspondence:

> On the phone the judge said that he will try to make it a fine, but that he was not sure if that would work out, due to your impressive police record. However, he'll consider it favorably.

Here the client is already positioned toward the expected outcome. The letter anticipates a strong position for the defendant, but in actuality this position is very fragile and therefore needs to be handled with care – especially so when it comes to the client who tends to overact and likes to talk his head off in court. In line with this rather difficult personality the lawyer also employs mild threats, such as that seen in this excerpt directed at the same client, but in a different case.

> As you know, only prison sentences up to two years can be set out on probation. Please, also take into consideration that you have previous convictions; that will influence the sentencing. Please, also take into consideration that, the higher the expected sentence the higher the anticipated risk of you fleeing when your warrant of arrest is concerned. I do not mean to scare you with this letter but rather mean to point out how narrow your room to maneuver is at the time. Please be careful! Do not destroy the last remaining chances of defense.

Here the lawyer anticipates for the client, who is quite confident and views himself as a victim of the harassment by the police, a position that forces him to act more cautiously. In this sense positionality meets with efforts to control the client by envisioning for him a position that can only be inhabited beneficially if he adheres to the rules.

What are we going to say?

Although the defendant cannot be heard as a witness in the German criminal procedure, the defense can make some crucial decisions with regard to who speaks. First of all the defendant can decide if he or she wants to give a statement (*Einlassung*) and answer questions or rather remain silent. From the observed cases it appears that this decision depends on three basic features: eloquence of the client, personal preference of the lawyer, and nature of the case.

Remaining silent in the court room is often preceded by remaining silent and in the background before the trial as well. In some cases a young lawyer I accompanied would literally stand in for the client, when he did not speak enough German to understand what was going on. In one case she wrote to the police, prosecution, and the court that all correspondence should be send to her office ("Ich bitte Sie, sich bei Problemen mit meinem Mandanten an mich zu wenden"). The client lost his voice in this case. Throughout the file there is no statement ascribed to him. Did he escape procedure? The client's or, better, the defendant's voice returns in the main hearing. He enters a statement that will ultimately harm his case. Hence, although silenced during preparation, the client does speak out in court.

The client's statement is not prepared in detail. Lawyer and client merely agree on the main line of argument. They share a version. In one case a lawyer–client conference was opened by the lawyer who formulated the main task as follows: "We need to get across why it was that your scooter did not work". Here it is not the lawyer who knows best. They design a counter-version 'on what really happened' together. This positions the client not only next to the lawyer in a cooperative sense but also for the anticipated examination by the judge and prosecutor. Two criteria guide the preparation here: firstly, the prepared version can be narrated by the client without further assistance; secondly, the line of argument holds against the judge's and the prosecutor's critical questions. Throughout preparation, the lawyer aims for such alliance and pretest. The defense lawyer needs to rely on the client and vice versa.

Another method of preparing the defendant-position in court is role play. The lawyer takes the position of the judge in order to identify weak points and to eliminate 'bad' surprises. This is why we find extended interrogation of the client in the law firm. The lawyer asks for nearly every detail mentioned in the allegations: "And there is really nothing else to this?" Such pre-interrogation is presented as a last warning not to change position and to remain consistent from now onwards. The lawyer makes sure that she can really sit next to the defendant as his representative during the trial. The function of preparation here is similar to that in the example with the broken scooter, but it addresses itself to a different kind of client. With this client, the lawyer needs to readjust the overall strategy of positioning during the trial. She needs to re-stabilize her client, to coach, to correct, and to educate her client: "You need to talk less. Two-three sentences, that's enough. Let them finish with what they want to say."

In all these examples the defense anticipates very different future positions: that of the silent bystander, that of the cooperative defendant with a strong account, and that of the defendant critiqued. All these positions are accommodated by the same procedural frame. They might change later on, when the prosecution shifts the allegations. The defense position is not fixed once and for all; it is kept tentative.

"What do you want?" – positioning before the trial

Differently from the adversarial system, there is no plea-bargain as an alternative route in the German criminal system. Once the defendant is indicted there will be a trial. This means that the trial identity of the defendant is decided almost immediately and is not subject to defense or prosecution negotiations, or procedural correctives as is the case in the American and, to a lesser extent, English systems.

Although the German criminal system allows for a procedural mechanism similar to plea-bargain, which is called a "deal" (*tatsächliche
Verständigung*), the deal cannot be made in advance but only during
the trial. The deal is made between the prosecution and the defense
and both parties suggest the negotiated outcome to the judge. By way
of a deal both parties will often claim to waive their right of appeal,
although this practice has been abandoned by the German federal court
(*Bundesgerichtshof*). Trials where a deal might be possible will often
be preceded by informal chats between the professional participants,
including the judge. These talks test the ground for alternative resolutions. For example, the lawyer's file of Mr. Becker's case contains the
following note:

> Judge calls/asks what the defense wants/suggests to restrict the appeal
> to the sentencing/says that he will try to move from a sentence of jail
> time on probation to fee/suggests to restrict to sentencing.

Here the lawyer prepares the ground for an appeal hearing by restricting the appeal to the sentence (rather than to the facts). This is in the
interest of the court as it saves time and money. In a client–lawyer meeting the lawyer presents this option to the defendant, who agrees to
the change of appeal. This arrangement, however, does not imply an
entirely different positionality for the client. Not only did his position
in the trial not change, his position in the proceeding will not be altered
either – he remains the defendant in a defense ensemble. What may be
rearranged is rather his position in the defense ensemble as the informal
arrangements move the defendant to the side – he becomes someone
who "just needs to agree" and follow advice. Positioning here is an
involved re-arrangement between the lawyer and the client. Although it
might have considerable influence on the actual case, it has no influence
on the procedural routes to be taken.

Position and positionality puring the trial – adjusting in situ

Asking what spatial position the defendant is being prepared for by the
lawyer seems to suggest that positioning ends with the beginning of the
trial where positionality becomes position. This supposition does not
hold true for the German context. The option to "deal" is something
that often presents itself during the ongoing trial and an experienced
lawyer will know when the moment is right to take that route, for example, most often right before the scheduled testimony of the victim in
order to spare him or her the distress.

When the moment comes, the lawyer talks briefly to the client about the possible outcome of the deal and will then retreat with the prosecution and sometimes the judges. Hence, the client is not part of the informal negotiation. As with the arrangements prior to the trial through communications between the judge and the lawyer, the client here takes a backseat in the case. The client needs to "only" agree to the outcome. It is not uncommon that the lawyer will have to attend to some sort of shuttle diplomacy, equalizing the possible outcomes with the defendant's wishes. Ultimately the lawyer has to sell the outcome to the client. When all of this happens during the trial, the process of repositioning happens without leaving documentary traces, detectable only in the protocol of the trial.

In sum, positionality in the German context can be observed with respect to the organization of the defense ensemble and with regard to the speech position the defendant takes in the preliminary phase as well as the trial. However, regardless of whether the defendant gives a statement or remains silent, the positioning is always aimed at the trial as the anticipated venue. This means that the trial-identity is assigned to the client from the beginning. At the same time, the trial can take many days and up to several weeks, even months, so positionality can change during the trial as the activities of preparation and enactment begin to co-affect each other. As the means of alternate resolution, the "deal" cannot be divorced from the trial as it is incorporated into it. Hence, positioning a client for a possible deal is, on the one hand, essential as he or she needs to be cooperative, but, on the other hand, the possibility for a deal can present itself only during the trial itself. Hence the need for the German lawyer to keep this position open for the duration of the process.

Conclusion

In the introduction, we postulated that positionality in the legal context responds to both the procedural environment of a particular legal system and the prescribed rituals and concrete practices attached to doing procedure within that system. More specifically, we have focused on (a) legally defined positions that guide these practices and activities; (b) practices and activities of realizing positions by both the defense attorney and his or her client in three legal regimes; and (c) implications of positionality for these procedural regimes. As a result, the positionality in the US context – here a DWUI defense – showed itself to be a product of various procedure-governed and case-oriented actions and activities (for example, informing/explaining; speaking-for/negotiating; documenting/filing), which led the person in question through the provisional positions of the suspect, client, and defendant toward the anticipated position of the criminal.

Localized in several cases that involved the same crime (DWUI), the US study pointed to the preference for an alternative procedural future to be realized: plea-bargain, which replaces trial once certain formal conditions are satisfied. These conditions are defined by the US State rules of evidence as well as the rules of the court. For the US context, this means that an outcome is anticipated before the actual outcome has been achieved at the stage of the preliminary hearing. It is at that stage that the US defense ensemble makes the decision about the defendant's future procedural status, as in "guilty by own admission". An investigation of some oral exchanges between the attorney and the client, as well as the documents generated in the course of case-making, showed how the attorney "moved" the client toward this future, how he made this outcome possible and alternative ones impossible. Among the systemic implications of this kind of positionality was the general preference of the US-American State court for plea-bargain when it comes to specific kinds of crime.

Surprisingly for a similar legal system (adversarial), positionality in an English Crown Court case diverged significantly from that of the US context. The decisive point in that context was the threshold that separated trial from pre-trial activities. In comparison to the US case, in the English Crown Court this threshold was pushed to the actual trial. In view of this extension, criminal cases are prepared in such a way as to keep the possibility of the trial – as the likely and demanding future – open for as long as possible. This does not mean, however, that during the preparation stage, cases remain in limbo. On the contrary, case-work accomplished a number of future positions. Some of them were barely traceable and tended to be taken for granted (for example, accumulation of documents for later use), while others manifested themselves explicitly both in interaction and division of labor: the solicitor, together with the client, collected ideas in a search for witnesses to appear in court on their behalf; the solicitor prepared written instructions for a barrister to be hired and to represent the matter in the Crown Court; the barrister prepared the brief and interviewed the defendant in anticipation of meeting his colleague right before the trial hearing; the barrister's meeting dealt with a simple procedural alternative for the immediate future: plea-bargain or trial. By allowing for the last minute decision to take or to refuse trial, the procedural rules of the English Crown Court favored a fully developed case, which would be sufficiently robust to stand trial. The implications of this set-up are far reaching. The English Crown Court extends its horizon for criminal cases despite the fact that only a small number of cases end up being tried. This kind of positionality means an in-depth treatment of evidence, which may somewhat explain extensive legal aid available to the needy defendants. In turn, group-working toward the trial until the very end encourages continuous probing into the strengths and weaknesses of each individual case. Here, the defendant's final position is postponed until the very end. He remains in a hopeful position for long time, while slowly learning how to adopt the barrister's pragmatic stance.

The German case study presented another kind of positionality, which illustrated the possibility of administering justice in a legal environment where the boundary between preparation and enactment was not as clear. In the German *Landsgericht* the option to "deal" did not present itself before the trial. Thus, the German system positions all cases as necessarily triable, and although the alternative route is not excluded by the process it is a much more rare occurrence than in the US-American regime. Moreover, the "deal" can be actualized only at the trial stage. At the same time, in most cases "dealing" begins early by way of informal exchanges and remains potent for the duration of the casework. The defense lawyer never misses an opportunity to test whether a particular case is good for a deal. This testing, however, is oriented more toward the prosecution case and its weaknesses than toward a relational weighing of two competing cases like in the English regime. The defendant's positioning toward the future hearing shifts in light of this strength and vulnerability of the allegations and the evidence supporting them.

In the German case, procedural positionality of the client is thus a one-dimensional phenomenon; not only does it always direct itself toward the trial but also actually arrives there. A level of complexity is added at the final stage. The defense lawyer will recommend to the client to either speak out in front of the presiding judge and the prosecution (testifying) or to remain silent (abstaining). For the trial hearing, the defendant can either be positioned as a core figure and forensic measure or as a bystander to their own trial. This positioning, again, is different from the adversarial scheme. The defendant cannot be presented as a witness; he or she can serve only as representative of their own interest, a partial figure. What is more, he or she cannot even be prepared or scripted since the prevalent counterpart, the judge, does not allow the anticipation of questions. The German positionality shows this double character most explicitly: a trial hearing is approaching while its course (its length, its core features, and so on) remains obscure.

In sum, in the course of our analyses, the three respective contexts revealed three different senses of positionality. They also refined the concept of positionality taken initially as the phenomenon of distance between the pre-trial preparation and the trial performance. The greatest distance between the two events was revealed in the US legal context; reduced to locally administered DWUI cases, this context showed a clear preference for the former. It was thus suggested that for specific crimes, especially those where evidence is observable and testable, the defense will opt for a quick and easy version of justice. The English case demonstrated a certain structural complexity which in contrast to the US case study created a prolonged path from the pre-trial preparations to judgment. The analyzed data also showed the measure to which the solicitor–barrister division of labor benefited the defense by having it fully assembled and tested before the decision about moving to either trial or plea-bargain was made. Positionality in the German criminal regime presented the interwoven model of preparation and trial. As trials can take from one day over weeks to months, there is ample room for preparation, as in adjusting and readjusting the anticipation of the client's position for the trial. Therefore, the defense lawyer, if he or she does not want to make false promises, prefers to keep the field of future options open. Following these limited observations to their overall significance allows us to propose that anticipation of the intersection between plea-bargain ("deal") and trial was the strongest in the US case and the weakest in the German case. Respective positionalities defined the US defendant as an early decider, while the English case pointed to the borderline way of decision-making.

5
Procedural Presence: Failing and Learning

Doing procedure, one may also suggest, is about repeating what has been previously established with and by the acts archiving *and* about arranging future positions from the case's potentials, within certain standardized arenas. But is doing procedure this simple? In the previous chapters that have dealt with the procedural past and the procedural future, we already complicated and re-specified the picture. We observed unbinding from the past and re-positioning in regard to the final stages. However, it is inadequate to reduce doing procedure to the extensions toward the two temporalities: back to the past and forward to the future. The temporal extensions need to take place at some point in time. They have to be situated.

Once we focus on the moments of doing procedure, socially stipulated forces, such as proximity, contingency, and eventfulness, move to the fore. A procedural past and a procedural future are necessary but insufficient conditions for enacting a case. To put it differently, case-makers turn toward extended procedural pasts and futures in certain procedural moments and settings: plea-bargaining sessions, client–lawyer conferences, pre-trial hearings, jury trials, and so on. However, the view on the procedural present – what is going on here and now – does not always or to the same extent include an orientation toward the procedural past and future. At times, the 'here and now' of casework is stripped of these extensions. At times, complex procedural temporalization appears disrupted. The phenomenon that allows for such disruption, and the sheer presence, to take place is failing. Let us consider the following instance from proceedings that took place in the English Crown Court:

> The prosecuting barrister asked the questions set out by the filed witness statement. How this man let the boys into the car, how

the driver drove off, how they demanded him to stop and let them go, how he became angry, and how he pointed a knife at them to make them stay, how they ran off in fear, etc. The version seemed clear and strong; all it needed was a good articulation from the witness stand. Just when the barrister's questions arrived at this crucial appearance of the knife something unexpected happened. "What happened then?", he asked and the boy would respond: "We ran off. We were afraid." The barrister tried again: "Yes, but what was so frightening?" "His voice, it was his voice!" The barrister remained calm and in control: "Yes, the voice and what else. Was there something else?" He went on asking about the knife, but the knife would not transpire in the testimony. The boy would not mention it. Even a break plus the explicit permission by the judge "to give it another try" did not suffice. The prosecution gave up: "We rest our case", the barrister announced. The judge released the jurors.

This episode is a good example of failing and its implications in terms of the procedural times. The prosecution case seemed suddenly cut off from the binding past. The written statement lost its promised impact. The same applies to the future. All anticipated steps were suddenly disrupted. The disappearance of one narrative item, the knife, was sufficient to cause such a breakdown. These disappearances make us reflect upon the procedural presence in rather radical terms. Disappearance of evidence, as an act of making this evidence irrelevant, takes place in various dimensions. An item can disappear as a locution, as something that introduces a fact, a description, or a statement about the world. A disappearing utterance is identical to the disappearance of the corresponding item, often excused as (accidental) forgetting or as (purposeful) deletion. An item fails insofar as it is no longer used or invested in. Another dimension of disappearance can be found with illocutions. Here an item disappears as a claim for a party or for the case. The item would no longer be used as a functional element of the case. Actually, it would no longer be of use *for* the case; it may be even used against it. Failing may arise in relation to another form of disappearance. A claim may disappear, thirdly, as a perlocutionary act. In this case, the witness would have mentioned the knife, the barrister would use the knife as a proof, and this function would have been accepted by the deliberating body. As a perlocution, the item disappears as a relevant argument for the relevant audience, judge or jury. We traced these versions of disappearance or irrelevance to pinpoint failing in the empirical data.

We observed failure in various versions. Some items would completely disappear in the 'locutionary' sense. They ceased to exist. We observed failure as well as some unexpected reversals in relation to good reasons that belonged to one party prior. Thirdly, it was comparably hard to observe an item's disappearance as a perlocution. This was due to the restricted access to the deliberating phase: to jury or judge. In either way, by disappearing or not reappearing, an item loses the ability to attain the promised relevance and to develop all of its potential. Albeit limited in scope, failures make participants aware of procedural contractions, meaning the loss of resources from the past and of future prospects. Participants learn that at times, even with professional help and advice, it is the present moment that counts most. From now on, the party will no longer claim it. From now on, the past and future mean something different. It is this *now* that this chapter is concerned with.

In law-in-action studies, the here and now of the courtroom hearing, the plea-bargaining session, or the lawyer–client conference has always been the primary arena of investigation. From an interactional standpoint, the moment of enactment did and does count more than anything. Throughout the previous chapters, we agreed that under the procedural conditions of extended pasts and futures, this primacy or bias becomes problematic. What is more, the vast majority of law-in-action studies share a success bias. They account for the themes that participants consider fit for the legal or procedural arena. What remains unsaid, for instance, does not enter the analysis. The opposite holds true for failure as disappearance. We render failures observable due to procedural properties articulated in the temporal extensions of "doing procedure". Only in light of the procedural past and the procedural future are we able to relate to what is lost and no longer subsists. Only through temporal extensions and distributions are we able to detect this contracted presence where binding and positionality cease to apply. In the moment of failure, participants can no longer count on their previous investments, on their binding resources, on their scripts and preparations. The same applies to the prospective dimension. The participant, once a statement, an idea, or a story vanishes, can no longer rely on the item's future positions and promising states. From the point of view of doing procedure, failing takes a specific meaning. A failed item will *not* travel further through the procedural course and toward the relevant audience. However, failures vary systematically in the way that they affect the overall case and the procedural outcome. What is more, failing is not necessarily negative or destructive. Failing can be viewed as productive because it invites learning. Learning in this context shall be understood following Luhmann (1969), who conceptualizes learning in the legal system as the reshuffling of expectations with respect to changed premises. We will look into connections of learning and failing, arguing that one finds different forms of failing in our respective fields.

In the following, we analyze those moments which see thematic items fail or disappear. From the outset, we presume failing to be an event that can occur both in the process of case preparation (in the back) and during public performances (in the front). Therefore, in contrast to the earlier chapters, we group cases from different regimes together providing yet another measure for comparison of the latter. What is more, we compare early and late failures from distinct procedural stages. We analyze the disappearance of case items during pre-trial, trial, and deliberation. This order allows us to distinguish between and among forms of failure and their extents in relation to our different procedural regimes.

Pre-trial failures – disappearing prior to appearance

The pre-trial is the period of massive locutionary losses. A lot of items get *completely* lost during case preparation. As a stage in the judicial process, pre-trial resists an all-encompassing definition. For the defense, it includes all the work that has been done prior to the trial; at the same time, it can be equated with a particular procedural stage, such as plea-bargaining. Here, we use the category of pre-trial in a broad sense as the case work that precedes and, at the same time, informs the court trial. For the defense, pre-trial functions to create strong statements, to avoid unbeneficial binding effects, and to prepare the case for the possible procedural futures.

It is widespread practice in all our fields that certain valuable items (claims or arguments) are put to the test prior to their actual deployment. The following gives an example of such testing and risk management:

> In this English case, the client is charged with indecent assault. The defendant is accused of having touched and kissed a woman against her will. While following the case with the solicitor, the researcher finds the following note in the solicitor's diary: "Look into the family history of the complainant." The note derives from shortly before the first Crown Court hearing. During a meeting with the client and his partner, the solicitor makes more notes about the plaintiff's background: "She (the complainant) split up with the ex-husband and

father of her daughter and with the boyfriend after." However, after the conference, by way of conclusion, the solicitor writes: "Family background is probably not relevant." Two months later, after more digging, the solicitor advises the barrister on this subject: "Risk of raising this is that a jury may think that our client took advantage of a vulnerable woman." The barrister concludes: "This information may not assist greatly at trial."

During pre-trial, the defense calls upon, examines, and then elaborates on certain claims. In this particular case, we can see how the solicitor introduces a theme and invites his client and his partner to invest in it: family history. The question of her (missing) consent is compared and contrasted to her previous life-style. The solicitor's notes also show how this theme is set aside for further mobilization. Deploying such standard themes and search strategies can be beneficial, but often evidence fails to sustain the test. This failure occurred, before much had been invested. The failure remained internal and did not contaminate the case. This case demonstrates the relation and difference between employing a theme and mobilizing strategic items, here in order to undermine the witness' credibility. Calling on the "family background" marks this as a valid point for now. It would enable the adversary to exploit the same topic, once it has been introduced. This is what both solicitor and barrister fear, when they abstain from further investigation into the topic.[1]

On closer inspection, what is actually failing here? It appears, judging from the barrister's comment, that in order to show that the plaintiff behaved "provokingly", it is required that the evidence indicates similar incidents in the past. The defense needed to evoke a behavioral pattern, one of a personal life style. Dealing with the person and personality, such evidence must be particularly strong. The provocation needs to be anchored beyond the defense bias. Otherwise, if poorly made, it could turn on the defendant and his counselor, creating the counter impression of "throwing in all and nothing", or even worse, committing another immoral act: one of sexism and insult.

Interestingly, the barrister's response does not indicate an outright rejection, but is sufficiently ambiguous to suggest that "This information may not assist greatly at trial" may easily mean "until later" or "under different circumstances", that is, plea-bargain. The theme is not failing in the sense that it cannot be acted upon anymore during the case. Rather it is set aside. It can still be taken up later on. This engages the particularities of the English legal system that encourage collecting somewhat unstable points doomed to fail at the trial but good enough to be used as bargaining chips for possible attorney–attorney negotiations. Another peculiarity lies in the relationship between the solicitor and the barrister in the English system proper. This relationship is based on an institutionalized dyad that allows for a dual check: the solicitor does research and comes up with tentative suggestions, while the barrister either accepts or rejects them by anticipating the stages to come. The dyad allows for different perspectives and for early and internal failures to take place. This also means that nobody else will realize that they undertook these inquiries at all.

During the pre-trial, the participant's commitment to certain items or claims lacks continuity. The heart of the case often changes various times. In the US context, we find similar moments of 'low' failure. There is, however, a risk of bigger failure once pre-tests or early warnings are ignored. In the following case, a client does not accept early failure and risks a much bigger one.

> The defendant, an elderly gentleman, was arrested for driving under the influence. He did not deny the charges, nor could he: the police video footage made at the scene and then in the county jail during the booking constituted sufficient evidence for conviction. In view of these complications, the defense attorney, in her own words, "had squat to go by." It was the defendant who then offered a story about "them damn cops harassing an old man." As it turned out, shortly before his arrest, the defendant filed an official complaint with the local police department, stating the police had followed him repeatedly and "for no damn reason whatsoever." The attorney accepted the harassment strategy and contacted the local PD with a subpoena for the complaint and other materials, such as video tapes and audio dispatches. Unexpectedly, the PD had no record of the complaint. During her subsequent meeting with the client, the attorney announced that "it would be a suicide to go to trial with what we have – zippo." Despite his counselor's advice, defiant, the client insisted on trying the case with the failed strategy.

This case appears to be as crude as it is subtle. We therefore take it to be a good illustration of the evasive character of pre-trial themes. An attorney may generate them on legal grounds. They may surface in the discovery, or come by way of the client's story, as is the case here. The above case shows how the defendant's story generated an uneasy theme. It is uneasy in several respects. On the one hand, in its cause-effect "blame it on the other" logic, it lacks sophistication. On the other hand, it exploits the outdated theme of police harassment; once popular, it has been largely exhausted by this point and, given the conservative local constituency, could have backfired producing the opposite effect on the jury even if the defense managed to present the actual complaint. Despite the ambiguous history of the theme of police harassment in the legal system the defense attorney, at first, considered it to be strong enough.

At the same time, the "damn cops" theme was clearly identified as a strategy of default. It was established as such by the attorney who, in the absence of an alternative strategy, accepted the client's mundane reason, hoping to turn it into a legally acceptable argument. This is not to say that the client's story could not have been stabilized. It could, but given his compromised credibility that played into the hands of the prosecutor, his testimony alone would not have done the trick. The defense needed a "record" as a valuable part of the claim. Its nonexistence turned the client's story into a misfortune, at best. It also put the entire strategy into question. With no record of the defendant's complaint found, facing an overwhelmingly strong case from the prosecution, the defense was correct to announce the premature demise for the harassment theme. Only the client's refusal to budge made the attorney exercise the "dog and pony show" move, that is, following the wish of the client despite her own judgment. So, the attorney did go to trial, waiting for "a fortunate turn", in her own words.

In a miraculous turn of events, at the trial, the harassment theme resurfaced: on the stand, one of the arresting officers mentioned that shortly before the defendant's arrest, the state police had issued a search warrant for a car that somewhat resembled that of the client's. Further questioning made it clear that the stopped car was different in its make, model, year, and color. When the picture of the car was presented and then matched with the description of the wanted car, it became obvious that the police had made a suspiciously serious misjudgment, suddenly reviving the harassment theme. The officer tried to explain that the arrest took place at night, so no exact identification was possible. But, it was too late: the seed of doubt was planted in the minds of the jury. Being a complete failure in itself, the harassment strategy generated a spin-off that allowed the attorney to win the case. In retrospect, we might say that carrying on as if there was no failure created a space for the defense. Anticipating the harassment failure, the prosecution attempted to avoid it. These efforts were exposed by the attorney who then led the witness to "fulfill" the failure with their own reasoning. From the side of the defense one might say that this theme failed beautifully, without creating any fuss.

In the German context pre-trial work is often invisible as some lawyer's essentially put nothing of their preparation in writing. At the same time, as bigger cases stretch over several days, weeks, months, and sometimes even years, pre-trial and trial can be interwoven. The following example shows a form of failing that is rather typical of the German procedure. It took place at a lawyer–client conference:

> Kevin Becker is charged with fraud. The prosecution says that he ordered goods via the internet using stolen id and credit card information. As a client he is considered rather unreliable and "difficult to control", as he tends to talk his head off in court. In the last lawyer-client conference before the trial, the lawyer goes through the file and checks basically what the client is going to say. In this conversation the client remarks on a number of keys that the police found in his apartment and that belong to a real-estate dealer and recent burglary victim. Three times Kevin Becker brings up the issue of "the keys", stating that there were "forty, fifty keys to apartments... with addresses on them and everything". The lawyer counters all attempts to discuss this issue with the remark: "But this does not play a role here". The client drops the topic.

The failing here occurs almost without any notice. The client marks a theme as important to talk about and to be prepared for trial. The lawyer abstains from engaging with this new theme. The client's attempt at reshuffling the trial-strategy by introducing a new theme fails in the secluded area of pre-trial preparation. Especially with this client, it probably was a blessing that the theme was only brought up with the lawyer and not with the judge in the courtroom.

Pre-trial failing is performed in very different ways. In all three instances one could doubt whether we are looking at examples of failing at all. In the English case, the theme did not fail entirely, but merely stepped back. In the US example, the theme did fail on the back stage, but reappeared in open court, somehow successfully, due to the prosecution's counterstrategy. Although these instances of failing profoundly differ, they seem to share one feature: backstage. Failing in pre-trial is not a disaster and does not even come as a big surprise – it is rather usual business. On the backstage, having the failure attributed to one's side or person is unproblematic. The damage caused depends on the investments put into it: If standard themes like the family background issue collapse early, the damage – in terms of lost time and work – is minor. The function of these themes is to relieve the process of preparation as they can be employed and discharged as routine search strategies. In contrast, the collapse of 'creative', 'original' themes like the harassment in the US case is frustrating since it nurtures significant resources including the hopes of the client. Despite these investments, the three failures did not harm the overarching argument that was to be employed by the defense. The defense case was rather enhanced because certain themes could be left behind as unimportant and other more promising themes could move to the core. What we see here is a form of collective learning limited to the case at hand. Implications for future cases seem minor.

Trial – between disaster and strategy

In systemic terms the trial phase[2] seems to be the privileged place for claims to 'properly' fail. However, since trial hearings are organized differently in our three procedural regimes, we may expect different forms of failing. In trial, failure can occur and be received by the judges as poor performance: all the chances of victory are then converging into the potentialities of a convincing show. No matter what the reason is, at this stage, items and claims get lost for the party and, at times, the latter even turn against the original claimant. The following excerpt from the US context shows a perturbing case of incestuous rape where this 'turning' takes place. We will focus here on the defense's investment in an essential, if reluctant, witness.

> The attorney who took the case had little to go on: the two young men were caught in the act of raping their mother. There was little doubt as to what had happened. The mother's screams made the neighbors call the police in the first place. The victim's internal bruising and bleeding was consistent with rape trauma. In sum, from the defense standpoint, the case was a sure loss. It was then that the boys offered an unexpected strategy. They claimed that being super drunk and high, they mistook their mother for a girlfriend. It was further confirmed that the girlfriend indeed existed and, until recently, visited both sons regularly, often staying overnight and having sex with both of them. The woman was thirty years old and was built like the victim. "She liked to scream", the son told the attorney, "and she sounded just like mother." With this, the attorney would go to trial. His opening statements reflected this

strategy: "ladies and gentlemen of the jury, please take pity on the victims of the circumstances…they had no idea what they were doing." For evidence the defense had only the girlfriend, but she was so reluctant to testify that the attorney had to subpoena her. The forced testimony turned out to be disastrous. On the stand, the girlfriend stated that the brothers took her by force many times and although the attorney argued that she kept on coming back, at the end, she damaged the defense beyond recovery.

The defense clearly failed – entirely. The theme of mistaken identity turned out to be a disaster. Instead of countering the accusation of rape, the sons' excuse rather strengthened it. By presenting the line of argument through calling the witness, the attorney committed himself to it in public. The defense had already given up the case for lost, but a good testimony could have reversed the situation. The witness had however an almost impossible task: she had to be convincing on an unknown theme. "She was questionable, at best", said the attorney, "I hoped she would dig herself in, make the boys look stupid." In a strange reversal, the witness' animosity produced exactly the opposite effect: instead of looking stupid, the defendants looked sinister, malicious. Unlike the usual scenario, there was no story to be rehearsed. The witness, in fact, did not even want to testify. This points out the danger attached to developing arguments. Here, the defense had not established a reliable procedural past with respect to the witness. This example also points to an interesting difference between the adversarial and the inquisitorial systems, residing in the different roles of the presiding judge. In the German criminal system, for example, this kind of failure would not be viewed as the worst case but rather as, although irritating, normal, because the defense does not prepare to the same extent as in the adversarial context. The German system is much more used to surprise during the trial.

The openness to surprise becomes even clearer when turning to a German case we have already briefly introduced in the beginning of this chapter. Here a young drug addict, who is accused of robbing elderly ladies off their handbags, uses the fact that he lives with his grandmother as a discharging theme. The following episode resembles a failing performance.

When being interviewed by the police, Henning insists that he is not guilty. As one reason why he would never do something like that, he states that he himself lives with his grandmother. How could he rob an elderly lady. This defense account is repeated and stabilized several times during pre-trial by Henning. It receives support from one of his friends as well. Also, his grandma is interviewed. She does not strengthen the "granny-theme" by what she says but rather by the fact that she speaks up for him. She stresses that Henning used to sleep in long (most of the robberies were committed during the morning hours). The lawyer highlights this theme (among others) in the file. He marks it as important for the defense. He views it as convincing himself.

In the main hearing, the theme is introduced by the defense lawyer. After Henning's plea (that he is not guilty), the lawyer asks him where he lives: "At my grandma's". Henning's grandmother is supposed to testify in court later on. However, on the second day of the trial, the lawyer learns from Henning's family that the grandma will not testify. She cannot stand to see her grandson in the dock.

Here, the theme dematerializes at trial when not being supported by a witness. The failure is evident for the defense and notable to some but not to the wider public, who will not recognize the theme's absence or loss. The theme does not fail because of a poor performance but because it is not performed at all. The blank in this case does not appear in public, but it is discernable for the participants of the trial who know the case history and the file. Thus, the failure's audience is restricted and this limits the damage, as it allows for readjustments. From the defense perspective, the theme's failure appears even more evidently than in the rape case: it is a plain gap. This gap, however, can still be filled before the final deliberation.

Furthermore failing in trial can take the form of backfiring. The performance is secondary or even insignificant as the argument brought forward. Like the one below in the case of a ticket-less ride:

Mr. Olluh is charged with fare jumping on a regional train. He is a young African asylum seeker who does not speak German, only his native language and some broken English. The communication in this case has been solely between his lawyer and the prosecution and court; his voice never appears in the pre-trial phase.

In court, after the evidence has been taken, the defendant points out, with the help of an interpreter, that he already paid. The judge: "Paid what?" The interpreter: "47€." The defendant refers to the fine he paid to the train company, not understanding the difference between civil and criminal charges. In his "last words"[3] the defendant again asks, in response to the demand for a penalty by the prosecution, if he still will be punished although he paid the fine already. In the verdict the judge counts the fine as a mitigating factor. Still, the defendant receives a warning and several hours of community service.

Stressing that the defendant paid the fine to the train company is beneficial, as it depicts him as responsible and rule-abiding. It was essential that this impression was produced accidentally. The defendant's complaint that he had already compensated the train company for the damages had an unexpected effect: it served as a moral fact, not as a defense. But the case went on:

> The lawyer and the defendant appealed the verdict. When, in the appellate hearing Olluh is asked to say something, he insists that he already paid the money. It becomes apparent that the appeal is not on factual grounds. As the sentence is very low and because it is a juvenile case, the judge points out that it might be good to retract the appeal as he won't change the sentence. The factual grounds are uncontroversial, especially as the defendant has paid the fine already, which he takes as an admission of guilt.

In the lower court, the payment theme benefited the defendant with a mild punishment. At the appeal stage, it turns into a failure: it changes sides as it blocks the way to arguing against the committal of the misdemeanor. The payment of the fine turns against its author: it disappears as an excuse and reappears as admission. The theme of compensation does not fail for its poor performance but for its essential features, susceptible to be appropriated by the adversary. Unlike the previous cases, in which the performance caused failing, here the theme could not succeed even if better enacted. It was determined to fail because of legal reasons.

The trial stage failures cause the strain of the theme. Themes fail following multiple modalities: bad acting, absence, and backfiring – at least as many modalities as cases. Many of them are related to performance, others are not. Performance, here, adjusts the theme to the procedural dynamics and, conversely, failure equates the lack of adjustment. Other failures are more basic: claims do not find any support or voice. Of course, the themes require support and enactment during the pre-trial phase, but in a very different way. First of all, the audience differs appreciatively, mostly limited to the defense ensemble, only occasionally including other participants. Second, during the pre-trial phase there is time for refining and changing. Failure here can lead to learning for the case at hand and can help to strengthen it. During trial, items fail because of bad translation sometimes already between the lawyer and the client. At other times, the failure derives from an awkward theme and witness combination. In the rape case, the witness enters the procedure as a Trojan horse, producing a hostile version despite being a defense witness.

Failing during trial is related to surprise due to expected conditions not materializing. Does failure in court involve learning as well? It implies professional learning for the lawyers, as trial failures are often the result of lack of knowledge and risk-taking. Only exceptionally will learning apply to the case on trial, when there is still time for the defense to change strategy well before the point of no return. Overall, at the trial stage, the procedural regimes expose the defenses to different audiences, or more correctly, to different judges of the facts. This leads us to the final stage.

Deliberation – black and not so black boxes

A third phase of failing appears during the final stages, or to be more precise, during what one could call deliberation. Here items may be no longer mentioned, claims may support the adversary case, or formerly good reasons seem no longer convincing. The phase of deliberation is officially opened once the evidence is fully presented and the deliberative body retreats: the cards are laid on the table, which implies a 'point of no return'. The cases are now to be assessed; they are at the mercy of what is meant to be evidence-based decision-making. One could expect that this inevitability distances the defense from the need to account for failures. Failing by deliberation is part of the game – at least for the professional representatives. The decision-making body – a judge, a group of professional or lay judges, or a jury – assesses the cases in light of the "discursive facts" and their legal values.

At this late stage, failures are commonly established in order to facilitate or to justify a decision. One failure-establishing instance is, in most procedures, the judge, who can from now on treat the employment of certain themes as bound to validity claims that are to be accepted or refuted. Evidence is subjected to an array of sub-decisions. The judge may render claims as (legally) irrelevant, unpersuasive, or outmaneuvered. The following establishment of failure took place in this way during the sentencing in a US federal court.

> Sitting in the county jail, the defendant was waiting for his sentencing in the Federal Court. His guilt was established beyond doubt. The charges included drug trade, assault and battery, extortion, intimidation, possession of illegal firearm, and tax evasion, among many others. During the attorney-client conference, the defendant disclosed his ignorance of the fact that his pre-calculated sentence (cited in the Pre-Sentencing Report) amounted to 35 years. In shock, the defendant pressured the attorney to design a last-minute strategy to help him reduce the sentence.
>
> After an involved discussion, the attorney singled out three points for a potential reversal: a) unregistered weapon; b) quantity of drugs; c) number of accomplices. On the basis of the "new information," the attorney filed an objection. The court granted an extension for deliberations. In the objection, the attorney argued that the confiscated weapon was a .22 caliber rifle that could not qualify to be a "deadly weapon." Therefore, the felon could technically possess it, and it should not be considered "a tool in assistance." The counselor also argued that the amount of drugs had been calculated incorrectly: the total of the drugs included those that were obtained by his accomplices on their own. Finally, the defendant's wife should not be viewed as an accomplice but rather as a witness.

Here pertinent themes are identified on the basis of a case that is nearly over at a point that could be called pre-trial in trial. In the seclusion of the lawyer–client relationship new themes are collected in order to change a sentence at the last minute. The lawyer, like in the above mentioned case of incestuous rape, risks failures because there is nothing to lose. The prosecutor, in fact, attacks the three arguments on the spot and the judge, following the reasoning by the prosecution, marks all three as failures. First, according to the prosecution, the rifle was the right kind of gun. It could have been used for committing a crime if only the defendant wished it to be so. The second point failed because the accomplices had bought drugs from the dealer who worked for the defendant. Once again, the criminally-inclined defendant ordered the drugs. Finally, the defendant's wife did not have to participate in the crime; it was sufficient if she abated it. Later, during the sentencing, the judge addressed the last-minute attempt as "what could have not affected the sentencing either way." The objections were doomed to failure.

The failures are established by the judge during his sentencing. The attorney saw them coming but could not help agreeing to his client's wish to 'try everything'. The attorney describes the points as being forced on him by the defendant. In an ethnographic interview that preceded the sentencing the attorney stated that "it is his [the client's] right to fight points but I could tell those were not strong ones". Apparently, the judge's quick rejection leaves the attorney with the need to explain 'whether something went wrong'. The mode of failing requires a local, undamaging explanation in order to neither count as misconduct nor as incompetence. The results are not *somebody's* failure: they are normal outcomes of the 'last-minute try'. The failures are related to the case's weakness – and as such to be accepted, no matter how severe the consequences for the client may be.

The premature deliberation described in the US example, is an informal sibling of deliberation proper. It shows how the temporal conditions of failing matter. Before the official deliberation is announced, any communicated refusal opens up space for modification and adjustment. Afterwards, the failing marks the final say that can only be interpreted, explained, and accounted for.[4] In both cases, the lawyers got an idea about why their cases failed. This knowledge is, in relation to the time of failing, one crucial condition of the possibility for any kind of learning. This learning can be understood in two ways: case-internal learning for the party receiving a judgment; judicial learning for all possible parties that inquire into the law. In line with this, the legal decisions refer to specific others and general others, the case-specific, co-present audience and a not yet existing future audience. Legal decisions are made for specific cases in light of the general implications. The first one provides the chance to improve the case before the final decision is fixed; the second one provides the opportunity to use a decision as a precedent for the coming cases that share the decided-upon features, and might thus even has effects on the common law system (Scheffer 2010: viii).

Deliberation is not always about giving reasons. In the Crown Court procedure, for example, the final decision "on the facts" is reduced to the bare minimum: "guilty or not guilty". There are no reasons given for an acquittal or for a conviction. The jury is backed up in the jury room, shielded from the public. Its deliberation is black boxed. In the following case, defense and prosecution received the verdict in the so called "sleep-walking case". The case was unusual in various aspects:

> The defendant was charged with indecent assault. The prosecution case reads like this: "The victim goes to bed with her boyfriend. She wakes up to discover the defendant fondling her vagina. The victim screams, and wakes her boyfriend. The defendant denies touching the victim and then leaves the room." The defense version was rather surprising. The defendant claimed that he had been sleepwalking. On the first possible occasion, during the police interview a day after the incident, he responded: "So how would you get from your own room into their bedroom? I think I might have sleep walked or went to use the bathroom or something and then gone back... "

> The prosecution countered this version by an expert report. The report, after going through all positive and negative sleep walking factors, rejected the 'excuse': "If the circumstances of the alleged offence were that Mr. Sleeper apparently stroked Victoria Victim in a sexual manner (with apparent sexual purpose) then... it is fair to comment that this would be a more unusual – more unlikely occurrence during sleep walking."

> The defense, however, insisted on the client's version. The defense presents its own expert: "It does appear to me to be entirely possible that Mr. Sleeper, whilst sleepwalking (and at the same time, still under the influence of a significant quantity of alcohol), without being aware of what he was doing, walked into his housemate's room and attempted to get into the bed there... "

Does the sleep walking account fail? In fact, we will never know. The jury acquits Mr. Sleeper. The barristers speculate why they did so. Was it the victim's story in the first place, as the prosecution barrister thought, or did the defense establish the sleep walking as a "reasonable doubt"? Only in the case of a conviction could the sleep walking story fail in the procedural public.

If the sleep walking defense failed, as the prosecuting barrister believed it did, then this failure emerged without an external audience during the jury deliberation. There is no information available on how the jurors deliberated on the theme of sleep walking. This lack of transparency gives rise to some speculation: who and what failed at what point in time? Was it the expert for the defense, the complainant's testimony, the expert for the prosecution, and so on? The failing spreads and makes it impossible to actually learn that sleep walking is an accepted 'excuse', that victims need to be more convincing, that there was a lack of detail, emotion, or substance. The black-boxing of deliberation has consequences in terms of loosing and learning. Cases are lost without getting to know why and where. Lost cases become infected with failure, no matter what the actual (minor) reason. The defense, in return, can treat the risky sleep walking account as a full success, since they won the case. The assistant of the expert witness already indicated that in the case of an acquittal, their institute would get more of these cases, meaning more lucrative appearances as an expert in criminal courts around the country. A full success of the sleep walking story could not surface differently: an acquittal is the most its user can hope for.

Interestingly, the sleep walking case can be seen in a broader framework. During the last years, the argument of sleep walking in cases of sexual harassment has spread in England and repeatedly juries have acquitted. Through repeated acquittals in similar cases with similar arguments one can assume that sleep walking now counts as a good reason. What we call a theme. The sleep walking in the analysis now has the defined term "sexsomnia" attached to it.

The degree of observability of failing carries consequences for the decision about whether or not an appeal should be lodged and on what grounds. Appeal hearings revise the allocation of failings. Did this point fail rightly; did that point succeed rightly? The documentary basis allows the appealing party a grounded revision. A critique may refer to wrong failing or missed failing. In the following case, the defense claims that the judge in the first instance determined the sentence on a wrong basis. What is more, the defense reintroduces a theme from the pre-trial phase in order to present the client as a victim rather than a perpetrator.

> The client, Kevin, is charged with obstruction of justice because he made false allegations in a case in order to protect a friend. During the pre-trial, the client hands his lawyer two bullets – he says, that he received them in an envelope without a note. The lawyer contacts the police, indicating that she and her client view this as a threat by some of his friend's acquaintances. She files a notice with the police against a person unknown. During the main hearing, Kevin sits next to his friend and his fear does not become an issue during the trial. Kevin is sentenced to twelve months on probation and lodges an appeal.

In the appellate hearing, the judge introduces the first instance verdict and states that the factual grounds are not questioned but the interpretation of the facts and that to his knowledge the defendant did not give a statement at the first instance because he was afraid of this co-defendant. The judge asks Kevin directly if he was, indeed, afraid of his friend. "Yes", Kevin responds. The prosecutor points out that Kevin never said anything and that he even could sit next to 'his friend'. Kevin insists: "But I was afraid, and nobody could take away that fear".

In the verdict, the sentence is slightly reduced, however not changed into a fine as hoped by the defense. The judge decides that no massive threat existed. However, some slight fear may have been the motivation for the defendant to remain silent.

The defense's attempt fails to turn a valid theme (fear) into a valid argument. The judge, as well as the prosecutor, clearly accepts that fear could be a reason to stay silent. However, they do not share the argumentative use this theme has been put to. This failing is peculiar in various respects: the point did not fail, as one would expect, by means of the judge's deliberation. It failed rather somewhere between pre-trial and trial by means of non-engagement. Neither the defense nor the police were willing to pick up on the theme. It was not fed or supported and never made it into court. This passive failing causes problems in the appellate hearing. The defense cannot show that the judge falsely rejected the theme. It cannot show that it was ignored or downplayed during the trial hearing. However, the theme still works to some degree. Since fear and anxiety may cause silence, any former silence can be subjected to reinterpretation. The defense tries to reframe the defendant's behavior during the trial hearing in exactly this way. The appellate court, careful enough, does not fully reject this reinterpretation but reduces the sentence. The failing here is not absolute but partial, the theme is too weak to have a strong impact on the decision.

Deliberation is a strong force for actually establishing failures but is not as clear cut as one would believe. Premature deliberation can suggest failures before time and allow parties to correct the failed point(s), not unlike some failures during the trial phase that occur without the evaluation of the deliberating body. Here, deliberation can be used as a pre-test, directed at the case's future. In general, deliberation marks failures on the basis of the evidence and, by doing so, establishes them once and for all. But their visibility differs. Some deliberation is black boxed and obtains no capacity to establish failures publicly. Black-boxed failures require speculative inferences for the judge's deliberation. These inferences choose themes and reasons that were emphasized during the trial. However, inferred failures are not less valid than others. They may even contribute to precedence for future cases, thus exceeding their original procedure.

Discussion

If we are to entertain failure in relation to doing procedure, we must attend to how the defendant's contributions fail in their locutionary, illocutionary, or perlocutionary dimensions or forces. They fail by losing their impact altogether, or by losing it for the original case, or in the final decision. As a result of our analyses, we establish failure as an essential part of legal procedure – as the vehicle to experience the procedural presence. Moreover, we found different performances of failing. For example, failure performs differently at different stages because the failing of a specific locution, illocution, and perlocution cuts through the binding forces and wipes out anticipated futures. It brings the contingencies of the here and now to the surface. At the same time, depending on the availability of the failure, the latter suggests learning. The failures during preparation and pre-trial are often considered as "normal failures". The inquiry into the family background in the English case, as it was described above, is a minor failure that was initiated by way of trial and error. The lawyer would stop further inquiries and investment of time and effort due to the missing illocutionary force of such a claim. Such a routine failure is disappointing and at times annoying, depending on how much work went into it, but it is also productive as it allows the defense to learn before it is too late.

The normalcy of failing during the pre-trial seems to hold true for all our cases. In the English system, this way of learning is built into the specific figuration of the defense ensemble that includes an inquiring solicitor and a performing barrister. In the German case study pre-trial failures on the side of the defense are fleeting and at best scarcely documented. This is the reason why, in German criminal cases, as little as possible is put into writing by a defense attorney. In this way, failures are available only to a narrow circle, sometimes even only to the defense lawyer him- or herself. In all our cases, failures during pre-trial casework are somewhat damaging; yet, they assist the overall construction of the case. With the help of failures, the defense conducts experiments (sometimes mental) with bold and adventurous claims that can be solidified and put to use.

Failures at trial occur differently in our cases. The audience here is the legal counterpart, the judge(s), witnesses, and a wider public. Some pre-prepared themes enter the public arena; some of them manage to realize their anticipated future. Others fail. The party cannot dispose of the latter any longer. Here failing appears as a "poor performance" (the incestuous rape case) or as a "no-show" (the grandmother case). The failure of performance rarely leaves room for improvisation and adjustment. It harms the case beyond repair. During the trial, failures are often surprising, meaning, in contradiction to what a party or even both parties expected to happen. It appears that tolerance for surprises differs in our procedural regimes. The Crown Court exhibits a preference for an enactment of scripts. A defense barrister never asks a question to which he or she does not have an answer. The inquisitorial design on the other hand puts more emphasis on narrative accounts, thereby including the "human factor". Some failures, especially those that occur on factual or technical grounds, imply that the defense did not do its homework. It did not test the arguments and rules rigorously. It did not rehearse enough. The notion of disaster points to the fact that failing in trial has no productive side effect for the defense. It is mainly destructive.

All the regimes have a separate deliberation phase that allows legal figures to decide the fate of themes, stories, and statements. The decision-making is rarely public. Failing here occurs differently and is communicated to different audiences: in the United States and England, the outcome of an assessment is announced, but does not have to be justified. The public and the participants of the trial can only guess what it was that actually failed. In the German context, the judges give reasons in public. The verdict is open to public assessment. In both systems failing is unavoidable and usual business for the lawyer (not for the client). This failing differs from pre-trial preparation, where failings are frustrating as plenty of resources have been invested in vain. On the other hand, the fact that the failing themes made it to the now and here proves that the defense was not completely mistaken in picking them. From this point on, the chosen theme cannot fail entirely anymore, only in relation to other themes. For the cases under consideration, failing at this stage could not be productive anymore. But that is not to say that no learning occurs. The lawyer will reshuffle his or her expectations of the specific participants for coming cases. What themes and arguments does this judge accept, how does this prosecutor react? Here local knowledge is attained; knowledge that is essential for the German system with its emphasis on the presiding judge.

Besides learning about patterns of local contingency, failing in deliberation also marks the point of system's learning. The failing here can create precedents. Hence, it marks instances in the process of the system's taking in new knowledge. Failing at this stage is not only addressed to the general public but simultaneously, by way of creating a precedent, to the juridical public, as a discipline. This kind of learning works at different speeds in the three regimes. The English system with its black-boxed decision process learns by failing in deliberation, but much slower that what *might* have failed needs to be put to the test of procedure again and again in order to establish its failure for sure. Thereby, although marking the presence in the flow of the proceeding, failing also produces futures as it informs the participants about what counts as a good statement, story, or argument for the future and thus can reorganize their expectations not only for the present cases but also for the cases to come.

6
Courts as Ways of Knowing

Procedure can be studied and theorized in yet another way. System theorists and scholars in organization studies, such as Niklas Luhmann, focused on procedure as a decision-making process. They asked how decisions were reached in every case and how these decisions were accepted by the parties, and by others. Linguists dealing with courtroom interaction or critical philosophers, such as Habermas, approached procedure from a different angle: they focused on communicative events or pragmatics of communication, in order to answer questions on voicing, participation, or representation. In this chapter we place an emphasis on the third strand of procedural analysis. We approach procedure with the focus on knowing or knowledge processes. We have already noted this property of procedure in the previous chapter when we talked about learning. Here, we would like to approach procedure as an epistemic organization. In this approach, the questions of method, proof, and case move to the fore. It is important to keep in mind that none of these foci is conclusive: decision, communication, and knowledge interrelate and cannot be studied in isolation.

The focus on knowing directly relates to those procedural temporalities that we discussed in the three previous chapters. Binding, positioning, and failing were analyzed and weighed in the light of certain procedural items: interview statements, recurring accounts, lost claims. These items, in turn, share the emphasis on fact-finding and knowing. In this chapter, we concentrate on the ways of knowing that are implied by procedure and the official procedural arena, that is, the court. We confront the three courtrooms, the English Crown Court, the German County Court, and the US-American State Court, with the following questions: How do (these) courts know?[1] How do they perform truth effects? What is the role of procedure in doing so? This focus is relevant in two directions: firstly, it shows the effects of procedure in terms of fact-finding and, ultimately, case; secondly, it emphasizes core differences by distinguishing among the epistemic cultures of the courts as *the* procedural venues par excellence. Therefore, we explore criminal courts in their fact-finding function. Before we do so, we would like to show why places and knowledge forms are linked at all. Does knowing not apply automatically to scientific methods and discourses? In an essay by Thomas Gieryn on "truth spots" (2002), we find a handy demonstration on how places and ways of knowing are interrelated. Gieryn distinguishes three truth spots. His typology on 'how places know' reads like a brief history of natural sciences:

> Thoreau's Walden Pont was *a place celebrated*: a sublime wilderness deftly concocted as a unique site from which one could – with sufficient patience, nativity, submission, and solitude – plumb the depths of eternal verities. The Howard's Indore Institute of Plant Industry was *a place on display*: designed and built to translate abstract theories about nature and about science into object lessons that could teach visitors the virtues of holism and organicism, truth that they would then carry outside to others. Princeton's Lewis Thomas Laboratory is *a place denied*: a space designed and built to control the vicissitudes of ordinary places by standardizing them into a cloned array of lab modules, allowing molecular biologists to presume equivalence in the conditions of their work and thus ignore them – no matter where it happens.
>
> (Gieryn, 2002, p. 130)

According to Gieryn, places are related to knowing in various ways. Places can promise deep truth through contemplation; they can tell the truth by ways of spatial and material demonstrations; and they can promise truth effects by the absence of deflection. There are, indeed, various ways to link an epistemic analysis to a theory of place. When understood through procedure, as it were, they come up as procedural places. Procedure activates and exposes these places. Gieryn's typology does not imply three different truth spots for our three courts. It rather implies three different points of view for our comparative endeavor. Hence, we do not claim that a courtroom fits one type and not the other by its architectural, normative, or interactional arrangement. Rather, each court could inhabit all three respects: it might be a place celebrated, a place on display, and a place denied. The answer to "how courts know" could therefore be elaborated by referring to symbolic specificities, to the dramaturgical orders, and to the wider knowledge processes. In this chapter, we will focus on the last two dimensions: the 'centered' interaction order and the 'decentered' knowledge process. The role of procedure in exposing both is obvious, albeit somewhat simplistic: withholding knowledge is one of the court's primary pragmatic functions. It is routinely requested that attorneys "stick to the argument" or "cut to the chase". Courts perform on a timer: proceedings begin at a certain time, break, and end at a certain time. More important, however, is the fact that the same means that are deployed to decenter some knowledge place other kinds of knowledge in the center.

Some references may suffice here to hint at the symbolic dimension of courts that is relevant as a foundation for the two others. We could not explain concepts of 'showing respect' in courtroom interaction or of 'promising a truth value' in the wider knowledge process without a symbolic reading of the court. In our three procedural regimes and their respective legal traditions, courts enjoy a high symbolic status as paradigmatic places comparable to cathedrals or parliaments. As symbolically charged venues, they enhance the status of the happening. They teach respect to those who enter their atmosphere. In the socio-legal and legal philosophy literature, courts are linked to authority, symbolic violence, and what Bourdieu and Derrida both call the "force of law" (Bourdieu, 1987; Derrida, 1999). It is no surprise that legal anthropologists who aim at capturing the spirit of a foreign legal culture study court hearings.[2] Political scholars who aim to demonstrate how courts invoke a communal sense,[3] a democratic culture,[4] or an idea of national eternity turn toward the courts' iconography.

The prominent and paradigmatic position of courts is accompanied by widespread concerns about their cultural standing. Courts, it is has been said, should refuse their authority, their moralizing power, their integrity. Major works in communication studies, socio-legal studies, and discourse analysis approach courts critically. The critique focuses on the lay people that are pushed into unfavorable and outright hurtful positions. The role of procedure in this respect is maintenance of these positions. In this line, criminal justice studies that focus on the 'lay perspective' of witnesses, defendants, juries, or victims claim that the court space is daunting and intimidating; cognitive studies on jury deliberations conclude that the court space is confusing and perplexing; feminist studies on rape trials criticize the "second victimization" that rises from within the procedural formalities; behavioral studies on judges criticize their technical (all too procedural) treatment of cases. Courts provide manifold cultural images based on their historic textuality, their inbuilt biases and asymmetries, and the inscribed power relations. In this context, cultural studies scholars interpret courts, for example, their spatial elevation of certain roles, the visual dominance of certain emblems or insignia, or the memories of social hierarchies mediated by procedural zones and barriers.

The court as a "place celebrated" would lead us as well to the representational economy of courts as representatives of a certain political community. As institutional spaces, courts *know* because they are ascribed such categories as sacredness and greatness. Courts, like cathedrals, promise truthfulness due to their proximity to the highest authority. Such nearness makes people suddenly act in a ritualistic way: lower their voice, duck their heads, and tiptoe around once they enter the 'sacred' courtroom. Durkheim, in his studies on religion, and later Goffman, in his studies on human behavior in public places, observed certain repertoires of the legal activity vis-à-vis the sacred one; both are rituals of respect and humility. Following Durkheim, one would study the symbolic order inscribed in the place and re-vitalized by collective performances that include "totems" as representations of the sacred and "priests" as agents of the sacred order. Courts know because their judges are equipped with 'the legal spirit' that oversees all the truth seeking performances in the court of law. Even the courts' architecture suggests that they belong to an unshakeable tradition:

> The symbolism of judicial structures can convey voluminous messages about classic themes in the study of law, history, and politics. Judicial images reflected in court architecture and art may reveal the importance of the rule of law, judicial independence, and judicial power in a political and legal culture.
>
> (Perry, 2001, p. 317)

In the following, we focus on the other two perspectives on truth spots: the "place denied" and the "place on display". It is within these analytical frames that we run our rounds of comparing the English Crown Court, the German District Court, and the US State Court. During our fieldwork, the courts came into view from two perspectives: as demonstrations of epistemic subjects and as passages for epistemic objects. The comparative rounds sketch answers to our main preoccupation with legal knowing and the role of the courts that are played in relation to the procedural frame. We conclude with a brief discussion on the exceptional status of the US-American State Court in comparison to the English and the German epistemic modes.

The court as interaction order

A court knows because of its infrastructure of visibility and articulation; or, leaning in on the dramaturgical perspective, we can say that the court knows because it separates front and back stage, presents participants as epistemic subjects, defines the footing of certain speech contributions, and engages co-present judges of the facts. Moreover, courts know due to the preferred mode of interaction: question and answer. The pervasiveness of this structure explains the key focus of the courtroom studies on interrogation, including its local management, and its effects in terms of institutional power and bias.[5] In one of the earliest accounts of the courtroom from the interactional perspective, Harvey Sacks identifies the basic mode of communication in the courtroom as the "production of answers to the 'why' questions" ([1964]1997, p. 46). In their subsequent examination of the courtroom order, Atkinson and Drew (1979) corrected Sacks by noting that the question and answer pattern functions differently in different contexts. A further specification of the question–answer structure can be stated as another reason for truth effects: courts know because of the ceremonial display of the witness testimony. Witness testimonies are framed as highly relevant – to the court as an institution – speech events. It is often the witness who is selected as the main bearer of moral and ethical obligations. Yet, the enactments of these obligations differ across different court systems and their procedural regimes: they are the main factors that determine court-specific interactive patterns.

The differences are significant enough for us to suggest that although the three courts selected for this study administer justice with the help of similar procedural means, the actual deployment of these means differs by degree and in kind. In this first round of comparison presented below, we highlight these differences as they manifest themselves in the respective interaction orders. We ask: *Are there certain elements that stand out? How do the courts know differently?*

US-American State Court: Elastic and fragmented

The US court can easily be analyzed as a "place on display": first, because it is mostly open to the general public; second, because it embraces both its actual (local) engagements on legal matters and its image for the mass media space, offering a wide variety of perspectives on criminal and civil processes; finally, the criminal trial is *the* public event of US criminal justice. The systemic components of the trial are set in such a way as to ensure that the US court continues to display itself.

It might be useful in this regard to examine these components starting with the key participants. In the State Court these include the judge, the US attorney, the defense attorney, the client, witnesses, the jury, the bailiff, and the transcriber. These and some other supporting figures are the only ones allowed into the amphitheatre which is generally off limits to the general public. All of the above participants are assigned a seat: the judge sits on the elevated platform behind a massive desk. Next to him sits an assistant or a secretary. Below sit the transcriber and the bailiff. Their jobs are to keep record and order, respectively. At the railing that separates the public and the judiciary, there are two desks facing the judge: one accommodates the defense attorney and her client, the other one is at the disposal of the prosecutor and his team. The two parties are the only ones who commonly cross the space that includes their respective "stations". They move in and out when they make a motion, interrogate a witness, confer with the judge, or consult with the client. The movements, whether they require the whole body or only speech, appear habitualized and well orchestrated. Not only the interaction between and among the participants is ordered, but also the content and direction of the subsequent argument.

The procedural rules drawn for the State Court (Figure 6.1) are as follows. Only the judge and the attorneys may address each other; the supporting figures and the audience remain silent during the proceedings; witnesses respond to the questions but are prohibited from asking them unless explicitly invited to do so. The symbolism of these rules

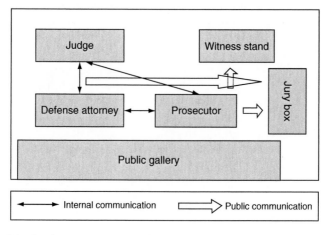

Figure 6.1   Graphic representation of a US courtroom

dovetails into their pragmatics: the court proceedings are a living record; only what needs to be recorded is put on display. The contents of the record function similarly to those of museum pieces which are put on display in the absence of the context of its production. However, the analogy between court and museum cannot help but give only a partial perspective. It cannot take away the theatrical side of "showing oneself". Figure 6.1 emphasizes performativity of court proceedings by showing the lines of communication between and among the participants. Despite its preferential status, examination of witnesses must be preceded by the formalities of introducing the adversary case. The contest space acquires the third dimension in the course of communications between and among the parties. Those communications are clearly vectored toward the two decision-making bodies: the jury and the judge. The courtroom space is specifically designed to accommodate this kind of communication dynamics.

As the figure shows, every person entering the courtroom, be it a visitor or a judge, has a pre-assigned position and is obligated to follow the rules of conduct, such as speaking in turn, or keeping silent and listening. Despite the explicitly stated court rules and the interaction order, activities in the courtroom are not smooth and continuous but jagged and interrupted: announcements from the judge, motions by the attorneys, witness testimonies, attorney–client conferences, recesses, and provisional decisions mold the courtroom space into a place of objection. In this regard, the US court sets unique standards compared to the German and the English exemplars. There is a certain freedom of movement which makes the space suitable for presenting arguments and conducting cross-examinations in the US court. This freedom extends to influencing the composition of the jury as well as the choice of the judge. The complicated process of jury selection before each trial helps the US State Court adjust the audience to the cases on display. This is different from the English criminal system, where the jury is gathered by way of a random lottery-like selection process, precluding handpicking of individual jurors. In comparison, the jury selection for the US criminal trial is case-specific, revealing the general accent on gearing the interaction order of the US court to the specifics of each case.

At the same time, the flexibility of the US interaction order does not imply a speedy and straightforward resolution of criminal matters. While the attorneys' body movements are fit into the sequential order of examinations and cross-examinations, they still contribute to the slow and interrupted pace of the hearings. There is always room for pauses and gaps. To a lay person, the US hearings seem fragmented, separated in two parallel discourses: here the accessible presentation of arguments are geared to the jury; there the technical motions are carried out in a formal and inaccessible jargon. The traffic rules standards help create the regularities in the case-by-case working of the courts. They promise and perform the so-called "equality before the law" by displaying the means for fulfilling this purpose. Other courts may pursue different objectives, thus aligning their spatial and interactional patterns toward exposing a particular facet of procedure: not that of equality, but of appropriateness; not of standards, but of specialization.

English Crown Court: Traditional and standardized

A lot of features of the US-American State Court are repeated in the English Crown Court. We find similar inner and outer circles. We find similar speech positions, such as the examined witness, the overlooking jury, or the refereeing judge. The positions identify who is who in the courtroom. The chairs, tables, barriers, and so on (see Figure 6.2), build compartments for all relevant players: judge, barristers, defendant, jurors, witness, the general public, and so on. Compartments and oppositions repeat in all Crown Courts, regardless of their individual setup.[6] These stabilities are supplemented by moving assistants who quietly deliver documents, messages, evidence, or persons. Social mechanisms repeat as well: similar to the State Court, the Crown Court displays identifiable interaction units due to a ceremonial order of movements and formats, for example, being brought to the witness stand, standing up

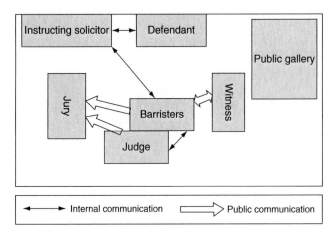

Figure 6.2   Graphic representation of an English courtroom

or sitting down after an 'instant' allowance by the judge. The Court displays itself as transforming speech into truth claims, appearances into accountabilities, interests into obligations. In both courts, major truth effects derive from the logic of competition. In both courts, two adversarial cases compete in front of an impartial and common sensual audience.

The spatial relations of speech positions and reception positions are schematized in Figure 6.2. First of all, the order of positions defines minimal conditions for trial hearings to commence. Secondly, it defines minimal conditions for truth claims to be processed. With one of the obligatory participants (judge, jury, prosecutor, and defendant) absent, the trial hearing could not commence.[7] What is more, the interaction order places speakers vis-à-vis the assigned recipients. The witness is meant to address, firstly, the examining barrister and, secondly, the generally interested jury. The judge controls whether or not "the court" is able to fully receive what is being said ("Would you raise your voice, please!"). Besides, the general audience and the defendant sitting in on the trial serve as an overhearing audience that does not, similarly to the jury, express their attitude in the course of witness examination. In this way, spatial positions are attached to a number of procedural restrictions and assignments.

More similarities materialize when one focuses on the major functions of the interaction order on display. The spatial features identify interaction units (such as the introduction, the witness examinations, or the closing speeches), epistemic relevances (such as testimonies or cross-examination) and modes of participation (defendant, witness, or legal representative, not, for example, victim) (see Philips, 1986). The court as a "place on display" organizes, furthermore, one focus of attention for the multi-party gathering (Atkinson and Drew, 1979). The interaction order centers the attention of the many by giving the floor to one speaker at a time. The court does so by explicitly highlighting important speeches. This includes the separation of contributions: on the basis of content and form, of "what happened" and of "the law". The latter is displayed as 'not of interest' for the audience, while the former is amplified as the all decisive statement.

Despite these similarities, the US-American State Court and the English Crown Court show some differences. These differences concern (a) the position of the defendant, (b) the position of the in-court lawyer, namely the barrister, (c) the movements of the latter in court, and (d) the degree of standardization concerning positions, movements, and cases. Competition, it can be argued in light of these differences, is geared toward and restricted by legal tradition. The barristers display, first of all, their public commitment to the court and, on this basis, their partisan commitment to the instructed case. This includes a comparably high degree of 'showing respect' and 'showing self-restraint' vis-à-vis the court. The latter displays itself as an arena, but more than that, as an arena that is meticulously organized and ordered by procedural standards and traditions.

The differences concern the defendant, the barristers, and their movements. (a) The defendant finds himself seated not next to his attorney, but apart from his legal representative. Neither the case-managing solicitor nor the case-performing barrister accompanies him or her through the trial hearing. The defendant is sidelined (and silenced)[8] and only contributes to the hearing when being asked to plea or when appearing as a witness for the defense. (b) The two barristers are placed interchangeably right in front of the judge. From the outset, they appear as being of the same kind: barristers for this or that side. Barristers take their role on a case-by-case basis. This time, a barrister could appear for the prosecution, the next time for the defense. Alternating between sides creates a shared *habitus* with an emphasis on the court, not on the party, on collaboration, not on winning. (c) This legalism reappears in another difference to the US-American State Court. Figure 6.1 shows fixed positions. The barristers are not moving around. They are not crossing the space, visiting the jury, the defendant, or the judge. Movements are restricted and only permitted once the judge releases the parties from their fixed positions. This fixation is consequential: the barrister would not exaggerate 'his position'; he would not argue the case in 'full person'; he would not act out 'his client's misery, tragedy, or innocence'. All this is displayed in a quiet, objective, respectful tone and atmosphere.

Overall, the Crown Court displays continuity that overarches singular cases and individual dismay. It overarches (nearly) all types of offences and serves as the general template for whatever crime is brought before it. What is more, the Crown Court presents itself as being traditional, rule-governed, and impersonal: by the wigs and gowns that cover individuality, by the dispassionate speeches that cover interest and passion, by the reduced and disciplined performances that cover the will to win. The roles are geared toward respect for the institution. Arguments seek allies in the past: in the precedence, the authorities, and the traditions. This backward orientation relieves local

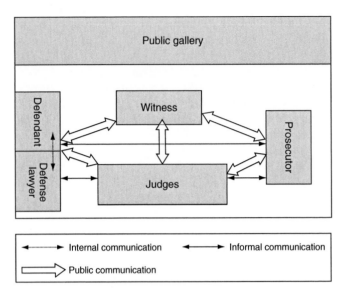

Figure 6.3 Graphic representation of a German courtroom

negotiations in favor of the court as a perpetual order of talking facts and cases.

German District Court: Relaxed and personal

Local negotiations and local decisions are required to a far greater extent in the German District Court. The District Court (Figure 6.3) separates the general public and the involved parties, but it does so with varying effects and in changing configurations. As a consequence, the resulting relations are largely different.

These differences can be demonstrated when comparing the placement of the defendant next to his or her lawyer (a) and the placement of the witness amidst judge, prosecution, and defense (b). Differently to the adversarial settings, the German court does not allow for detailed anticipation and preparation of the testimonies during pre-trial (c).

(a) The defendant sits next to his or her lawyer and enters a visible, case-related unit or party. The defendant can refrain from answering questions and turn to his or her right to speak to their legal representative. But he or she can also speak for himself or herself, including asking questions to the witnesses, thus turning the defense ensemble into a multiplicity of voices. The defendant, moreover, cannot appear as a witness. He or she remains seated next to the lawyer throughout the proceeding. Another difference is straightforward. There is no overhearing jury. Instead, we find another unit: the judge. The bench comprises, depending on the chamber, one to three professional judges and two lay judges, with the latter, although formally on equal footing with the professional judges, only rarely appearing as active players in the trial hearing.

(b) The witness is placed in a rectangle, opposite the three sites of interest: the presiding judge, the prosecutor, and the defense team. The judge sits facing the witness, while the "opposing parties" (prosecution and defense) face the witness from each side. These positions reflect lines of interest that put the presiding judge at the center: the witness is face-to-face with the judge. The defendant seems to be removed from the center of attention, similar to the English Crown Court. However, he or she is rather sheltered by the defending lawyer and is able to withdraw from the judge's gaze. The judge, defense/defendant, and prosecutor have stable positions assigned for the entire trial. Like in the other courts, only the witnesses are called from the outside to the witness desk for the duration of the testimony.[9]

(c) The interaction order combines informal/internal talk on the one hand and public interaction on the other hand. The transition from one to the other is often abrupt and intransparent, compared to the Crown Court. Only internal negotiation between the two parties is clearly marked by moving it outside the court into the corridor. Another variation appears when the judge switches from his or her presiding mastery to a rather oversight role for derivative interactions between lawyers and witnesses or the concerned persons. In general, the interaction order is orientated toward the judge. The judge starts questioning the witnesses. Subsequently, the two parties take over to ask further questions. The same is true for the separate interrogation of the defendant, who is examined not as a witness but as a party. Again, the first to take their turn is the judge. The lawyers are set back as being mere recipients for the time being; only subsequently will they suggest themes that have not, or not sufficiently, been touched on by the judge. Commonly, prosecutor and defense lawyer leave the floor to the judge. This division of labor carries vast consequences for the predictability and the possibility for witness preparation. Compared to the barrister directed "friendly examination" in the English or the US context, the German hearing disallows detailed anticipation and preparation.

This openness and localism expands to the overall trial hearing. The German court leaves room for local specificities to a much higher degree than the ordered and ritualized exemplars in England and the States. For example, unlike its Anglo-American siblings, it allows much talk between various participants. There is a whole communicative web finely-spun in the courtroom. The presiding judge defines barriers and gives allowances, depending on the nature of the case and within the spirit of the procedural rules. Similarities emerge when comparing the three criminal courts with respect to the positioning of the witness right in front of the truth-determining body: in all three cases, the epistemic subject is placed either in front of the jury or the judge or both. Besides, the openness and localism may explain why preparation, scripting, and even coaching play a bigger role in the English and US contexts. The German hearing systematically defies control and direction prior to it.

In sum, we find a preference for "scripted talk" (Goffman, 1981) in the Crown Court, a preference for embodied speech in the US court, while in the German court, the ongoing inquiry and search for truth is preferably undertaken by means of "fresh talk" (ibid.). The German court is managed rather locally and in due course, while the American and the English courts are characterized by "chains of rituals" (Collins, 2004). The German court invites a wait-and-see attitude, while the adversarial courts seem to invite a detailed preparation. Not knowing what to expect becomes a regular condition of legal case-work in the German context. Hence, although the case is prepared in the offices by defense counsel and prosecution, the interaction order of the court allows and asks for case-making, not case-representation, in court. This, however, relates to a different perspective: from here, we place the courts and compare them within extended knowledge processes.

The court as epistemic site

The following chapter identifies courts with knowledge processes. This perspective emphasizes a different truth effect of courts. How, we ask, is it that the courts' particularities are swallowed in the knowledge process? How is this achieved and how is this achieved differently? Authors from *Science and Technology Studies* and *law and Society*, respectively, can be named as particularly useful in order to grasp this perspective on law:

for example, Valverde (2003) because of her interest in various objects and ways of legal knowing; Damaska (2003) because of her epistemic interpretation of legal norms; Shapin (1988) because he links the history of adversarial trials to the organization of modern scientific knowing. None of these scholars, however, has provided us with a comparative frame. This lack is overcome by a comparative ethnography by Karin Knorr (1999) who compared "epistemic cultures" in general and their knowledge processes in particular. For Knorr, laboratories differ in their truth effect depending on their different epistemic positions in knowledge processes.

Knorr (1999) studied laboratories in biology and physics. She claims that ethnographic laboratory studies made wrong generalizations concerning the status of labs. Specifically, laboratory studies, due to certain presumptions, have not accounted for various epistemic functions of labs. The same holds true for a wide range of law-in-action research: for a long time, courtroom studies, by focusing on the communicative aspects of courtroom interaction, tended to flatten profound differences amongst courts.[10] What are the differences between the laboratories that Knorr observed? Knorr distinguishes three laboratory–experiment relations:

(1) "Experiments (almost) without laboratories: objects that stage real-time events" (Knorr, 1999, p. 33). Important characteristics of this type can be found in the concepts of simulation, correspondence, and non-intervention. "Like a stage on which plays are performed from time to time, the laboratory (in social science) is a storage room for the stage props that are needed when social life is instantiated through experiments" (ibid.). The experimented objects "are called upon to perform everyday life in a competent manner and to behave under laboratory conditions true to the practice of real-time members of daily life" (ibid.).

(2) "Laboratories come of age: the construal of objects as processing materials" (ibid., p. 36). Here laboratories are engaged in an ongoing processing of objects as partial versions of phenomena. The objects are subjected to "procedural manipulations" (ibid.). These workbench laboratories carry on without experiments. They resemble ongoing tinkering processes. They put together objects that did not exist before. They do not prove or falsify, but invent a truth.

(3)   "Laboratories vs. Experiments: when objects are signs" (ibid.,
p. 39). Here, the objects feature as signatures of past events. As
psychoanalysis "disengages patients from everyday situations"
(ibid., p. 40), so does this experimental relation disengage the
object from its processual occurrence – as mere signs of something outside its current existence. The laboratory, with the
psychoanalytical couch or the biological workbench, becomes
the habitat or infrastructure that frames and hosts the "signifying" experiments. In the last section of this chapter we apply
these distinctions to the German District Court, the US State
Court, and the Crown Court.

Similarly to Knorr, we weigh the work of courts by placing them in their
respective knowledge process. The hearings contribute in different ways
to the rather extended formation of facts and cases. This can be observed
by focusing on witness statements and how they come about in the
course of pre-trial and trial.[11] Witness statements undergo various mod-
ulations. They reappear at different sites and moments of the criminal
procedure. Tracing the careers of statements as truth claims includes
various procedural sites, material forms, articulations, and modes of
reception.[12]

German District Court: Laboratory hosting series of experiments

How can we understand the District Court in terms of Knorr's three
laboratory–experiment relations? Which of the three relations may fit
best? We claim that the District Court bears a close resemblance to the
third version: a laboratory hosting a series of experiments. The court
as laboratory enables the scientist to "bring home" natural processes
and to confront them with "the conditions of the local social order"
(Knorr, 1999, p. 28). Knorr characterizes this laboratory by three features
of natural objects that it does *not* need to accommodate: (1) it "does not
need to put up with an object *as it is*" (ibid.); (2) it "does not need to
accommodate the natural object *where it is*" (ibid.); (3) it does not need
to accommodate an event "when it happens" (ibid., p. 27).

Like the laboratory, the courtroom provides procedural regimes with
a forum for something that happened outside and before. In court, the
participants of the procedure gather signs or traces of these external
occurrences and utilize these traces as reasons for a conviction or an
acquittal. This mode of knowing acknowledges that there is no direct
access to the "truth out there". It acknowledges that whatever happened can only be guessed in the light of the cues and signs that are

conveyed by eye witnesses, by hearsay, or by designated experts. This general skepticism leads the court toward a strategy of triangulation, of collecting more of the same, of gathering numerous cues and interpretations. From the perspective of the English Crown Court, the German court seems excessive when it comes to the facts. The collection of – more or less significant – details is part of an open and explicit evaluation process, pursued until the judge considers some kind of epistemic saturation has been reached, his or her readiness to decide.

German judges regularly verbalize the limited or even unattainable accessibility of truth when they question various types of witnesses (with direct or indirect knowledge about what happened or who the defendant really is). They tackle the principal problem stepwise, by integrating the 'partial' versions and accounts from outside. They produce a sense of certainty by enhancing their experimental production of even more signs or symptoms. They excuse the impossibility of 'proof beyond doubt' by weighing different certainties: from eye witnesses to gossip and hearsay, from forensic traces taken from the crime scene to probabilities stated by experts, from personal statements to biographical hints on someone's good or bad character. The inquisitorial system follows a flexible paradigm of discovering (parts of) the truth, much less of testing or producing truth claims. The driving force is not a "fair" contest between equal parties, but the "impartial" and "distanced" evaluation by an authoritarian judge.

The presiding judge runs the laboratory and undertakes various experiments. The judge aims for 'more' signs and symptoms in the name of certainty. He or she extracts 'more of the same', under the critical eyes of prosecution and defense. While the responsive witnesses or the silent vestiges, such as a murder weapon or a footprint, do not allow for any direct access to "what happened", the court engages arrays of experiments that provide (more) hints about the past, more jigsaw pieces. A lack of hints does not, first of all, trigger an acquittal, but it results in the prolongation of the trial to reach a stronger clarification of facts. In comparison, from an adversarial point of view, the prolongation would be conceived as an indication of a bias against the defendant. It would be conceived as the judge's desire to convict.

At the same time, the prosecutor and lawyer are not passive in the course of the open-ended experiment. Although the presiding judge is clearly in charge of the experiment, the lawyer and prosecutor can motion before as well as during the trial for certain evidence or the testimony of certain witnesses. The presiding judge then will decide whether or not this specific detail is relevant for the knowledge process and why.

Here, two interesting aspects emerge: first, what constitutes a useful and good experiment in the trial at hand can be up for discussion – the process of knowledge production is linked to a methodological discourse on what constitutes good knowledge and sufficient knowledge *in the given case*. Second, should the judge turn down motions for evidence, this opens a door to a motion for revision of the verdict, that is, for an appeal on procedural grounds. Hence, the notion of collecting as many signs and symptoms as possible about "what really happened" is not only motivated by the judge's search for truth but also by his or her willingness to reach a lasting verdict.

We arrive at a picture that seems contradictory to the common view on inquisitorial trials. The German court does *not* verify the single dossier that has been accumulated during the pre-trial by the police and the prosecution in the search for truth (and guilt). The court uses the dossier as a map that provides orientation, traces, possibilities, and so on. It suggests where to inquire further and where to watch out for more signs and symptoms. Made possible by an interaction order that allows for informal talk, the court can design and run its experiments during trial, including experiments that turn out to be inconclusive. Unlike adversarial judges, the German judge knows the case – plus the defendant's criminal career – backwards and forwards. The court hearing is the dense and finalizing continuation of an extended inquiry, supervised by the judge. The German District Court is not a standardized laboratory, but the sovereign territory of the presiding judge. This authority is not isolated though: it rather assumes that every 'responsible' and 'capable' judge would look for the truth until it transpires from the trials. This is why the court-laboratory can promise a truthful verdict: every independent and responsible judge carries out 'sufficient' experiments.

English Crown Court: Experiments away from the laboratories

The Crown Court is positioned differently in the overarching knowledge process. In light of the case and decision-making, the Crown Court does not serve as laboratory. It rather presumes the existence of independent laboratory work – involving witnesses, statements, and files – away from and prior to it. The Crown Court, it seems, hosts experiments in discontinuation from the case-making laboratories that are operated by the defense and the prosecution. Discontinuation indicates that the parties can by no means go on with the tinkering work, their trial and error processes, or their mobilization of ideas and hypotheses. The lawyers need to demonstrate their conclusive results with the help of recruited witnesses in friendly examination. They demonstrate their conclusive results vis-à-vis the judges of the facts that are confronted with the case – including the scripts, the cast, and the presenter – for the very first time.

There are some additional reasons why the Crown Court fits the first of Knorr's real types: there, we observed a high degree of standardization, both in terms of rituals and in terms of form. As we argued in the last chapter, the trial follows a fixed sequential order of opening speeches, friendly and cross-examination of prosecution witnesses and defense witnesses, the closing speeches, and the judge's summary. Interruptions caused by technical or legal problems are factored out from the standard stream of episodes – and dealt with in the inner circle of the court. The "interaction ritual chain" (Collins, 2004) signifies equal chance and transparency for both sides. One important side effect of ceremonial standardization is the possibility of anticipating what comes next. It allows for a strong trial- and case-orientation already in the early pre-trial phases. Each party can put together statements, narratives, and a case envisioning the future conditions of the ultimate trial hearing in court. Each party can concoct 'admissible' and 'promising' arguments and facts in their confidential laboratory away from court.

Different to the District Court in Germany, the Crown Court is not the place to put to test new ideas or hypotheses. The invention of new insights is principally removed from the court to extra-procedural sites: the law firms, the client's neighborhood and home, the barrister's meetings in restaurants or coffee shops, the solicitor's filing cabinet, and so on. Again, this is different in the German context, where the court is involved in much longer phases of 'truth-finding' processes. An ethnographer who studies the epistemic process of Crown Court procedures would not undertake a classical laboratory study. He or she would (hopefully) not stay at court to await the next appearances of new epistemic subjects and objects. They would rather follow the lawyers, the files, and the circulation of documents to the various sites of case-making.

The tentative laboratories and the ultimate court shed light on the interim products of case-making. What is put on stage does not derive – at least not primarily – from laboratory work "in court", but from distributed laboratories outside it: the police, the law firm, the hallways and interview rooms, and so on.[13] What is staged in court has developed prior to the court hearing and outside it. This does not mean that the hearing aims for a representation of the crime. There is, actually, no attempt whatsoever to make the "crime" appear before the eyes and ears of the jurors. There is no attempt to stage a simulation of the crime. Rather, adversary cases are simulated by defense *and* prosecution in a public contest. Or more precisely: simulated are the statements that were entered and confirmed by the witness (including the defendant), that were requested, received, drafted and disclosed by the solicitor as a caseworker (Scheffer, 2003), and that were, finally, studied, assessed, and put into work by the barrister as an in-court lawyer (Scheffer, 2006b). Only carefully chosen statements that passed the various pre-tests would arrive at court and be put on stage.

For our characterization of the court hearing as an experiment away from the laboratory, the relation of simulation and the simulated are crucial. The two are not just siblings, or matters of repetition. Simulation in the context of criminal trials is a risky endeavor. The experiment remains a contingent situation full of pitfalls and problems. Staging a scripted statement vis-à-vis the judges and the opponent can fail. The statement may be harmed by the conditions of staging, by the witness' lack of memory, by the anger caused by systematic intimidation or confusion, or by the uncertainties about the adversary's challenges in cross-examination. The court hearing, as a standardized "trial of strengths", is kept open for something new and unexpected to happen. In the English jury trial, the parties will not be able to simply repeat what they fabricated in advance. They must recall, accentuate, defend, or simplify 'what they planned to deliver'. The participants in the experiment have to attune their messages to the experiment's local, interactive dynamics.

Throughout the pre-trial, the lawyers anticipate what something may look like and whether or not it may matter in court. They do so in line with their practical knowledge on the workings of experiment's sequential and relational set up 'in this case'. Following the lawyer through pre-trial and trial shows how the case-making includes this temporal reversal. Statements are completed (as script, in memory, and so on) as something that can be translated/staged under the Crown Court conditions for all practical purposes. The relation of simulation and the simulated allows another reversal: the parties can simulate the expected trial hearing beforehand and settle the debate by weighing carefully selected statements. This takes place in, what we call, trial oriented plea-bargaining sessions. This is different in the US context, where plea-bargaining is deal oriented right from the start, which involves deviant – in the sense of unofficial and tacit – rules of evidence, deviant methods of case-completion, and deviant criteria of judgment (see Sudnow, 1964). Before the actual experiment-event, careful predictions about the case's likely outcome are exchanged. Hence, even without the trial taking place the court remains highly influential. The court selects and structures what is presented before it.

The court allows legitimate expectations and detailed anticipations. The court, while being separated from the knowledge producing and case-making laboratories, provides the model and the frames by which the case-in-the-making is repetitively assessed, contrasted, and finalized. The "experiment away from the labs" draws on ceremonial and ritual patterns, less on professional ethics. It forms general trust in *one* procedural future, no matter about the actual court and the actual personnel. The court's epistemic force derives from this positionality: its absence (as singularity) and presence (as generality) in the competing, target-oriented case-making projects.

US-American State Court: Laboratory without experiments

Proceeding with Knorr's distinction between laboratories and experiments, as well as the variations on the relationship between these two components, we would like to single out the US-American State Court as a phenomenon with an uneasy relation to either. The key peculiarity in this respect lies in the strong preference for plea-bargain in the context of the US criminal justice system, meaning an extra emphasis on joint laboratory work (Maynard, 1984). This work is pre-set and adheres to a complicated set of procedural rules, implicitly governed by the rules of evidence. Evaluation of evidence is the central point of the proceeding (Conley and O'Barr, 1990). Once evidence is deemed suitable for presentation, *id est*, is considered as contestable and debatable, it comes to be enacted as an experiment by way of the trial (in that sense, the US-American State Court reminds us of the English Crown Court). Otherwise, it forms the ground for either dismissal (experiment not possible) or deal (experiment not needed). In both cases, matters such as the available resources of the court, possible social impact, and the probability of the desired outcome fall under consideration. Once all these considerations come into play, the need for an experiment as "the construction of new knowledge" becomes paramount. By putting its object of interest on display the experiment "translates abstract theory into palpable evidence for all to visit and see" (Gieryn, 2002, p. 122). If there are no conflicting theories and the evidence base is sound, the experiment is replaced by plea bargaining, which is basically a feasibility study. Although it necessarily involves the court, plea-bargaining should not be taken for a partial experiment, for not only does it change the general procedural course (by skipping procedural stages), it also changes its outcome (by making it predictable); in addition, it becomes a stage itself in the process of administering justice, by following its own procedural protocol. Following the panopticum metaphor to the extreme, plea-bargaining can offer a completely new way of encountering the law.

For example, in the case of plea-bargaining, the essential component of the US criminal justice system, trial by jury, is no longer required. This not only excludes the jury as the decision-making body, it also replaces the jurors as the participants in the experiment with the plea-bargain protocol. In turn, the protocol spawns a settlement to be achieved by the adversary parties through a series of face-to-face negotiations either in a semi-formal setting (for example, inner circle of the courtroom) or an informal exchange (for example, e-mail and telephonic interactions). Once plea-bargaining has been chosen as the route to be taken, administration of justice becomes merely a matter of archiving: the defendant admits guilt; the probation officer compiles a pre-sentence report; the judge uses the report to make a decision. From this perspective, the laboratory work blends with experimentation, redefining it in terms of evaluating its probability.

This hypothesis coincides with a certain stage outlined in the German Court section, namely, the engagement of competing private "labs", so to speak. The consensus reached by these labs is sufficient to avoid conducting an actual experiment in favor of a rough estimate of its effects. By allowing for this route, the US State Court, as the laboratory, does not cease to produce results but continues to function as a laboratory. This is consistent with the Derridian notion of archive as a place which, by continuously calling to itself, exhibits a centripetal drive. Gilles Deleuze notes that a signifying regime must be able to reassemble itself. The record becomes an event after the event. Hence the paradox of the archive: a closed collection of facts, it must be open for generating further possibilities. In addition to the new events (for example, violation of the terms of probation), one means of addition is the actual reassembly of the old (for example, appeals). The court case material is accessible and can always be called for review.

The legal epistemic products that emerge from this design are, therefore, not only facts, tactics, and arguments but precisely the modes in which all these epistemic products are conceived, produced, and presented or not presented. By offering a choice between these two modes, the US-American State Court proffers them as legal epistemes in their own right. The trial mode is one such episteme; it underlies the ability of the legal machinery to engage new materials for the production of the unanticipated results. It therefore stages experiments that have been approved for presentation. In comparison, the plea-bargain mode puts at the forefront the predictability of a criminal event, not in terms of "what really happened" but rather as "what could have happened for all practical purposes". It is, therefore, the capacity of the laboratory not to bother with staging experiments that are not worthy of being staged that creates a legal episteme of an entirely different kind. It is here that the plea-bargaining does not need to anticipate the court's experiment; it does not need to contemplate how the jury would decide if this case was put in front of it. As an alternative procedure, plea-bargain differs fundamentally from the trial-directed procedure. We suggest that this difference should make us reconsider not only the casework but also the idea of the case.

Indeed, unlike the event of trial, plea-bargaining has no close analogue in the scientific world. From the scientific point of view, plea bargaining would equal fraud. It is for this reason that Knorr's typology provides a poor fit here. Although it might be disappointing compared to a clean-cut insertion into the presented typology, this aberration should be taken as a benefit rather than a shortcoming. After all, it shows both the complexity and diversity of different social systems,[14] as well as their irreducible local pragmatics.

Summing up

In this chapter we have compared the English Crown Court, the German District Court, and the US-American State Court first as interaction order and second as a pragmatic function that deals with wider knowledge-producing processes. The role of procedure here is to regulate the production of some knowledge versus some other. As interaction orders, courtrooms show preferences for varying multi-party constellations and different ways of speaking, listening, acting, and assessing. The American court appears flexible when it comes to the spatial positioning of its major protagonists: the lawyers can walk around and address the jury freely and directly. This freedom is limited only by situational "objections" and by the refereeing role of the judge. In contrast, the English sibling of the US-American State Court, the Crown Court, presents itself as a highly ritualized and strictly governed space. The barristers' bodies are placed vis-à-vis the judge. They turn toward the jury once they obtain the space according to the ritual sequential order of speech. Here, again, the judge remains rather passive. He or she can delegate much of his or her refereeing to the court's decorum. The German District Court, moreover, shows another preference. It appears as a local or personal interactional order insofar as its regulation depends far more on the presiding judge. The interaction order seems relaxed and individual. Order emerges through the procedural character of the proceedings, which privilege the centrality of the judiciary who not only preside over the others' interactions but also embody this interaction by serving a paragon of impartiality, objectivity, and fairness.

As for the comparison of the epistemic status, we began by detaching the notion of court from that of case because a case may be pretty fixed prior to the court hearings. It may come reduced to a number of hypotheses to be tested (England). A case may still be in construction even during the court hearing (Germany). In these lines, we positioned the courts within larger knowledge processes that exceed or even substitute the finalizing trial. Again, the three criminal courts showed various preferences when it came to the construction and assessment of cases. In order to mark their different roles, we employed the experiment–laboratory relations as developed by Knorr. The application of science studies literature made us aware once again of various preferences for legal knowing and preferences of utilizing the court for this knowing. The epistemic perspective referred to other facets of the legal process – such as keeping records, the division of labor amongst caseworkers and case-performers, the preferred and the disallowed modes of knowing – that, no doubt, should be further explored and expanded. As a result, while the English Crown Court resembles an experiment away from the laboratories of defense and prosecution, the German District Court looks rather like an all-embracing laboratory, improvising one "experiment" after the other. While the English Crown Court puts to test the cases that were assembled prior to the hearing, thus placing an extra emphasis on the work of the procedural regime outside of the court hearings, the German court provokes signs and symptoms of past involvements in an ongoing and, to some extent, open-ended process that blends the pre-trial regulation with the trial one.

This might explain why the interactional standards in the German District Court are comparably relaxed and informal. The State Court in the United States, however, seems to represent a court in crisis, insofar its inner structure and regulatory procedure is concerned. The latter does not provide strong measures of anticipation outside of the courtroom. Its hegemony seems to be questioned. This weakened state, we suggest, is reflected in the synchronic performances in the court. Rather than being a rupture and a finalizing (decisive) experiment, the US-American

State Court hosts series of hearings that allow for early departures from the lawyers' case-making laboratory work. The "place on display" is turned into an exceptional, exemplary, and impressive spectacle.

Outlook: Vanishing trials and vanishing truth spots?

Courts are more than truth spots. They do more than just displaying facts or processing cases. They are procedural, that is, pragmatically functional places. Next to the epistemic function, one should also find in the court a certain technical function that comes with the activity of administrating cases. One should find the societal or communal function that rises from directly or indirectly moralizing on the issue of guilt for a wider audience. One also finds legal functions that come with the continuation of the authorities or with the interpretation of the law. We did not, however, relate the promise and the truth-making operation by the courts with their functions as case-managing organizations, morality-speaking institutions, or as parts of the judicial division of labor. This final discussion provides some intimations about how and why the truth functions may dissolve (in favor of other functions) due to processes that lie outside the thick walls of courtrooms in the procedural regime as a whole. We will focus on the American example because it is here that the truth function seems to dissolve most rapidly and radically.

On the basis of our comparison, we would like to suggest three reasons that may explain the preference for deals in the US-American State Court procedure compared to the German District Court and the English exemplar. We group the reasons in order to offer an overview of the empirical range that is covered here. In sum, the US inclination for deals may occur due to procedural, professional, or legal-cultural preferences. The preferences have a bearing on the weight of different courts and their virtual forces.

(1) The procedural preference for plea-bargaining refers to the conditions of possibility to actually meet up for a bargaining session, be it on the phone or in face-to-face encounters. There are a number of formal and informal interim meetings before any trial hearing commences. There are, moreover, direct and indirect consultations right from the start that invite the parties to reduce the room for disagreement and to negotiate toward some shared positions. As a result, the US courthouse, its corridors, and interview rooms give space for ongoing negotiations, often extending over

several meetings. On the contrary, the English and German procedures open up fewer opportunities for negotiation. Major time-slots,
moreover, are scheduled shortly before the trial hearing. Since the
case construction is merely completed at this late point in the
procedure, the incentive to actually not use the ready-made case
in court is small compared to the American procedure.

(2) The professional preference refers to the inbuilt division of labor
that separates in-court lawyers and caseworkers. In the English system, the barristers monopolize the right to represent cases in the
Crown Court. They receive cases in the form of condensed materials
and instructions called 'the brief'. The instructing figure is not the
defendant (or the victim), but the defending solicitor or the solicitor in the CPS (Crown Prosecution Service). Once the barrister has
received the brief, he or she is inclined to do what they are meant
to do. The profession of barrister finds its mastery here, in the heat
of the jury trial debate. This inbuilt desire for a trial proper cannot
be thwarted even by financial incentives because it touches the very
identity of the profession. In other words, without trial hearings the
profession of barrister would disappear. The situation is comparable
in Germany. Here we also find a division of labor amongst caseworkers (the prosecution) and the main performer of the case, the judge.
For the judge, the case is a case proper once it is enacted in the
court of law. The deal, in contrast, decenters the judge's authority
and redefines his or her impact on the outcomes in both positive
and negative terms: on the one hand, the attorney has much control of the preliminary stage of the process; on the other, by virtue
of having to do it all, he or she tends to expedite the matters, even
if it means selecting plea-bargain in favor of trial. In the US context
the identity of the lawyer is not bound to the trial hearing, allowing
him or her to control and manipulate the procedural machinery to
an extent far greater than that common for the English and for the
German courts.

(3) The legal-cultural preference may be the most abstract. The courts
differ in the ways they inhabit and embody different cultures of
playing the game and doing the job. In the American context we
encountered ways of representation that would be questionable, in
the literal sense of the word, in the English context and unthinkable
in the German context. As a matter of habit, the American lawyer
contacts his adversary right from the start in order to check for and
assess the room for prospective negotiations. The structure of these
negotiations is less defined by the case and more so by the position

of the lawyer in the socio-cultural network of the local court. The lawyer would invest his connections and his good name in order to enter promising negotiations right from the start. Case-making plays a minor role, compared to the English dealings. Here, cases are developed, testimonies are mobilized, and weak links are identified and supplemented before a counterpart would even get to know about it. Earlier attempts to enter negotiations would be conceived as playing soft and betraying the client's interests. This hesitation corresponds, moreover, with the professional preference since the barrister would not enter negotiations with caseworkers and vice versa. The caseworkers would wait to take such steps until a barrister is hired, informed, and persuaded to do so. The minor role of negotiation in the German legal culture relates to what one could call the authoritative role of the state. The state has a case while the defense controls central inquiries. This is to say that the overall procedure is maintained by the state, while moves inside it are performed by both the defense and prosecution. This kind of unequal footing does not easily lead toward fair negotiations. Moreover, the German defense lawyer is not accustomed to negotiating his or her case right from the start.

At the very end, we would like to ask, why does the US-American courtroom lose its significance as a truth spot? And why do the German or the English not? In the States, there is much written about "vanishing trials" (Friedman, 2004) and why the American jury trial is about to lose or has already lost its power in this specific and globally dominant adversarial legal culture. So far we have chosen to bypass the discussion of what is taken to be the main reason for this transformation, namely, that the trial is too costly for all the parties to be held on a regular basis. Be that as it may, our observations show that there is no reason to believe that the trial hearing will ever be fully replaced by plea-bargaining. If anything, technological advances are going to "purify" the delivery of evidence to such a degree that, in a lot of criminal cases, plea-bargaining will be the only reasonable resolution of the case. The implications of this are far-reaching: the knowing court that displays and processes accounts, positions, and cases, is itself not a cultural constant. The courts as knowing apparatuses in wider epistemic processes are not needed or wanted all the time. In fact, most of the time, the court is considered a costly and unnecessary effort, which should be avoided. Even in relatively rich modern welfare states, the knowing court is considered a luxury that may better be replaced by cheaper alternatives; after all, plea-bargaining includes bargaining with the facts. Instead of displaying or processing facts through courts, the criminal procedures fabricate deals either right from the start, sometimes on the basis of indications and guesswork only, or, much later, in light of competing cases in a simulated trial. These different procedural orientations are as relevant as the epistemic events and processes that take place in different courts. Moving toward a deal or a trial decides whether this or that knowing court and its cases will remain to be a truth spot or not.

Postscript

Why should we, as scholars of law-in-action, bother about procedure? Why not focus on conversation, interaction, or social situation as so many others have done before? Why did we depart from traditional law-in-action approaches? The structure of our comparative ethnography already reveals the answer to these framing questions. By focusing on the procedural past, the procedural future, and some moments of sheer procedural presence we have reached beyond the situational boundaries to an extent that required a radical elaboration. As we demonstrated in the previous chapter, our three divergent criminal courts each resemble a specific temporal fusion of procedural past, future, and presence. All in all, legal activities are retrospective, prospective, and momentous in ways that cannot be accommodated in conventional interactional frames such as rounds, talk, or exchange. Procedure as a distinct meaning producing frame involves more than a single temporality and one sequential succession. Especially professional participants of procedure cultivate another temporal sense and orientation, another look-out back and forth in time. It is this other mode of participation that we have tried to capture and detail throughout our comparative ethnography.

The retrospective and prospective orientation of social activity is nothing new in itself. It lies at the heart of micro-sociological approaches such as symbolic interactionism or ethnomethodology. According to scholars like Schegloff or Goffman, members do it all: they memorize, recall, re-narrate, and repeat. All these past oriented activities are routine features of everyday life. Reaching out into the past does not demonstrate a systematic divergence from the procedural frame. The same applies to future orientations. People anticipate what comes next, tomorrow, or in one month time on an everyday basis. They perform the future by way of planning, making appointments, or closing contracts. The future orientation does not make a case for a unique procedural property either: and the sheer presence? Is it part of the natural attitude?

Do people realize the contingencies they live by in everyday life? The everyday orientation on the here and now is perhaps best grasped in the moments when things get out of hand, when the possibility of failing calls for immediate adjustment. The minor and bigger accidents, the crises and confusions make people aware of the contingencies they live by, inside as well as outside institutional frames.

The procedural frame puts these time dimensions to work in a different fashion to that in our everyday dealings. Contributions to the procedural frame stretch toward wider temporal horizons, and they do so continuously and systematically. One would fail to attend the frame without facing these horizons, without reaching out continuously. One would ignore relevant obstacles, if just sticking to what one would call the lifeworld attitude. A systematic extension toward the past, future, and present is demanded by any routine "doing procedure" – and it is demanded and done differently depending on *the* procedure in question. The procedural horizons carry extra relevance and force that the participants had better account for. In the same token, the procedural horizons introduce critical means of reception and corroborative means of demonstration that are unobtainable in everyday contexts. In the procedural frame, members frequently fail to attend to the demanding extra relevancies. Members perform these kinds of short-circuits frequently. By doing so, they accidentally assist the adversary and undermine their own case. Legal decision-making benefits from these accidents and failures.

The everyday and the procedural are not mutually exclusive. They rather mingle. The procedurality demands attention and care, while involving the participants in ongoing mundane activities such as talking, telling stories, answering questions, being polite, giving reasons, and so on. Everyday expressions are not overcome, but recoded and translated. In our ethnographic fields, we did not find informality in contrast to formality, but informality at the outset of case-making and formalization processes. Placing something in the procedure means to fit it into what has happened thus far and what can be anticipated at this stage. Past and future contributions are within reach due to a number of mediations: orderly inscriptions (for example, a police protocol), the separated and shared archived (for example, the disclosed prosecution file), ritualized speech (for example, a testimony from the witness stand), an interaction order (for example, the overall jury trial). In this way, nearly everything, including silence, may become a valid contribution to the procedure and its case(s). Doing procedure means to attend to parallel and extended sequences of mediated speech or writing acts.

The procedural past and future are not enforced on the current dealings by rule or doctrine, but by ways of keeping – certain versions of – contributions in play and available. Protocols, files, or interactional stages – they all render statements at hand for the longer duration of procedure. Contributions from various space-times are kept in play. They exist in different modes, reach various audiences, and outlive a number of contexts. Doing procedure, this is the shared intuition of our three ethnographic explorations, is about acting upon and enacting these extended contributions. The parties reach out in order to keep up with 'what is going on'. 'Falling behind' the procedural succession means that a participant misses facts and relevancies that have been already established; 'falling behind' means that a participant fails to take impending stages into account; 'falling behind' causes unintended consequences right here, right now. Procedure is, in these respects, a discursive and a disciplining force. It pushes (formerly) local utterances into response distance to distant others, meaning into extended relations, while excluding 'local others' by the same token.

Getting involved in a procedure and living up to its challenge means that every act, every utterance, and every contribution 'better' takes these 'extra' relations into account. Doing procedure realizes these extensions and dramatizations and contributes to them. Accordingly, competent members attend to the case's archive, to other witnesses, to the wider public, to categorical implications, to speech positions, to procedural conventions – all of which potentially propel the contribution's relevance. Not all the participants are able to do this. Not everybody is equally capable of attending to this multiplicity. There are certain limits to it, especially for lay people or for novices who have not learnt yet how to do procedure. This unequal capacity is built into all our procedural regimes and into the modern judiciary. Lay people are represented by professions; those affected are voiced by official spokespersons; those accused or charged are protected by accredited lawyers. The procedural activity frame turns professionalism and amateurism into a well grounded distinction. Being one or the other is a matter of know-how, of procedural fluency, of practical experience. Much of what is going on in the procedural frame rests on this basic complementary relation. Lay people are easily trapped, seduced, misled, abused, and so on simply by way of asymmetrical knowledge distribution. This asymmetry characterizes the procedural speech and writing events. Procedural events do not resemble plain, uniform, and universally accessible frames. Due to this asymmetry, legal representation is not merely a profitable market or a functional resource to discipline defendants or victims. Advocacy is not simply a vehicle for the force of law or a means to break the people's resistance in the name of justice. It is, from the point of view of participation, a simple necessity to move in the confusing and powerful procedural terrain.

The procedural outreach fundamentally alters the participants' situated estimation on what does count up to this point in time and what does not count any longer. It alters their distinction between what is in play and what is not. A statement performs in these temporal extensions and, thus, differs sharply from a singular spatio-temporal articulation. Its procedural mode of existence turns it into a discourse analytical item that remains in play, threatening, challenging, and haunting those who (have to) take the floor and act upon all of these discursive items. The same applies for the future calculus: a statement might receive its full relevance in relation to yet unknown others in the generally anticipated procedural arena. In this line, a local utterance that seems acceptable or reasonable vis-à-vis *this* police officer or with reference to *this* unfavorable barrister may turn out to be unacceptable and unreasonable later as a contribution to *this* procedure. Procedure stretches the field wherein statements make sense and gain relevance. It is this procedural productivity and our attempts to meet it that moved our comparative ethnographies close to some discourse analytical concepts.

Meeting the procedural outreach cannot be equated with meeting the natives' point of view. One can perfectly attend the current meeting, interview, or hearing without realizing the procedural dimensions. One can respond in good faith, without grasping the wider implications of this response. One can comment and argue about what is going on, without realizing some further implications. All our procedural regimes allow for or even invite connections, crosscuts, and measures that exceed the current overview of lay people in particular and professionals in general. However, the common participant meets the procedural outreach in various ways: by listening to his or her lawyer; by studying his or her written statement; by realizing his or her partial position; by repeating former versions; by keeping silent. Procedure allows for and imposes these basic orientations.

Doing procedure is not a universal structure. Differently to conversation or, better, a game of chess, it is not easy to identify a "simplest systematics" (Sacks *et al.*, 1974) or common ground rules that govern the procedure. Each procedural regime applies different regularities, different languages, and thus different grammars to the members' contributions and cases. From a comparative perspective, reaching toward the future is encouraged and demanded by the English regime with its highly standardized and ritualistic court interaction order, while the outreach seems rather short due to the judges' autonomy and the hearings' local pragmatics in the German regime. The stretch toward the procedural future is even shorter in the US-American regime. This is due to an 'early' preference for plea bargaining (in contrast to the English and German preference for trial) that impedes the full maturity of cases. Similar differences apply to the procedural past: the English procedure allows for extended binding, but only on the basis of 'selected' (from a German point of view) statements, while the German procedure allows for extended retrospection including even 'poor' evidence (from the perspective of the English system). Such an extension of the procedural past does not fully apply to the American regime, at least not when routinely opting for early plea-bargaining. Here, it is only the prosecution that invested much in archival facts, while the defense invested rather in their critical review.

The procedural presence offers another component that contrasts the procedural frame with natural occurring frames. In procedures, contingencies multiply. Early statements, basic claims or full accounts can fail in the most diverse and sometimes unexpected moments. However, these moments are spread differently. They appear in different rhythms in the procedural courses. They appear, moreover, with or without warning in our three regimes. While the English Crown Court procedure allows for failing as a pre-testing device, the German context renders failing often invisible due to a lack of binding and positionality. The US-American procedure narrows down the effects of failing. Its focus is on contrasting imagined (standard) cases, since – in the preferred mode of plea-bargaining – the procedural past and future reach out comparably little. Practically speaking, the US procedure offers comparably little risk of faliure since the few procedural events presume continuity of resources and positions.

Doing procedure does not show in its full significance when sticking to procedure just as case, or procedure just as a set of rules. Rather, the temporal outreach shows with a view on the singularity and generality of procedure. Procedure becomes both in our ethnographic explorations: the individual course and history of *a* unique case (or two competing cases in an adversarial setting); the general stages and trajectory for *all* cases (or all competitions of two cases in the adversarial system). Doing procedure is about this case(s) and about a distinct regime of handling cases. This dualism of individual and general is a plea for a novel understanding of procedure. Procedure has often been mistaken as a container in which a caseload rustles and stirs, as if it were a magnetic field that attracts and turns into a series those tasks or problems that need to be solved; as an operational chart that moves cases from one stage to another. In order to serve as a meaning producing frame for the law-in-action inquiry, procedure should come out of the picture and be a part of the picture, as Goffman put it. The duality leads to the core plea of this postscript: law-in-action should regard procedure as being the *primary* mode of participation that is inseparable from what is going on now, then, and shortly before. Procedure serves as an activity frame due to its potency of constantly shifting the figures and the grounds. This shift shows in the procedural items, statements full of claims, and the turns by which participants contribute to procedural junctions. Doing procedure does not work by way of mere ideas, feelings, or emotions; it does not even operate by sheer utterances or by speech only. Doing procedure hinges on statements that parties nurture, attack, keep in play, and, by doing so, render available for all practical purposes. This might explain why our ethnographic take on defense work brought us so close to discourse analytical themes and concepts, such as discourse, archive, text, and talk. Procedure defines – more than who is allowed a voice, a representation, and a motion – what counts as a lasting contribution to the ongoing exchange. Procedure shapes the current activities so that subsequent activities can relate to by "doing procedure".

Doing procedure should not be reduced to discourse mechanics or operational rules. Doing procedure resembles a craft. On the one hand, it appropriates the mundane tongue by encouraging common sense concepts, everyday expressions, storytelling, and moral intuitions. It appropriates, on the other hand, technical meanings and relevancies that promise replication, equality, and machine-like operations. Meticulous definitions, fixed criteria, interpretative traditions – all this discipline across cases and toward general programs add to the procedural outreach. The technicalities allow for even further extensions toward past and future. Due to the law-in-procedure, accounts are amplified beyond the members' everyday experience. Meeting the procedural outreach turns into a demanding task even for the participants, not to speak about the ethnographers.

We found a lot of extra legal amplification of words and accounts. It is not just law-in-procedure that turns words into weapons and accounts into mine fields. Discursive amplification, or relevance-production, proceeds due to mediated availabilities. Speech, documents, files, archives, speech positions, and so on, introduced the extra-legal amplifiers that are necessary conditions for these highly productive and consequential temporal extensions. Binding, positioning, and failing are performed by competent participants who are searching for options and alternatives at a given procedural junction. Binding, positioning, and failing are, what is more, synonym for the procedural forces that turn these participants into objects of knowledge and decision-making processes. They restrict options sometimes down to sheer adherence. All these framed practices and effects are embedded in a procedural infrastructure consisting of systematic mediations ranging from ritual orality (for example, giving testimony vis-à-vis the presiding judge) to multi-texts in files (for example, the brief to Counsel).

Doing procedure opens up for differences that are commonly out of sight from either law-in-action or law-of-the-books perspectives. The outreach of the past-in-the-presence or the future-in-the-presence or the sheer contingencies of failing – all these are just invitations to engage with the mechanics and the layers of procedure as *the* meaning-producing frame. Binding, positioning, or failing do not resemble these time dimensions. The procedural past, future, and presence are more than uniform forces. The opposite is true. Binding, positioning, and failing proposed certain versions of the respective temporal dimensions. Each force counts in light of an opposite drift: toward unbinding, toward the inability to position, toward learning. Procedure is not a force that pushes cases in a certain direction. It is not a biased force per se. As a process, procedure accomplishes cases that provide sufficient reason to decide once and for all. As a chain of events, it accomplishes a degree of irreversibility in order to provide stable grounds for whatever conclusion.

Unbinding, inability to position, and learning did not just introduce antipodes. They are more than oppositions to open up a comparative spectrum. They imply local criteria of justice and evaluation. This critical dimension was pushed aside due to the ethnomethodological stance of the overall project. We, the three authors of this book, analyzed what is going on in 'our' three procedural regimes. Our studies of "doing procedure" were not without position. The opposite is true. Especially in our internal group discussions each author showed signs of "going native". Each took a stance in favor of his or her procedural field. Each started to justify what is going on "here", different to how it works "there". Our debates concerned analytical, micro-sociological, and methods' questions on the one hand; they concerned questions of proper or just procedure on the other hand. "Going native" means that we as the fieldworkers identified with the fields' diverse concepts. Other procedural regimes seemed illogical at the start and unjustified later on. The

American procedure seemed too fast, from the English perspective; the German procedure seemed too messy, from the American standpoint; the English seemed to ritualistic and superficial, from the German perspective; and so on. Each started to identify with protections and safeguards of *his or her* procedure, such as space for unbinding, chances to learn, or possibilities to deliberately position one-self. But what we advocated, differently to lawyers or human rights scholars, were less universal rights, rather local rules. We had to realize that what we supported was an integral part of the game under study: protections that respond to certain threats of *my* procedure; openness that respond to certain specifications of *my* procedure; chances to learn that respond to certain risks of *my* procedure. Does all this apply to a more general principle, to some ethics even? A narrow answer to this question would be no. A wide answer would be yes. Yes, because the doubts and critique relate to a sense of balance. This balance is not so much about balancing the parties or defense and prosecution, but procedure as an amplifying force and its participants as frequent members. The shared ethics of our comparison seems to implicate this: procedure is a strong force that achieves a whole lot that could not be achieved by other meaning production frames, but it does so at the expense of the members' (limited) capacities. Doing procedure, in this view, is a methodical activity by members that, at the same token, systematically exceeds the know-how of these members.

As a meaning producing frame, doing procedure is not restricted to law and legal procedure. It applies as well to other systemic contexts such as parliamentary legislation, managerial innovation projects, administrative participatory planning, or scientific knowledge production. Recent efforts to apply the procedure frame to institutional politics could show that political activities proceed in similar contexts of 'extended' and 'frequent' meaning production. The same applies to studies on knowledge production in scientific procedure, on deliberation in legislative procedure, or decision-making in economics. Doing procedure deserves attention far beyond law-in-action, for example, by social researchers, activists, or potential participants who are interested in what is going on, why, and to what powerful effect. In other words, procedure as meaning producing frame is an analytical *and* practical concept. It gives insights to everybody who needs to understand what it means to speak out or remain silent at this very point in time, meaning at or on this procedural stage.

Notes

1 Introducing Procedure

1. The data were collected during two phases of fieldwork in three private defense firms and three respective courts in the United Kingdom, Germany, and the United States. The fieldwork was a part of international comparative project 'Comparative Micro-Sociology of Criminal Proceedings'. The project was hosted by Freie Universität Berlin and funded by DFG (Deutsche Forschungsgemeinschaft).
2. For an elaboration of this point, see Banakar and Travers (2002).
3. The same principle was vocalized by Garfinkel in a different way: 'if the matter is meaningfully consistent, it may be correctly treated as the thing which actually occurred' (1967, p. 106).
4. Qualitative scholars with an inquisitorial or continental background show a stronger affinity to the judges' activities (for example, Wolff/Müller, 1979; Schmid et al., 1997; Komter, 2003; Stegmaier, 2008).
5. When speaking about 'epistemic cultures', Karin Knorr (1999) issued a similar critique of ethnomethodological laboratory studies lead by such scholars as Latour, Woolgar, Lynch, and others. The differences amongst natural scientific laboratories are underrated due to the resulting emphases on the situated and pragmatic dimension of science-in-action often referred to as the scientists' tinkering. As a consequence, Knorr offered a comparative account of the diverse roles and organization of laboratories in different knowledge processes.
6. For more on this connection, see Ehrlich (2001).

2 Field Access as an Ongoing Accomplishment

1. In an exemplary narrative of the kind, Geertz (1973) narrates his access into the field with the thick description about "the cock fight". He thus stresses the discovery aspect of access by relating his and his wife's journey towards the backstage of the local event that stands at the gate of the Balinese culture.
2. There are important cultural variations to what appears to be a general rule concerning public access. In their conversational analytic study of the production of credibility in court, Wolff and Müller (1997) address the issue of access with regard to the difficulty of conducting recordings of trials in German court rooms. They ascribe their successful access to the field to fortunate circumstances as well as insider consent, namely, permission by the judge in question. Here, one judge functioned as the door opener by naming potentially willing and interested colleagues. The second prerequisite concerns negotiating access at the site of the trial with all the participants.

Although some defendants and witnesses denied consent to the recording (interestingly none of the professionals did), Wolff and Müller obtained permission to collect as much data as they hoped for.

3. Suffice to mention Wilhelm Dilthey, Heinrich Rickert, Martin Heidegger, Hans Gadamer, and, more recently, Northrop Frye, Hayden White, Roland Barthes, Paul Ricoeur, Alaisdire McIntytre, and Tzvetan Todorov. Emphasizing different dimensions of narrative, all these scholars argue for its centrality in creating meaningfulness.

4. According to Blackstone's Criminal Justice, the trial should be public, meaning "the doors of the courtroom are expected to be kept open, the public are entitled to be admitted, and the trial is to be public in all respects" (1998, p. 1050).

5. In a Practice Direction issued in 1981, the use of tape recorders is classified as "contempt of court" unless they are used "for purposes of official transcripts or proceedings" (Archbold, 2000, p. 2341).

6. He operated the only authorized tape recorder in the room. He had to switch it on and off when the judge entered court and left it. Additionally, he scribbled case-number and case-title on the tape. An official transcription service would use these tapes in order to prepare verbatim records on demand.

7. One judge – by help of a Chinese Whispers – asked his clerk to ask the usher to ask the recorder to address politely the issue of being appropriately dressed in court. He was worried about me sitting there without any jacket. My neighbor did not know how to put it: "The judge would appreciate if you could leave your jacket on during the hearing." "Or shall I better come in a suit?" "Well, yes that would be excellent." He seemed a bit embarrassed at first (like myself) and relieved later. "This is very kind of you", he added satisfied. The same day I got myself a dark blue suit.

8. Here are some of their nosy questions: "How can you study this without any knowledge of the law?" "Which system is better: the German or ours?" "What do you think: guilty or not guilty?"

9. Just one year later, I experienced more flexibility. I accompanied a barrister and sat as his (kind of) apprentice right behind him.

10. There is, of course, much more to say about these social relations in the field. The barristers were generally interested in the academia, the research project, the work of sociologists, our career path, and so on. They turned my research themes easily into "hooks" for long cultivated conversations – as if they were constantly after "general knowledge". They treated my co-presence with professionalism and curiosity.

11. Hence, the sequentiality here is reversed in a way. In order to understand the sequential build-up of a criminal case I started with the (possible) final stage of this process.

12. This points at an important feature of the criminal procedure in Germany: lawyers of the defense are not a constitutive part of the procedure in smaller cases – often it can be financially reasonable for a defendant to come without a lawyer. At the same time I encountered quite a few defendants who were on their own and obviously failed to understand the dealings in their own trial.

13. They are persons receiving practical training in legal work after having passed the first state exam.

14. My closest academic companions included Hammersley and Atkinson (1983), Maanen (1988), Weiss (1994), and Emerson *et al.* (1995).
15. This is how Marlow, the protagonist from Joseph Conrad's *Heart of Darkness* expressed this moment of self transformation: "For a time, I felt that I belonged still to a world of straight-forward facts, but that feeling would not last long. Soon it would become nostalgia" (Conrad, 1902, p. 20).
16. We wish to thank our informants and guides, the attorneys as well as all the clients who allowed us to follow the often private matters. Moreover, we respect the reasons given by those lawyers and clients who did not grant us access because of other, more pressing matters at hand.

3   Procedural Past: Binding and Unbinding

1. See McBarnet (1981), Devlin (1985), or Ashworth (1998) on silence and its legal implications in the criminal process.
2. See Sudnow (1964), McIntyre (1987), and Cunningham (1991).
3. Durkheim (1897) referred to the "the social bond" in order to explain how individuals adapt to social collectives. The social bond can be either loose or tight. It leaves either little room or much room for individual self-rule. A similar idea can be found in Elias' sociology of figurations. "Individuals" are kept within groups by "elastic bonds" (Elias, 1965). In economical sociology, the notion of binding is used in relation to contracts and decisions. Depending on the cultural conditions, contracts are more or less binding to transaction partners (Maneschi, 2004).
4. Goffman (1959) describes the building of social identities or personhood similarly. Self-presentations add up to a relatively consistent image that the person gets bound to. Not sticking to the image can cause confusion and perplexity, at a minimum.
5. See, for the case of asylum hearings, Scheffer (2002).
6. We investigated into concepts such as career, mobilization, and becoming in order to stipulate some sequential accounts of the procedural course. By *career* (Scheffer, 2003a), we referred to the increasing or shrinking social relevance of arguments or stories. We focused on the social value that they acquired in smaller and larger procedural publics. By *mobilization* (ibid.), we referred to the investigations into these arguments or stories in order to make them fit for the legal contest. Each mobilizing move involves new points of attack and, in this line, risks being undermined by the adversary. By *becomings* (Scheffer, 2004), we emphasized that arguments are not fully valuable right from the start. The analysis encounters a series of halfproducts on the way to court. These three temporal concepts point towards the fact-producing capacity of procedures.
7. Crown Court cases derive from lower Magistrates' Courts. The Magistrate, assisted by a legally trained clerk, delegates the matter to the higher court, because (1) the offense is triable only on indictment (such as murder, manslaughter, or rape); (2) the defendant of an "offence triable either way" (such as theft, obtaining by deception, or burglary) chooses trial by jury; (3) the Magistrate decides that the maximum adequate penalty exceeds their powers.

8. The Criminal Procedure and Investigation Act 1996

> imposes a staged process, shifting between the parties: first upon the investigator of the crime a duty to record and retain relevant material; then for the prosecutor to make primary disclosure to the defense of material which it is not proposed to use, but which in his judgement might undermine the case for the prosecution, and a schedule listing other unused non-sensitive material; then for the accused to disclose the nature of the defense; then for the prosecutor to make secondary disclosure of any material, not so far disclosed by him, which in the light of its disclosure might reasonably by expected to assist the defense; and finally in the event of a dispute for the defense to raise it, and the court to dispose of it. The situation must be kept under review, and the prosecutor must continue to disclose further material which comes to his attention. . . .
>
> (Tapper, 1999, p. 251)

9. Lynch refers to this practice critically.

> To attempt to exhibit 'contradictions' in the above fashion, however, is to miss an important distinction between talk in pre-trial sessions, and the presentation of arguments in court. For one thing, participants in pre-trial sessions were never shown to accuse one another of 'contradicting' themselves in the course of the current interaction. Furthermore, the extraction of temporally removed assertions and the comparison of those assertions under the rubric of 'consistency' fail to recognize the ways in which the assertions were responsive to the local course of Argument in which they occurred.
>
> (1999, p. 304)

10. In court, there are no police officers asking unwelcome questions. There is no hangover causing distress. The anger and rage has disappeared. This time the defendant's account is initiated by the "friendly examination" in front of judge, jury, and opponent. This time, it is his defense barrister who guides him through "his account," subsequently probed in the name of "consistency" during the cross-examination.
11. A close comparison shows that the account here is more streamlined, less ambiguous, more definite, and so on. It is condensed to the very performance of resemblance or repetition. This is, however, not a word-by-word repetition, but rather a repetition of features that can be reshuffled and contrasted.
12. See for instance the governmental Auld-Report from 2001.
13. PC: Did you feel any remorse for what you'd done or anything?
    Striker: No, I wasn't finished.
    PC: That would you have done to him?
    Striker: I don't know.
    PC: continues to recap the interview.

PC: I take it from talking to you, you're not sorry for what you've done, are you?

Striker: No.

PC: I take it as far as you're concerned he deserved it?

Striker: Yeah.

14. The prosecuting barrister made some triumphal comments right before the trial hearing: "You were *not finished*! What exactly were you about to do!"

15. We do not know whether Steve knew at all and realized that "the court or jury, in determining whether the accused is guilty of the offence charged, may draw inferences from the failure (to) mention when so questioned, charged or informed as appear proper." This at least is fixed in the Criminal Justice and Public Order Act from 1994, paragraph 34. Evaluative studies observed "a significant, but only partial shift in practice" (Ashworth, 1998, p. 104) after this Act was introduced. The percentage of interviews with "all questions answered" rose from 77 percent to 84 percent (Bucke and Brown, 1997, chap. 4).

16. Ashworth reports a similar case:

> The complainant in a rape case discovered that, although the offender had pleaded guilty, he pleaded guilty only on the basis that she consented to intercourse when it began and subsequently changed her mind. On inquiring how this version of facts was put forward, she learnt that this was the basis on which the plea of guilty was negotiated – in effect, to a version of the offence which was much less serious.
>
> (Ashworth, 1998, p. 276)

17. Only a minority of the accused is actually accompanied by a solicitor. In 1994 "some fifty-two percent had received no legal advice, nine percent had received only pre-interview advice, whereas some thirty-nine percent had a legal adviser present during the interview" (Bucke and Brown, 1997, chap. 4).

18. The solicitor wrote to her barrister,

> We have asked our client whether she can provide us with any information that might assist *us* in tracing Kim to see if she was prepared to give a statement. We appreciate her assistance is perhaps unlikely, but in any event client has not provided any information which could lead to tracing her.
>
> (p. 61/28.3.1)

19. Notice the persistent use of the introductory phrase "I understand", which not only refers to the defendant's story in a segment-by-segment fashion, but also cites the defendant as the co-author for the subsequent strategy.

20. Besides these two courts, two higher courts concern themselves with criminal cases – the *Oberlandesgericht* and the *Bundesgerichtshof*. In the cases the researcher followed during the fieldwork, both courts only featured as instance of complaint (the former) or as the addressee of appeals of verdicts from the *Landgericht* (the latter).

21. Of course, there are several rules that refine these rather broad descriptions. For the objective of this chapter, the given characterization is sufficient.

22. The case was presented to the field researcher when the lawyer started preparing for the appeal hearing. All information thus derives from the shared file and from talks with the lawyer. The case under consideration is a very complex one. We focus only on one thread of the proceeding.

23. Although referring to the client just by last name might seem impolite, it reflects the practice of the participants in the proceedings.

24. The accused has the right to be heard during the investigation, but one can also remain silent. Remaining silent comes in two forms: one can either follow the summons for a police interview and state the intention to remain silent in the interview, or one can just ignore the summons. If the summons is not from the police but the prosecution, however, attendance is mandatory.

25. This is similar to the DUI cases insofar as it includes, by definition, that the accused is caught in the act. The lawyer's work is reduced to interpreting and legally weighing the facts.

26. Again, the ethnographer encountered this case at the advanced stage of preparation for the appeal hearing. The material, thus, is drawn from the file and from the information given by the lawyer.

27. We add quotation marks to facilitate the reading. As for the protocols of the trials, an important difference exists between the *Amtsgericht* and the *Landgericht*. The protocol of the trial at the *Amtsgericht* is not a close transcript of the trial (the trial is not and must not be taped) but a summary that reflects the central statements. In trials at the *Landgericht* even central statements of testimonies, and so on, do not go into the protocol: only the procedural aspects are recorded. Interestingly, at the *Landgericht*, in order to make a statement accessible for the future (for example, for appeals), one has to get the statement into the file; that is, handing it over in writing.

28. The trial in the first instance shows an intriguing detail – one of the witnesses was a police officer who was involved in the first "scooter case." He testified that the scooter was running, and even driving fast at that time. Hence, the story of the defendant is not only introduced informally through prior interpersonal relationships or formally by reading the list of prior convictions, but a preceding case is also explicitly cited as an analogy to the actual case at hand. The lawyer was furious about this.

29. In the German criminal law system, the documents in the file can be introduced to the trial as a *Vorhalt*. The judge, attorney, or prosecutor will read out parts of a document and ask the witness or defendant to relate to the passage. This may function to freshen up a witness' memory. It may also function to confront the witness or defendant with former, conflicting versions. Only a judicial interrogation prior to the trial can be read out in court and thereby introduced as binding to the trial.

30. It might seem that the question marks are missing here. This judge "asked her questions" by making statements that often reformulated the former utterance. She rather demanded responses.

4 Procedural Future: The Politics of Positioning

1. In his examination of the Miranda Rule, Allen (2006) noted that the hasty adaptation of the rule for the wording of the Fifth Amendment created incongruent interpretations, such as, for example, "being incapable of rational understanding..." in contrast to "being inconsistent with the personal preference" (p. 72). The, thus, created ambiguity makes the Miranda rule a rather ineffectual mechanism of civil protection: only a gross violation of the rule as, for example, its non evocation may be useful to the defense, but still in a partial way, as it points to the ineffectiveness of the law enforcement rather than the absence of a cause.
2. The transcription conventions include (a) *italics* for designating actions and activities; (b) <u>underline</u> for emphasis; and (c) stretch marks for prolonged sounds. Wherever the tape is not clear, I have written "unintelligible".
3. On the effects of the arrest on the suspect, see Williams (1991).

5 Procedural Presence: Failing and Learning

1. When using the term "topic" we hint at a possible connection between the notion of failing and the rhetorical concept of *topos*, especially in its epistemological dimension. See Hannken-Illjes *et al.* (2007) and Hannken-Illjes (2007).
2. In the following, we will exclude plea-bargain from our analysis for the pragmatic reason that it does not occur in all our systems.
3. In German criminal trials the defendant has the last word, before the judges retreat for deliberation. These last words are commonly used for apologies and promises to lead a better life. Cautious defendants often say only that they follow their lawyers in their remarks.
4. This does not exclude, but opens up the regular aftermath of criminal trials: the parties' assessments of whether or not they should lodge an appeal. Any appeal hearing rests on public knowledge about what was decided and how during the hearing. There is, hence, an in-built rationale to expose failures publicly at one point or another during the trial.

6 Courts as Ways of Knowing

1. This is a specific reformulation of Valverde's question "how law knows" (2003). See also, Sarat *et al.*, 2007.
2. Only a few would consider the "space celebrated" as being part of the law: "Whilst it is sometimes argued that the familiar image of oak chambers, leather seats, judicial benches, jury boxes, witness stands and docks, may add to the magisterial aura of law, these are considered to be merely extraneous features – they are not in and of themselves Law" (Haldar, 1994, p. 187). Quite similarly, Scheffer (2004) described the courtroom as a relatively solid object that is at the same time co-productive and unavailable in relation to the current dealings.

3. One example: in 1849, Prussian law admitted the public to trials. Suddenly, courtrooms were meant to accommodate a public. The architects arranged for entrances and exits, and for public corridors that would channel the ordinary men right to the proceedings without much disturbance (see Bednarek, 2003).

4. The Design Guide for English Crown Courts suggests: "The building should be seen less as a symbol of authority than as an expression of the concept of justice and equality before the law. The scales of justice are a more appropriate symbol than the sword of retribution" (1.2., quoted in Mulcahy, 2006).

5. These courtroom studies include ethnographic and conversation analytical work by scholars such as Travers, 1997; Drew, 2003, 1992; Bogoch, 2000; Ulmer, 1994; Atkinson, 1992; Lynch, 1982; Komter, 1998; Stygall, 1994; Maynard, 1982, 1984; Danet, 1984; Pollner, 1979. These rich and detailed contributions to the study of the courtroom interaction have advanced it far enough to be capable of bringing our attention to unique orders of producing system-relevant knowledge.

6. The Crown Court standards are inscribed in "design templates". While some standards remained "constant from at least the fifteenth century until the present day" (Mulcahy, 2006, p. 10), others such as the role of lawyers in court have changed significantly over the last decades. The barristers were elevated to the central "rows of seating... [which] served to vertically separate the judge and defendant and horizontally separate the jury and the witnesses" (ibid.).

7. These obligatory participants are not identical with the members of the inner circle of the court. Rock (1993) distinguishes between four concentric circles with the judges forming the center and grouped around them being "the team" (consisting of the court staff), the professionals from outside the court, and, as a fourth removed circle, the public.

8. See Langbein on how the "accused became silenced" (2003), while the trial became increasingly lawyer-dominated.

9. An exception is the *In-Augenscheinnahme*. Some evidence needs to be looked at in situ, often because there is only one copy of the document, photo, or other item. The items to be identified or explained are placed on the judge's bench. Participants are invited to walk up to the bench and "take a look". This huddle allows informal chats.

10. We do not claim a full resemblance here. Jasanoff contends, rightly, that a "careful account would find congruence as well as clashes in the processes of law and science" (2005, p. 51).

11. Shapin understands experimental knowledge by showing the "connections between empiricist processes of knowledge making and the spatial distribution of participants, pointing to the ineradicable problem of trust that is generated when some people have direct sensory access to a phenomenon and others do not" (1998, p. 374).

12. As explicated above, our "trans-sequential analyses" (Scheffer, 2010) combine the "here and now" of events with the "there and then" (Katz, 2004) of processes. We suggest that "event and process" (Scheffer, 2007) be related differently in different court procedures.

13. For some exceptions, see the micro-analysis of the barrister's casework (marking, drafting, noting, scripting, and so on) on the day of the trial hearing (Scheffer, 2006b). Some of this work would be finished only minutes before his or her closing speech.
14. Jasanoff highlights crucial differences: "The formal spaces of both institutions – courts no less than labs – are claimed to be dedicated to finding the truth, though with different ends in view: the law needs facts as necessary adjuncts to doing justice; science seeks facts more as an end in itself. Legal fact-finding therefore generally remains within the framework of a specific case or controversy, whereas scientific facts must speak to wider audiences" (2005, p. 51).

References

Abel, R. L. (1997) *Lawyers: A Critical Reader* (New York: The New Press).

Abel, R. L. and Lewis, P. S. C. (1995) *Lawyers in Society: An Overview* (Berkley: University of California Press).

Allen, G. (2006) 'The Crime of Driving Under the Influence', *Crime and Society* 12(3), 237–259.

Anderson, B. (2006) *Imagined Communities* (New ed.) (London, New York: Verso).

Archbold. (2000) *Criminal Pleading, Evidence and Practice*, P. James Richardson (ed.) (London: Sweet and Maxwell).

Arlt, G. (1993) 'Der Mensch als Macht', *Philosophisches Jahrbuch* 100(1), 114–130.

Arminen, I. (2008) 'Scientific and "Radical" Ethnomethodology. From Incompatible Paradigms to Ethnomethodological Sociology', *Philosophy of the Social Science* 38, 167–191.

Ashworth, A. (1998) *The Criminal Process. An Evaluative Study* (New York: Oxford University Press).

Atkinson, P. (1983) 'The Reproduction of the Professional Community', in R. Dingwall and P. Lewis (eds) *The Sociology of the Professions. Lawyers, Doctors, and Others* (London: The Macmillan Press).

Atkinson, M. (1992) 'Displaying Neutrality: Informal Aspects of Informal Court Proceedings', in P. Drew and J. Heritage (eds) *Talk at Work: Interaction in Institutional Settings* (Cambridge: Cambridge University Press).

Atkinson, J. and Drew, P. (1979) *Order in Court: The Organization of Verbal Interactions in Judicial Settings* (London: The Macmillan Press).

Banakar, R. (2002) 'Reflections on the Methodological Issues of the Sociology of Law', *Journal of Law and Society* 27, 1–34.

Banakar, R. (2003) *Merging Law and Sociology. Beyond the Dichotomies of the Socio-Legal Research* (Berlin: Glada and Wilch).

Banakar, R. and Travers, M. (2002) *An Introduction to Law and Social Theory* (Oxford: Hart Publishing).

Barzilai, G. (2003) *Communities and Law: Politics and Cultures of Legal Identities* (Ann Arbor: University of Michigan Press).

Baum, L. (1997) *The Puzzle of Judicial Behavior* (Ann Arbor: University of Michigan Press).

Bednarek, A. (2003) *Gerichtsbauten in Schlesien 1815–1945* (Görlitz-Zittau: Verlag Gunter Oettel).

Benneworth, K. (2007) ' "Just Good Friends": Managing the Clash of Discourse in Police Interviews with Paedophiles', in J. Cotterill (ed.) *The Language of Sex Crimes* (Basingstoke: Palgrave).

Benson, D. and Drew, P. (1978) ' "Was there Firing in Sandy Row that Night?": Some Features of the Organization of Disputes about Recorded Facts', *Sociological Inquiry* 48, 89–110.

Black, D. (1971) 'The Social Organization of Arrest', *Stanford Law Review* 23(6), 1087–1111.

Black, D. (1999) *Law in Film. Resonance and Representation* (Urbana: University of Chicago Press).

Blumberg, A. (1967) 'The Practice of Law as Confidence Game: Organizational Co-optation of a Profession', *Law & Society Review* 1, 15–39.

Bogoch, B. (1990) *The Dynamics of Power: Lawyer-Client Interaction in a Legal Aid Setting*. Paper presented at The Sixth International Colloquium of the International Association of the Semiotics of Law, 7–10 July in Onati, Spain.

Bogoch, B. (1994) 'Power, Distance and Solidarity: Models of Professional-Client Interaction in an Israeli Legal Aid Setting', *Discourse & Society* 5(1), 65–88.

Bogoch, B. (2000) 'Discourse Dilemmas and Courtroom Control: The Talk of Trial Judges', *Law and Social Inquiry. Journal of the American Bar Foundation* 25(1), 227–247.

Bogoch, B. and Danet, B. (1984) 'Challenge and Control in Lawyer-Client Interaction: A Case Study in an Israeli Legal Aid Office', *Text* 4(1–3), 249–275.

Bohannan, P. (1997) 'Ethnography and Comparison in Legal Anthropology', in L. Nader (ed.) *Law in Culture and Society* (London: University of California Press).

Boon, A. and Levin, J. (1999) *The Ethics and Conduct of Lawyers in England and Wales* (Oxford: Hart Publishing).

Bourdieu, P. (1987) 'The Force of Law: Toward a Sociology of the Juridicial Field', *The Hastings Law Journal* 38, 805–853.

Bourdieu, P. (2000) *Pascalian Meditations* (Cambridge: Polity Press).

Bradney, A. and Cownie, F. (2000) *Living Without Law. An Ethnography of Quaker Decision-Making, Dispute Avoidance and Dispute Resolution* (Aldershot: Ashgate).

Brewer, J. D. (1990) 'Sensitivity as a Problem in Field Research. A Study of Routine Policing in Northern Ireland', *American Behavioural Scientist* 33, 578–601.

Brown, P. and Levinson, S. C. (1993) 'Linguistic and Non-linguistic Coding of Spatial Arrays: Explorations in Mayan Cognition', *Working Paper of the Cognitive Anthropology Research Group*, No. 24 (Nijmegen: Max Planck Institute of Psycholingistics).

Bucke, T. and Brown, D. (1997) *In Police Custody: Police Powers and Suspects' Rights under the Revised PACE Codes of Practice* (Home Office Research Study 174).

Burawoy, M. (1991) 'The Extended Case Method', in M. Burawoy *et al.* (eds) *Ethnography Unbound: Power and Resistance in the Modern Metropolis* (Berkeley: University of California Press).

Burke, P. (2004) 'Identities and Social Structure: The 2003 Cooley-Mead Award Address', *Social Psychology Quarterly* 67(1), 5–15.

Burke, P. (2006) 'Identity Change', *Social Psychology Quarterly* 69(1), 81–96.

Burns, S. (2004) 'Pursuing "Deep Pockets" Insurance-Related Issues in Judicial Settlement and Work', *Journal of Contemporary Ethnography* 33, 111–153.

Burns, S. (ed.) (2005) *Ethnographies of Law and Social Control. Sociology of Crime, Law and Deviance* (New York: JAI Press).

Burns, S. (2008) 'Demonstrating "Reasonable Fear" at Trial: Is it Science or Junk Science?' *Human Studies* 31, 107–131.

Burns, S. and Peyrot, M. (2001) 'Sociologists on Trial. Theoretical Competition and Juror Reasoning', *The American Sociologist* 32, 42–69.

Burns, S. and Peyrot, M. (2003) 'Though Love. Nurturing and Coercing Responsibility and Recovery in California Drug Courts', *Social Problems* 50, 416–438.

Butler, J. (1993) *Bodies That Matter* (London: Routledge).

Butler, J. (1997) *Excitable Speech: A Politics of the Performative* (New York: Routledge).

Cain, M. (1983) 'The General Practice. Lawyer and Client: Toward a Radical Reconception', in R. Dingwall (ed.) *The Sociology of the Professions* (London: Palgrave Macmillan).

Cain, M. (1994) 'The Symbol Traders', in M. Cain and C. B. Harrington (eds) *Lawyers in a Postmodern World* (Buckingham: Open University Press).

Cambrosio, A., Limoges, C. and Pronovost, D. (1990) 'Representing Biotechnology: An Ethnography of Quebec Science Policy', *Social Studies of Science* 20, 195–227.

Carlen, P. (1976) *Magistrates' Justice* (London: Martin Robertson).

Carr, D. (1973) *Explorations in Phenomenology* (The Hague: Martin Nijhoff).

Chase, O. (2002) 'American Exceptionalism and the Comparative Procedure', *The American Journal of Comparative Law* 50(2), 277–301.

Christensen, R. and Kudlich, H. (2001) *Theorie richterlichen Begründens* (Berlin: Duncker & Humblot).

Cicourel, A. V. (1968) 'Police Practices and Official Records', in R. Turner (ed.) *Ethnomethodology: Selected Readings* (Harmondsworth, Middlesex: Penguin).

Clifford, J. and Marcus, G. E. (1986) *Writing Culture* (Berkley: University of California Press).

Coffrey, A. (1999) *The Ethnographic Self. Fieldwork and the Representation of Identity* (London: Sage).

Colbert, D., Paternoster, R. and Bushway, S. D. (2002) 'Do Attorneys Really Matter? The Empirical and Legal Case for the Right of Counsel at Bail', *Cardozo Law Review* 23, 101–165.

Collins, R. (2004) *Interaction Ritual Chains* (Princeton: Princeton University Press).

Conley, J. and O'Barr, W. M. (1977) 'Behavioral Analysis of the American Criminal Courtroom', *Research Report* No. 4, Law and Language Project, Duke University.

Conley, J. and O'Barr, W. M. (1990) *Rules Versus Relationships: The Ethnography of Legal Discourse* (Chicago, IL: University of Chicago Press).

Conley, J. and O'Barr, W. M. (1998) *Just Words. Law, Language and Power* (Chicago: University of Chicago Press).

Conley, J., O'Barr, W. M. and Lind, E. A. (1978) 'The Power of Language: Presentational Style in the Courtroom', *Duke Law Journal* 78, 1375–1399.

Conrad, J. (1902) *Heart of Darkness* (London: Penguin).

Couric, E. (1990) *The Trial Lawyers: The Nation's Top Litigators Tell How They Win* (Boston: St. Martin's Griffin).

Coutin, S. (2002) 'Reconceptualizing Research: Ethnographic Fieldwork and Immigration Politics in Southern California', in J. Starr and M. Goodale (eds) *Practicing Ethnography of Law* (New York: Palgrave Macmillan).

Cownie, F. (2004) *Legal Academics: Cultures and Identities* (Oxford: Hart Publishing).

Cunningham, C. D. (1991) 'The Lawyer as Translator, Representation as Text', *Cornell Law Review* 77, 1298–1387.

Damaska, M. (2003) 'Epistememology and Legal Regulation of Proof', *Law, Probability and Risk* 2, 117–130.

Danet, B. (1980) 'Language in the Legal Process', *Law & Society Review* 14(3), 445–564.

Danet, B. (1984) 'Studies of Legal Discourse', *Text* 4, 1–3.

Danet, B. and Rafin, H. J. (1977) 'Strategies of Control in Courtroom Questioning', presented at the *Annual Meeting of the American Sociological Association*, Chicago.

Danet, B., Hoffman, K. and Kermish, N. C. (1980a) 'Obstacles to the Study of Lawyer-Client Interaction: The Biography of a Failure', *Law & Society Review* 14, 905–922.

Danet, B., Hoffman, K., Kermish, N. C., Rafn, H. J. and Stayman, D. G. (1980b) 'An Ethnography of Questioning', in R. W. Shuy and A. Shnukal (eds) *Language Use and the Uses of Language* (Washington, DC.: Georgetown University Press).

Danielsen, D. and Engle, K. (eds) (1994) *After Identity: A Reader in Law and Culture* (New York: Routledge).

Dann, M. (1997) 'Waking Up Jurors, Shaking Up Courts, Trial Magazine', *Public Affairs & Education Committee of the American Trial Lawyers Association* 33(7), 20–28.

Danto, A. (1985) *Narration and Knowledge* (New York: Columbia University Press).

DeCerteau, M. (1984) *The Practice of Everyday Life* (Berkeley: University of California Press).

Depraz, N. (2001) 'The Husserlian Theory of Intersubjectivity as Alterology', *Journal of Consciousness Studies* 8(5–7), 169–178.

Derrida, J. (1996) *Archive Fever*, E. Prenovitz (trans.) (Chicago: Chicago University Press).

Derrida, J. (1999) 'Force of Law: The "Mystical Foundations of Authority"', *Cardozo Law Review* 11, 919–1045.

Derrida, J. (2000) *Of Hospitality*, Rachel Bowlby (trans.) (Stanford: Stanford University Press).

Dershowitz, A. (1983) *The Best Defense* (New York: Vintage).

Devlin, P. (1985) *Easing the Passing – The Trial of Dr John Bodkin Adams* (London: The Bodley Head).

Diamond, S. and Vidmar, N. (2001) 'Jury Room Ruminations on Forbidden Topics', *Virginia Law Review* 87, 1857–1915.

Dingwall, R. (1980) 'Ethics and Ethnography', *Sociolegal Review* 28, 871–912.

Dingwall, R. (2002) 'Ethnomethodology and Law', in R. Banakar and M. Travers (eds) *An Introduction to Law and Social Theory* (Oxford: Hart Publishing).

Doering, H. and Hirschauer, S. (1997) 'Die Biographie der Dinge. Eine Ethnographie musealer Repräsentation', in K. Amann and S. Hirschauer (eds) *Die Befremdung der eigenen Kultur. Zur ethnographischen Herausforderung soziologischer Empirie* (Frankfurt am Main: Suhrkamp).

Doyle, J. M. and Grace, K. (2007) 'Are Racial Identities of Multiracials Stable? Changing Self-Identification Among Single and Multiple Race Individuals', *Social Psychology Quarterly* 70(4), 405–423.

Drew, P. (1992) 'Contested Evidence in Courtroom Cross-Examination: The Case of a Trial for Rape', in P. Drew and J. Heritage (eds) *Talk at Work: Interaction in Institutional Settings* (Cambridge: Cambridge University Press).

Drew, P. (1997) 'Contested Evidence in Courtroom Cross-Examination', in J. Manzo and M. Travers (eds) *Law in Action. Ethnomethodological and Conversation Analytic Approaches to Law* (Aldershot: Ashgate).

Drew, P. (2003) 'Comparative Analysis of Talk-in-Interaction in Different Institutional Settings: A Sketch', in P. J. Glenn, C. D. LeBaron and J. Mandelbaum (eds) *Studies in Language and Social Interaction: In Honour of Robert Hopper* (Mahwah, NJ: Erlbaum).

DuBois, J. (1980) 'Beyond Definitiveness. The Trace of Identity in Discourse', in W. Chafe (ed.) *The Pear Stories* (Norwood: Ablex Publishing Co.).

Dupret, B. (2005) 'The Practice of Judging. The Egyptian Judiciary at Work in a Personal Status Case', in M. K. Massud, R. Peters and D. Powers (eds) *Dispensing Justice in Muslim Courts. Qadis, Procedures and Judgements* (Leiden: E. J. Brill).

Dupret, B. (2006) 'Morality on Trial. Structure and Intelligibility System of a Court Sentence Concerning Homosexuality', *Qualitative Sociology Review* 2(2), 7–31.

Duranti, A. (1992) 'Language and Bodies in Social Space: Samoan Ceremonial Greetings', *American Anthropologist* 94(3), 657–691.

Durkhein, E. (1933) *The Division of Labor in Society*, G. Simpson (trans.) (New York: The Free Press).

Durkheim, É. (1897) *Le Suicide: etude de sociologie* (Paris: Alcan).

Edwards, D. (2006) 'Facts, Norms and Dispositions. Practical Uses of the Modal "Would" in Police Interrogations', *Discourse Studies* 7(1), 5–29.

Edwards, D. and Stokoe, E. (2008) ' "Did You Have Permission to Smash Your Neighbour's Door?" Silly Questions and their Answers in Police-Suspect Interrogations', *Discourse Studies* 10(1), 89–111.

Ehrlich, E. (2001) *Fundamental Principles of the Sociology of Law* (New Brunswick (US), London (UK): Transaction Publishers).

Elias, N. (1965) *The Established and the Outsiders: A Sociological Enquiry into Community Problems* (London: Frank Cass & Co. Ltd).

Emerson, R. (1994) 'Constructing Serious Violence and its Victims. Processing a Domestic Violence Restraining Order', in G. Miller and J. Holstein (eds) *Perspectives on Social Problems* 6 (Greenwood: JAI Press), 3–28.

Emerson, R., Fretz, R. I. and Shaw, L. L. (1995) *Writing Ethnographic Fieldnotes* (Chicago: University of Chicago Press).

Emmelman, D. S. (1993) 'Organizational Conditions that Facilitate an Ethical Defense Posture Among Attorneys for the Poor: Observations of a Private Nonprofit Corporation', *Criminal Justice Review* 18, 221–235.

Emmelman, D. (1994) 'The Effects of Social Class on Adjudication of Criminal Cases: Class-Linked Behavior Tendencies, Common Sense, and the Interpretive Procedures of Court-Appointed Defense Attorneys', *Symbolic Interaction* 17(1), 1–20.

Engels, F. and Marx, K. (1976) *Collected Works, Vol. I–VI* (London: Lawrence and Wishart).

Erickson, F. and Schultz, J. (1982) *Counselor as Gatekeeper* (New York: Academic Press).

Ewick, P. and Silbey, S. S. (1998) *The Common Place of Law. Stories from Everyday Life* (Chicago: The University of Chicago Press).

Feeley, M. M. (1992) *The Process is the Punishment: Handling Cases in a Lower Criminal Court* (New York: Russell Sage Foundation).

Felstiner, W. (1998) 'Justice, Power and Lawyers', in B. G. Garth and A. Sarat (eds) *Justice and Power in Sociolegal Studies* (Evanston, IL: Northwestern University Press).

Felstiner, W. F. and Sarat, A. (1992) 'Enactments of Power: Negotiating Reality and Responsibility in Lawyer-Client Interactions', *Cornell Law Review* 77(6), 1112–1156.

Flemming, R. B. (1986) 'Client Games: Defence Attorney Perspectives on their Relations with Criminal Clients', *American Bar Foundation Research Journal* 11(2), 253–277.

Flood, J. (1981) 'The Middlemen of the Law. An Ethnographic Inquiry into the English Legal Profession', *American Bar Foundation Research Journal* 6(2), 377–398.

Flood, J. (1983) *Barristers' Clerks. The Law's Middlemen* (Manchester: Manchester University Press).

Flood, J. (1987) *Anatomy of Law. An Ethnography of a Corporate Law Firm* (PhD dissertation, Northwestern University).

Flood, J. (1991) 'Doing Business: The Management of Uncertainty in Lawyer's Work', *Law and Society Review* 25(1), 43–71.

Flood, J. (2005) 'Socio-Legal Ethnography', in R. Banakar and M. Travers (eds) *Theory and Method in Socio-legal Research* (Oxford: Hart Publishing).

Flood, J. (2006) 'Law Firms', in D. Clark (ed.) *Encyclopedia of Law and Society* (American and Global Perspectives, London: Sage Publishing).

Foucault, M. (1972) *The Archaeology of Knowledge and the Discourse of Language* (London: Tavistock).

Foucault, M. (1997) *Discipline and Punish: The Birth of the Prison*, A. Sheridan (trans.) (New York: Vintage).

Foucault, M. (2003) *Die Wahrheit und die juristischen Formen* (Frankfurt am Main: Suhrkamp).

Friedman, L. M. (2004) 'The Day Before Trials Vanished', *Journal of Empirical Legal Studies* 1(3), 689–703.

Garcia, A. (2000) 'Negotiating Negotiations. The Collborative Production of Res-olution in Small Claims Mediation Hearings', *Discourse & Society* 11, 315–343.

Garfinkel, H. (1956) 'Conditions of Successful Degradation Ceremonies', *American Journal of Sociology* 61(5), 420–424.

Garfinkel, H. (1962) 'Common-Sense Knowledge of Social Structures. The Docu-mentary Method of Interpretation', in J. Scher (ed.) *Theories of Mind* (New York: Free Press).

Garfinkel, H. (1964) 'Studies of the Routine Grounds of Everyday Activities', *Social Problems* 11, 225–250.

Garfinkel, H. (1967) *Studies in Ethnomethodology* (Englewood-Cliffs, NJ: Prentice-Hall).

Garfinkel, H. (1986) *Ethnomethodological Studies of Work* (London: Routledge).

Garfinkel, H. (1996) 'Ethnomethodology's Program', *Social Psychology Quarterly* 59, 5–21.

Garfinkel, H. (1997) 'Practical Sociological Reasoning. Some Features in the Work of the Los Angeles Coroner's Office', in M. Travers and J. Manzo (eds) *Law in Action* (Aldershot: Ashgate).

Garfinkel, H. (2005) *Seeing Sociologically: The Routine Grounds of Social Action* (London: Paradigm Publishers).

Geertz, C. (1973) *The Interpretation of Cultures. Selected Essays* (New York: Basic Books).

Geertz, C. (1983) *Local Knowledge: Further Essays in Interpretive Anthropology* (New York: Basic Books).

Genn, H. (1999) *Paths to Justice. What People Do and Think About Going to Law* (Oxford: Hart Publishing).

Gergen, K. J. (1991) *The Saturated Self: The Dilemmas of Identity in the Contemporary Life* (New York: Basic Books).

Gephart, W. (1992), 'Versteinerte Rechtskultur. Zur kultursoziologischen Analyse von Gerichtsbauten', in H. Mohnhaupt and D. Simon (eds) *Vorträge zur Justizforschung*, Bd.1 (Frankfurt am Main: Klostermann).

Gieryn, T. F. (2002) 'Three Truth Spots', *Journal of History of the Behavioral Sciences* 38(2), 113–132.

Giddens, A. (1991) *Modernity and Self-Identity* (London: Polity Press).

Gluckman, M. (1955) *The Judicial Process among the Barotse of Northern Rhodesia* (*Zambia*), 2nd edn (Manchester: Manchester University Press).

Goffman, E. (1955) 'On Face-Work: An Analysis of Ritual Elements in Social Interaction', *Psychiatry: Journal for the Study of Interpersonal Processes* 18, 213–231.

Goffman, E. (1959) *The Presentation of Self in Everyday Life* (New York: Doubleday).

Goffman, E. (1963) *Behavior in Public Places: Notes on the Social Organization of Gatherings* (Glencoe, IL: Free Press).

Goffman, E. (1967) *Interaction Ritual* (New York: Pantheon).

Goffman, E. (1981) *Forms of Talk* (Oxford: Blackwell).

Goodale, M. (ed.) (2002) *Practicing Ethnography in Law* (New York: Palgrave Macmillan).

Goodrich, P. (1984) 'Legal Techniques and Legal Texts', *Droit Prospectif* 2, 177–186.

Griffiths, A. (2002) 'Doing Ethnography: Living Law, Life Histories, and Narratives from Botswana', in J. Starr and M. Goodale (eds) *Practicing Ethnography in Law* (New York: Palgrave Macmillan).

Griffiths, J. (1986) 'What Do Dutch Lawyers Actually Do in Divorce Cases?' *Law and Society Review* 20, 135–175.

Gusfield, J. R. and Michalowicz, J. (1984) 'Secular Symbolism: Studies of Ritual, Ceremony, and the Symbolic Order in Modern Life', *Annual Review of Sociology* 10, 417–435.

Habermas, J. (1984) *The Theory of Communicative Action, Vol. 1: Reason and the Rationalization of Society*, T. McCarthy (trans.) (Boston: Beacon Press).

Habermas, J. (1990) *Moral Consciousness and Communicative Action* (Cambridge, MA: MIT Press).

Habermas, J. (1992) *Faktizität und Geltung. Beiträge zur Diskurstheorie des Rechts und des demokratischen Rechtsstaates* (Frankfurt am Main: Suhrkamp).

Haldar, P. (1994) 'In and Out of Court: On Topographies of Law and the Architecture of Court Buildings', *International Journal for Semiotics of Law* 7(20), 185–200.

Hallsdottir, I. (2006) 'Orientations to Law, Guidelines, and Dosed in Lawyer-Client Interaction', *Research on Language and Social Interaction* 39(3), 263–301.

Hammerseley, M. and Atkinson, P. (1983) *Ethnography. Principles in Practice* (London: Tavistock Publications).

Hannaford-Agor, P. L., Hans, V. P. and Munsterman, G. T. (2002) 'Speaking Rights: Evaluating Juror Discussions during Civil Trials', *Judicature* 85, 237–243.

Hannken-Illjes, K. (2007) 'Im Fall. Zum Scheitern von Produkten im Werden', in A. Traninger and K. Hempfer (eds) *Dynamiken des Wissens* (Freiburg: Rombach).

Hannken-Illjes, K. (2010) Making a comparative object. In: T. Scheffer and J. Niewöhner (eds) *Thick Comparison. Reviving the Ethnographic Aspiration.* (Leiden, Boston: Brill).

Hannken-Illjes, K., Holden, L., Kozin, A. and Scheffer, T. (2007) Trial and Error – Failing and Learning in Criminal Proceedings, *International Journal for the Semiotics of Law*, 20(2), 159–190.

Hans, V. P. (2001) 'The Power of Twelve: The Impact of Jury Size and Unanimity on Civil Jury Decision Making', *Delaware Law Review* 4, 1–31.

Hans, V. P. and Vidmar, N. (1986) *Judging the Jury* (New York: Plenum Press).

Hans, V. P., Hannaford-Agor, P. L., Mott, N. L. and Munsterman, G. T. (2003) 'The Hung Jury: The American Jury's Insights and Contemporary Understanding', *Criminal Law Bulletin* 39, 33–50.

Haraway, D. (1991) *Simians, Cyborgs, and Women: The Reinvention of Nature* (London: Free Assoc. Books).

Harding, S. (1991) *Whose Science? Whose Knowledge?* (New York: Cornell University Press).

Harre, R. and Moghaddam, F. (2003) *The Self and Others: Positioning Individuals and Groups in Personal, Political, and Cultural Contexts* (Westport, CN: Praeger Publishers).

Harris, S. (2001) 'Fragmented Narratives and Multiple Tellers. Witness and Defendant Accounts in Trials', *Discourse Studies* 3, 78–92.

Hazard, J. N. (1962) 'Furniture Arrangement as a Symbol of Judicial Roles', *ETC: A Review of General Semantics* 19(2), 181–188.

Heinz, J. P., Nelson, R. L, Sandefur, R. L. and Laumann, E. O. (2005) *Urban Lawyers: The New Social Structure of the Bar* (Chicago: University of Chicago Press).

Heritage, J. (1984) *Garfinkel and Ethnomethodology* (Cambridge: Polity Press).

Hester, S. and Eglin, P. (1992) *A Sociology of Crime* (London: Routledge).

Heumann, M. (1977) *Plea-Bargaining* (Chicago: The University of Chicago Press).

Hirschauer, S. (1994) 'Towards a Methology of Investigations into the Strangeness of One's Own Culture', *Social Studies of Science* 24(2), 335–346.

Holstein, J. (1993) *Court-Ordered Insanity. Interpretive Practice and Involuntary Commitment* (New York: Aldine de Gruyter).

Hooks, B. (2000) *Where We Stand: Class Matters* (New York, Routledge).

Hosticka, C. (1979) ' "We Don't Care About What Happened, We Only Care About What is Going to Happen": Lawyer-Client Negotiations of Reality', *Social Problems* 26(5), 599–610.

Hoy, J. (1995) 'Selling and Processing Law: Legal Work at Franchise Law Firms', *Law and Society Review* 29(4), 703–730.

Husserl, E. (1970) *The Crisis of European Sciences and Transcendental Phenomenology* (Evanston, IL: Northwestern University Press).

Husserl, E. (1973) *Zur Phänomenologie der Intersubjektivität. Texte aus dem Nachlass. Dritter Teil: 1929–1935* (The Hague: Martinus Nijhoff).

Husserl, E. (1977) *Cartesian Meditations*, D. Cairns (trans.) (New York: Springer).

Husserl, E. (1983) *Ideas Pertaining to a Pure Phenomenology and to a Phenomenological Philosophy*, F. Kersten (trans.) (Dordrecht: Kluwer Academic Publishers).

Hymes, D. (1981) *In Vain I Tried to Tell You. Essays in Native American Ethnopoetics* (Lincoln: University of Nebraska Press).

Hutchinson, A. (1998) 'Legal Ethics for a Fragmented Society: Between Professional and Personal', *International Journal of the Legal Profession* 5(2/3), 175–192.

Jaquemet, M. (1996) *Credibility in Court: Communicative Practices in the Camorra Trials* (Cambridge: Cambridge University Press).

Jarvis, R. and Joseph, P. (1989) *Prime Time Law. Fictional Television as Legal Narrative* (Durham: Carolina Academic Press).

Jasanoff, S. (2005) 'Law's Knowledge: Science for Justice in Legal Settings', *American Journal of Public Health* 95(1), 49–58.

Jönsson, L. and Linell, P. (1991) 'Story Generations: From Dialogical Interviews to Written Reports in Police Interrogations', *Text* 11, 419–440.

Jörg, N., Field, S. and Brants, C. (1995) 'Are Inquisitorial and Adverserial Systems Converging?', in C. Harding (ed.) *Criminal Justice in Europe: A Comparative Study* (Oxford: Clarendon Press).

Kafka, F. (1956) *The Trial*, E. L. George (trans.) (Boston: Glover Books).

Kagan, R. (1991) 'Adversarial Legalism and American Government', *Journal of Policy Analysis and Management* 10(3), 369–406.

Katz, J. (2004) 'On the Rhetoric and Politics of Ethnographic Methodology', *The Annals of the American Academy of Political and Social Science* 595, 280–308.

Kelly, M. J. (1994) *Lives of Lawyers: Journeys in the Organization of Practice* (Ann Arbor: University of Michigan Press).

Kendon, A. (1973) 'The Role of Visible Behavior in the Organization of Face-to-Face Interaction', in M. von Cranach and I. Vine (eds) *Social Communication and Movement* (London: Academic Press).

Kennedy, J. S. (2002) 'Victims of Crime and Labelling Theory: A Parallel Process?', *Deviant Behavior: An Interdisciplinary Journal* 23, 235–265.

Kidder, R. L. (2002) 'Exploring Legal Culture in Law-Avoidance Societies', in June Starr and Mark Goodale (eds) *Practicing Ethnography of Law* (New York: Palgrave Macmillan).

Kidwell, M. (1987) '"Calm Down": The Role of Gaze in the Interactional Management of Hysteria by the Police', *Discourse Studies* 8(6), 745–770.

Knorr, K. (1999) *Epistemic Cultures. How the Sciences Make Knoweldge* (Cambridge, MA: Harvard University Press).

Knott, P. (1999) 'Training the Next Millennium's Lawyers: Is There a Case for Joint Professional Legal Education?', *The Law Teacher* 33, 50–65.

Komter, M. (1994) 'Accusations and Defences in Courtroom Interaction', *Discourse and Society* 5, 165–187.

Komter, M. (1995) 'The Distribution of Knowledge in Courtroom Interaction', in P. ten Have and G. Psathas (eds) *Situated Order: Studies in the Social Organization of Talk and Embodied Activities* (Washington, D.C.: University Press of America).

Komter, M. (1997) 'Remorse, Redress and Reform. Blame-Taking in the Courtroom', in J. Manzo and M. Travers (eds) *Law in Action. Ethnomethodological and Conversation Analytic Approaches to Law* (Aldershot: Ashgate).

Komter, M. (1998) *Dilemmas in the Courtroom: A Study of Trials of Violent Crimes in the Netherlands* (Hillsdale, NJ: Lawrence Erlbaum Associates).

Komter, M. (2003) 'The Construction of Records in Dutch Police Interrogations', *Information Design Journal* 11(2/3), 201–213.

Komter, M. (2005) 'Understanding Problems in an Interpreter-Mediated Police Interrogation', in S. Burns (ed.) *Ethnographies of Law and Social Control* (New York: JAI Press).

Komter, M. (2006) 'From Talk to Text: The Interactional Construction of a Police Record', *Research on Language and Social Interaction* 39(3), 201–228.

Komter, M. L. (1998) *Dilemmas in the Courtroom: A Study of Trials of Violent Crime in the Netherlands* (Mahwah, NJ: Erlbaum).

Konradi, A. and Schmidt, M. (2003) *Reading Between the Lines: Toward Understanding of Current Social Problems* (New York: Mayfield).

Koppen, P. van and Penrod, S. (2003) 'Adversarial or Inquisitorial: Comparing Systems', in P. van Koppen and S. Penrod (eds) *Adversarial versus Inquisitorial Justice* (New York: Kluwer).

Kozin, A. (2010) On Positionality and its Comparability in the Legal Context. In: T. Scheffer and J. Niewöhner (eds) *Thick Comparison. Reviving the Ethnographic Aspiration.* (Leiden, Boston: Brill).

Kritzer, H. M. (1984) 'The Dimensions of Lawyer-Client Relations: Notes Toward a Theory and a Field Study', *American Bar Foundation Research Journal*, 409–428.

Kritzer, H. M. (1998) 'Contingent-fee Lawyers and their Clients: Settlement Expetations, Settlement Realities, and Issues of Control in the Lawyer-Client Relationship', *Law and Social Inquiry* 23, 795–822.

Kritzer, H. M. (2002) 'Stories from the Field: Collecting Data Outside Over There', in J. Starr and M. Goodale (eds) *Practicing Ethnography of Law* (New York: Palgrave Macmillan).

Kritzer, H. M. and Krishnan, J. (1999) 'Lawyers Seeking Clients, Clients Seeking Lawyers: Source of Contingency Fee Cases and their Implications for Case Handling', *Law and Policy* 20, 347–375.

Kunda, Z. (1990) 'The Case for Motivated Reasoning', *Psychological Bulletin* 108, 480–498.

Langbein, J. H. (2003) *The Origins of Adversary Criminal Trial* (Oxford: Oxford University Press).

Lasswell, H. D. (1979) *The Signature of Power: Buildings, Communication, and Policy* (New Brunswick: Transaction Books).

Latour, B. (1996) 'On Interobjektivity', *Mind, Culture and Activity. An International Journal* 3(4), 228–246.

Latour, B. (1999) *Pandora's Hope. Essay on the Reality of Science Studies* (Cambridge MA, London: Harvard University Press).

Latour, B. (2002) 'Scientific Objects and Legal Objectivity', in A. Pottage (ed.) *Making Persons and Things* (Cambridge: Cambridge University Press).

Lebaron, C. D. (1996) 'Looking for Verbal Deception in Clarence Thomas's Testimony', in S. L. Ragan *et al.* (eds) *The Lynching of Language: Gender, Politics, and Power in the Hill-Thomas Harings* (Chicago: University of Illinois Press).

LeBaron, C. D. and Streeck, J. (1997) 'Built Space and the Interactional Framing of Experience During a Murder Interrogation', *Human Studies* 20, 1–25.

Lemert, E. (1969) 'Records in the Juvenile Court', in S. Wheeler (ed.) *On Records: Files and Dossiers in American Life* (New York: Russell Sage Foundations).

Levi, J. N. and Walker, A. G. (eds) (1990) *Language in the Judicial Process* (New York: Plenum Press).

Levinas, E. (1998) *Otherwise than Being or Beyond Essence*, Alfonso Lingis (trans.) (Pittsburgh: Duquesne University Press).

Litt, F. (1957) 'Sociological Thinking of a Philosopher: Helmuth Plessner', *Sociology* 23, 45–78.

Lloyd-Bostock, S. (1988) *Law in Practice: Applications of Psychology to Law in Action* (London: Routledge).

Lubet, S. (2001) *Nothing But the Truth: Why Trial Lawyers Don't, Can't, and Shouldn't Have to Tell the Whole Truth* (New York, London: New York University Press).

Luhmann, N. (1989 [1969]) *Legitimation durch Verfahren* (Frankfurt am Main: Suhrkamp).

Luhmann, N. (2006) *Law as a Social System* (Oxford: Oxford University Press).

Lynch, M. (1982) 'Closure and Disclosure in Pre-Trial Argument', *Human Studies* 5, 285–318.

Lynch, M. (1993) *Scientific Practice and Ordinary Action* (Cambridge: Cambridge University Press).

Lynch, M. (1994) 'The Impropriety of Plea Agreements: A Tale of Two Counties', *Law and Social Inquiry* 19, 115–133.

Lynch, M. (1999) 'Archives in Formation: Privileged Spaces, Popular Archives and Paper Trials', *History of the Human Sciences* 122, 65–87.

Lynch, M. (2002) 'The Living Text: Written Instructions and Situated Actions in Telephonic Surveys', in D. W. Maynard, H. Houtkoop-Steenstra, N. C. Schaeffer and J. van der Zouwen (eds) *Standardization and Tacit Knowledge: Interaction and Practice in the Survey Interview* (New York: John Wiley & Sons).

Lynch, M. and Bogen, D. (1996) *The Spectacle of History: Speech, Text, and Memory at the Iran-Contra Hearings* (Durham: Duke University Press).

Lynch, M. and Bogen, D. (1997) 'Lies, Recollections and Categorical Judgements in Testimony', in S. Hester and P. Eglin (eds) *Culture in Action: Studies in Membership Categorization Analysis* (Washington, D.C.: University Press of America).

Machura, S. (2001) 'Interaction Between Lay Assessors and Professional Judges in German Mixed Courts', *International Review of Penal Law* 72, 451–479.

Maine, H. S. (1822) *Ancient Law* (Oxford: Oxford University Press).

Maneschi, A. (2004) 'Noneconomic Complementarity in the History of Economic Thought', *American Journal of Economics and Sociology* 63(4) October, 12–24.

Mann, K. (1985) *Defending White Collar Crime: A Portrait of Attorneys at Work* (New Haven: Yale University Press).

Manzo, J. (1993) 'Jurors' Narratives of Personal Experience in Deliberation Talk', *Text* 13, 267–290.

Manzo, J. (1997) 'Ethnomethodology, Conversation Analysis, and the Sociology of Law', in M. Travers and J. Manzo (eds) *Law in Action: Ethnomethodological and Conversation Analytic Approaches to Law* (Brookfield, USA: Ashgate).

Manzo, J. and Maynard, D. (1993) 'On the Sociology of Justice: Theoretical Notes from an Actual Jury Deliberation', *Sociological Theory* 11, 171–193.

Manzo, J. and Maynard, D. (1994) ' "You Wouldn't Take a Seven-Year-Old and Ask Him All These Questions": Jurors' Use of Practical Reasoning in Supporting their Arguments', *Law and Social Inquiry* 19, 601–626.

Manzo, J. and Maynard, D. (1996) 'Taking Turns and Taking Sides: Opening Scenes from Two Jury Deliberations', *Social Psychology Quarterly* 59, 107–125.

Manzo, J. and Maynard, D. (1997) 'Justice as a Phenomenon of Order. Notes on the Organization of a Jury Deliberation', in J. Manzo and M. Travers (eds) *Law in Action. Ethnomethodological and Conversation Analytic Approaches to Law* (Aldershot: Ashgate).

Marcus, G. E. (1995) 'Ethnography in/of the World System: The Emergence of Multi-sited Ethnography', *Annual Reviews* 24, 95–117.

Marcus, G. E. (1998) *Ethnography Through Thick and Thin* (Princeton: Princeton University Press).

Martinez, E. (2005) 'The Organization of Talk in "Immediate Trial" Hearings', *The International Journal of Speech, Language and the Law* 12(1), 125–127.

Martinez, E. (2006) 'The Interweaving of Talk and Text in a French Criminal Pretrial Hearing', *Research on Language and Social Interaction* 39(3), 229–261.

Martinez, E. (2007) *Flagrantes Auitions. Echanges Langagiers lors d'Interactions Judiciaires (Flagrant Hearings: Talk during Judicial Interactions)* (Berlin: Peter Lang).

Marx, K. and Engels, F. (1976) *Collected Works, Vol. I–VI* (London: Lawrence and Wishart).

Mather, L., Mc Ewen, C. A. and Maiman, R. J. (2001) *Divorce Lawyers at Work: Varieties of Professionalism in Practice* (New York: Oxford University Press).

Matoesian, G. M. (1993) *Reproducing Rape: Domination Through Talk in the Courtroom* (Chicago: University of Chicago Press).

Matoesian, G. (1997) ' "I'm Sorry We Had to Meet Under these Circumstance[s?]." Verbal Artistry in the Kennedy Smith Rape Trial', in J. Manzo and M. Travers (eds) *Law in Action. Ethnomethodological and Conversation Analytic Approaches to Law* (Aldershot: Ashgate).

Matoesian, G. (1999) 'Intertextuality, Affect and Ideology in Legal Discourse', *Text* 19(1), 73–109.

Matoesian, G. (2000) 'Intertextual Authority in Reported Speech: Production Media in the Kennedy Smith Rape Trial', *Journal of Pragmatics* 32, 879–914.

Matoesian, G. (2001) *Law and the Language of Identity. Discourse in the William Kennedy Smith Trial* (Oxford: Oxford University Press).

Maughan, C. and Webb, J. (1995) *Lawyering Skills and the Legal Process* (London: Butterworths).

Maynard, D. (1982) 'Aspects of Sequential Organization in Plea Bargaining Discourse', *Human Studies* 5, 319–344.

Maynard, D. (1983) 'Language in Court', *American Bar Foundation Research Journal* 1, 211–222.

Maynard, D. (1984) *Inside Plea Bargaining: The Language of Negotiation* (New York: Plenum Press).

Maynard, D. (1985) 'The Problem of Justice in the Courts Approached by the Analysis of Plea Bargaining Discourse', in T. A. van Dijk (ed.) *Handbook of Discourse Analysis, Vol. III* (London: Academic Press).

Maynard, D. (1988) 'Narratives and Narrative Structure in Plea Bargaining', *Law & Society Review* 22(3), 449–481.

Maynard, D. (1989) 'On the Ethnography and Analysis of Discourse in Institutional Settings', *Perspectives on Social Problems* 1, 127–146.

Maynard, D. (2006) 'Comment: Bad News and Good News: Losing vs. Finding the Phenomenon in Legal Settings', *Law & Social Inquiry* 31(2), 477–497.

Maynard, D. and Clayman, S. (1991) 'The Diversity of Ethnomethodology', *Annual Reviews* 17, 385–418.

Maynard, D. and Manzo, J. (1993) 'On the Sociology of Justice: Theoretical Notes from an Actual Jury Deliberation', *Sociological Theory* 11, 171–193.

Maynard, D. and Manzo, J. (1997) 'Justice as a Phenomenon of Order: Notes on the Organization of a Jury Deliberation', in M. Travers and J. Manzo (eds) *Law in Action: Ethnomethodological and Conversation Analytic Approaches to Law* (Brookfield, USA: Ashgate).

McBarnet, D. (1981) *Conviction – Law, the State and the Construction of Justice* (Wolfson College, Oxford: SSRC Centre for Socio-Legal Studies).

McConville, M., Hodgson, J., Bridges, L. and Pavlovic, A. (1994) *Standing Accused. The Organisation and Practices of Criminal Defence Lawyers in Britain* (Oxford: Clarendon University Press).

McIntyre, L. J. (1987) *The Public Defender: The Practice of Law in the Shadows of Repute* (Chicago, London: University of Chicago Press).

Mead, G. H. (1934) *Mind, Self and Society* (Chicago: University of Chicago Press).

Medcalf, L. (1978) *Law and Identity: Lawyers, Native Americans, and Legal Practice* (London: Sage).

Meehan, A. (1989) ' "Assessing the Police Worthiness of Citizens" Complaints: Accountability and the Negotiation of Facts', in D. Helm, W. T. Anderson, A. J. Meehan and A. W. Rawls (eds) *Interactional Order: New Directions in the Study of Social Order* (New York: Irvington Press).

Meehan, A. (1992) ' "I Don't Prevent Crime I Prevent Calls": Policing as Negotiated Order', *Symbolic Interaction* 15(4), 455–480.

Meehan, A. (1993) 'Internal Police Records and the Control of Juveniles: Politics and Policing in a Suburban Town', *British Journal of Criminology* 33(4), 504–524.

Meehan, A. (1995) 'Policing and the Chronically Mentally Ill', *Psychiatric Quarterly* 66(2), 163–184.

Meehan, A. (1997 [1986]) 'Record-keeping Practices and the Policing of Juveniles', *Urban Life* 15, 70–102. [Reprinted in M. Travers and J. Manzo (eds) *Law in Action: Ethnomethodological and Conversation Analytic Approaches to Law* (Aldershot, UK: Dartmouth Publishing Co.)].

Meehan, A. (1998) 'The Impact of Mobile Data Terminal (MDT) Information Technology on Communication and Recording in Patrol Work', *Qualitative Sociology* 21(3), 225–254.

Meehan, A. (2000) 'The Transformation of the Oral Tradition of the Police Through the Introduction of Information Technology', *Sociology of Crime, Law and Deviance*, 2, 107–132.

Merry, S. E. (2002) 'Ethnography in the Archives', in M. Goodale and J. Starr (eds) *Practicing Ethnography in Law* (New York: Palgrave).

Michelson, E. (2006) 'The Practice of Law as an Obstacle to Justice: Chinese Lawyers at Work', *Law & Society Review* 40(1), 1–38.

Moerman, M. (1987) *Talking Culture. Ethnography and Conversation Analysis* (Philadelphia, PA: University of Pennsylvania Press).

Moore, S. F. (1987) 'Explaining the Present: Theoretical Dilemmas in Processual Ethnography', *American Ethnologist* 14, 727–736.

Morison, J. and Leith, P. (1992) *The Barrister's World and the Nature of Law* (Buckingham: Open University Press).

Morrison, K. (1995) *Formations of Modern Social Thought* (London: Sage).

Mulcahy, L. (2006) 'Architects of Justice: The Politics of Courtroom Design', *Reading Law School Research Seminar Series* (Reading, UK: University of Reading).

Mulkay, M. (1986) 'Conversations and Texts', *Human Studies* 9, 303–321.

Mungham, G. and Thomas, P. A. (1983) 'Solicitors and Clients: Altruism or Self-Interest?', in R. Dingwall (ed.) *The Sociology of the Professions. Lawyers, Doctors and Others* (London: The Macmillan Press).

Musterman, V. (1986) *Judging the Jury* (New York: Plenum Press).

Nader, L. (1965) 'The Ethnography of Law', *American Anthropologist* 6(2), 141–165.

Nader, L. and Yngvesson, B. (1973) 'On Studying Ethnography of Law and its Consequences', in J. J. Honigmann (ed.) *Handbook of Social Cultural Anthropology* (Chicago: Rand McNally).

Nekvapil, J. and Leudar, Ivan (2006) 'Sequencing in Media Dialogical Networks', *Ethnographic Studies* 8, 30–43.

Neustadter, G. (1986) 'When Lawyer and Client Meet: Observations of Interviewing and Counselling Behaviour in the Consumer Bankruptcy Law Office', *Buffalo Law Review* 35, 177–284.

Nicolau, G. (1997) *Approche ethnométhodologique des pratiques d'un juge des enfants* (Paris: Publications de l'université Paris 7 – Denis Diderot).

O'Barr, W. and Atkins, B. K. (1978) 'When Silence is Golden – An Inquiry into the Nature and Meaning of Silence in an American Trial Courtroom', *Research Report* No. 18, Law and Language Project, Duke University.

O'Barr, W. and Conley, J. (1976) 'When a Juror Watches a Lawyer', *Barrister* 3(2), 8–11.

Osvaldsson, K. (2002) *Talking Trouble: Institutionality and Identity in a Youth Detention Home* (Linkoping: Linkoping Studies in Arts and Science).

Parsons, T. (1949) *Essays in Sociological Theory* (Free Press: New York).

Perry, B. A. (2001) 'The Israeli and United States Supreme Courts: A Comparative Reflection on their Symbols, Images, and Functions', *The Review of Politics* 63, 2317–2339.

Peyrot, M. and Burns, S. (2001) 'Sociologists on Trial: Theoretical Competition and Juror Reasoning', *The American Sociologist* 32, 42–69.

Philips, S. (1986) 'Some Functions of Spatial Positioning and Alignment in the Organization of Courtroom Discourse', in S. Fischer and A. D. Todd (eds) *Discourse and Institutional Authority: Medicine, Education and Law – Advances in Discourse Processes* (Norwood: Ablex).

Philips, S. (1992) 'The Routinization of Repair in Courtroom Discourse', in A. Duranti and C. Goodwin (eds) *Rethinking Context: Language as Interactive Phenomenon* (Cambridge: Cambridge University Press).

Philips, S. (1998) *Ideology in the Language of Judges: How Judges Practice Law, Politics, and Courtroom Control* (New York: Oxford University Press).

Pickering, A. (1995) *The Mangle of Practice. Time, Agency, and Science* (Chicago and London: The University of Chicago Press).

Pizzi, W. T. (1999) *Trials Without Truth. Why Our System of Criminal Trials Has Become an Expensive Failure and What We Need to Do to Rebuild It* (New York, London: New York University Press).

Plessner, H. (1999) *The Limits of Community* (Bloomington, IN: Indiana University Press).

Polkinghorne, D. (1988) *Narrative Knowing and the Human Sciences* (Albany: SUNY Press).

Pollner, M. (1979) 'Explicative Transaction: Making and Managing Meaning in Traffic Court', in G. Psathas (ed.) *Everyday Language: Studies in Ethnomethodology* (New York: Irvington).

Pollner, M. and Emerson, R. M. (2001) 'Ethnomethodology and Ethnography', in P. Atkinson, A. Coffey, S. Delamont, J. Lofland and L. Lofland (eds) *Handbook of Ethnography* (London: Sage).

Pomerantz, A. (1984) 'Evidence in Court', *Proceeedings of Analisi del Discorse e Retorica Naturale* (Padua, Italy: Cleup University of Padua Press).

Pomerantz, A. (1987) 'Descriptions in Legal Settings', in G. Button and J. Lee (eds) *Talk and Social Organisation* (Clevedon, UK: Multilingual Matters).

Pomerantz, A. and Atkinson, J. M. (1984) 'Ethnomethodology, Conversation Analysis, and the Study of Courtroom Interaction', in D. J. Mueller, D. E. Blackman and A. J. Chapman (eds) *Psychology and Law* (New York: Wiley).

Raffel, S. (1979) *Matters of Fact. A Sociological Inquiry* (London: Routledge).

Rawls, J. (1971) *The Theory of Justice* (Cambridge, MA: Harvard University Press).

Richardson, P. J. (ed.) (2002) *Criminal Pleadings, Evidence and Practice* (London: Sweet and Maxwell).

Robertson, M. and Bittner, E. (1982) 'The Availability of Law', *Law and Policy Quarterly* 4(4), 399–434.

Rock, P. (1991) 'Witnesses and Space in a Crown Court', *British Journal of Criminology* 31(3), 266–279.

Rock, P. (1993) *The Social World of an English Crown Court. Witnesses and Professionals in the Crown Court Centre at Wood Green* (Oxford: Clarendon Press).

Rose, G. (1997) 'Situating Knowledges: Positionality, Reflexivities and Other Tactics', *Progress in Human Geography* 21(3), 305–320.

Rosenthal, D. (1974) *Lawyer and Client: Who's in Charge?* (New York: The Free Press).

Rüschemeyer, D. (1973) *Lawyers and their Society: A Comparative Study of the Legal Profession in Germany and in the United States* (Cambridge, MA: Harvard University Press).

Sacks, H. (1972) 'Notes on Police Assessment of Moral Character', in D. Sudnow (ed.) *Studies in Social Interaction* (Glencoe: The Free Press).

Sacks, H. (1975) 'Everyone Has to Lie', in B. Blount and M. Sanches (eds) *Sociocultural Dimensions of Language Use* (New York: Academic Press).

Sacks, H. (1997) 'The Lawyer's Work', in M. Travers and J. Manzo (eds) *Law in Action: Ethnomethodological and Conversation Analytic Approaches to Law* (Brookfield: Ashgate).

Sacks, H., Schegloff, E. and Jefferson, G. (1974) 'A Simplest Systematics for the Organization of Turn-taking for Conversation', *Language* 50, 696–735.

Sarat, A. and Felstiner, W. (1986) 'Law and Strategy in the Divorce Lawyer's Office', *Law and Society Review* 20, 93–134.

Sarat, A. and Felstiner, W. L. (1988) 'Law and Social Relations: Vocabularies of Motive in Lawyer-Client Interaction', *Law and Society Review* 22, 737–769.

Sarat, A. and Felstiner, W. (1989a) 'Law and Social Relations: Vocabularies of Motive in Lawyer/Client Interaction', *Law and Society Review* 22, 737–769.

Sarat, A. and Felstiner, W. (1989b) 'Lawyers and Legal Consciousness: Law Talk in the Divorce Lawyers Office', *Yale Law Journal* 98(8), 1663–1688.

Sarat, A. and Felstiner, W. (1990) 'Lawyer-Client Communication', in Judith N. Levi and Ann Graffam Walke (eds) *Language in the Judicial Process* (New York: Plenum Press).

Sarat, A. and Felstiner, W. (1995) 'Law and Social Relations: Vocabularies of Motive in Lawyer-Client Interaction', in R. L. Abel (ed.) *Law and Society Reader* (New York: New York University Press).

Sarat, A. and Felstiner, W. (1996) *Divorce Lawyers and Their Clients: Power and Meaning in the Divorce Process* (New York: Oxford University Press).

Sarat, A. and Felstiner, W. (2007) 'File Work, Legal Care, and Professional Habitus: An Ethnographic Reflection on Different Styles of Advocacy', *International Journal of the Legal Profession* 14(1), 57–81.

Sarat, A. and Kearns, T. R. (eds) (1999) *Cultural Pluralism, Identitiy Politics, and the Law* (Amherst Series in Law, Jurisprudence, and Social Thought).

Sarat, A., Douglas, L. and Umphrey, M. M. (eds) (2007) *How Law Knows* (Stanford: Stanford University Press).

Sartre, J.-P. (1956) *Being and Nothingness*, H. Barnes (trans.) (New York: Washington Square Press).

Sbisà, M. (2001) 'Illocutionary Force and Degrees of Strength in Language Use', *Journal of Pragmatics* 33, 1791–1814.

Scheffer, T. (2002) 'Zur Kritik der Urteilskraft – Wie in Asylanhörungen Unentscheidbares in Entscheidungen übersetzt wird', in J. Oltmer (ed.) *Migration und Verwaltung* (Göttingen: Vandenhoeck & Ruprecht).

Scheffer, T. (2003a) 'Die Karriere rechtswirksamer Argumente. Ansatzpunkte einer historiographischen Diskursanalyse der Gerichtsverhandlung', *Zeitschrift für Rechtssoziologie* 24, Heft 2, 151–181.

Scheffer, T. (2003b) 'The Duality of Mobilisation. Following the Rise and Fall of an Alibi-Story on its Way to Court', *Journal for the Theory of Social Behavior* 33, 313–346.

Scheffer, T. (2004) 'Materialities of Legal Proceedings', *International Journal for Semiotics of Law* 17, 356–389.

Scheffer, T. (2005) 'Courses of Mobilisation: Writing Systematic Micro-Histories on Legal Discourse', in Max Travers and Reza Banakar (eds) *Theory and Method in Socio-Legal Research* (Oxford and Portland Oregon: Hart Publishing).

Scheffer, T. (2006a) 'On Procedural Discoursivation – or How Local Utterances are Turned into Binding Facts', *Language & Communication* 27, 1–27.

Scheffer, T. (2006b) 'The Microformation of Criminal Defence: On the Lawyer's Notes, Speech Production, and the Field of Presence', *Research on Language and Social Interaction (ROLSI)* 39(3), 303–342.

Scheffer, T. (2007) 'Event and Process. An Exercise in Analytical Ethnography', *Human Studies* 30(3), 167–197.

Scheffer, T. (2010) *Adversarial Case-Making. An Ethnography of English Crown Court Procedure* (Leiden: Brill).

Scheffer, T., Hannken-Illjes, K. and Kozin, A. (2006) 'Bound to One's Own Words? Early Defences and Their Binding Effects in Different Criminal Case', *Law & Social Inquiry* 32(1), 5–39.

Scheffer, T. and Niewöhner, J. (2010) *Thick Comparison. Reviving the Ethnographic Aspiration.* (Leiden, Boston: Brill).

Schmid, J., Drosdeck, T. and Koch, D. (1997) *Der Rechtsfall – ein richterliches Konstrukt* (Baden-Baden: De Gruyter).

Sears, D. O., Fu, M., Henry, P. J. and Bui, K. (2003) 'The Origins and Persistence of Ethnic Identity Among the "New Immigrant" Group', *Social Psychology Quarterly* 66(4), 419–437.

Seibert, T.-M. (1996) *Zeichen, Prozesse: Grenzgänge zur Semiotik des Rechts* (Berlin: Duncker & Humblot).

Seibert, T.-M. (2004) *Gerichtsrede. Wirklichkeit und Möglichkeit im forensischen Diskurs* (Berlin: Duncker & Humblot).

Shapin, S. (1988) 'The House of Experiment in Seventeenth-Century England', *ISIS* 79, 373–404.

Sherr, A. (1986) *Client Interviewing for Lawyers: An Analysis and Guide* (London: Sweet & Maxwell).

Sherwin, R. (2000) *When Law Goes Pop. The Vanishing Line Between Law and Popular Culture* (Chicago: The University of Chicago Press).

Schumann, K. F. (1977) *Der Handel mit Gerechtigkeit* (Frankfurt am Main: Suhrkamp).

Shuy, R. (1993) *Language Crimes* (Oxford: Blackwell).

Shuy, R. (2001) 'Discourse Analysis in the Legal Context', in D. Schiffrin, D. Tannen and H. E. Hamilton (eds) *Handbook of Discourse Analysis* (London: Blackwell).

Sidnell, J. (2004) 'There's Risks in Everything: Extreme Case Formulations and Accountability in Inquiry Testimony', *Discourse and Society* 15(6), 745–766.

Silbey, S. (1981) 'Making Sense of the Lower Courts', *Justice System Journal* 6(1), 13–27.

Silbey, S. and Ewick, P. (2003) 'The Architecture of Authority: The Place of Law in the Space of Science', in A. Sarat, L. Douglas and M. Umphrey (eds) *The Place of Law* (Ann Arbor: University of Michigan Press).

Simon, R. (1999) *The Jury & the Defense of Insanity* (New Brunswick: Transaction Publishers).

Simon, W. H. (1991) 'Lawyer Advice and Client Autonomy: Mrs. Jones's Case', *Maryland Law Review* 50, 213–226.

Sloan, M. (2007) 'The "Real Self and Inauthenticity": The Importance of Self-Concept Anchorage for Emotional Experiences in the Workplace', *Social Psychology Quarterly* 70(3), 305–318.

Smith, D. (2005) *Institutional Ethnography. A Sociology for People* (Lanham: Altamira Press).

Smith, D. E. (1985) 'Textually Mediated Social Organisation', *International Social Science Journal* 99, 59–76.

Smith-Lovin, L. (2007) 'The Strength of Weak Identities: Social Structural Sources of Self, Situation and Emotional Experience', *Social Psychology Quarterly* 70(2), 106–124.

Southworth, A. (1996) 'Lawyer-Client Decisionmaking in Civil Rights and Poverty Practice: An Empirical Study of Lawyer' Norms', *Georgetown Journal of Legal Ethics* 9, 1101–1155.

Spradley, J. P. (1980) *Participant Observation* (New York: Holt, Rinehart and Wilson).

Starr, J. and Goodale, M. (eds) (2002) *Practicing Ethnography of Law* (New York: Palgrave Macmillan).

Stegmaier, P. (2008) *Wissen, was Recht ist: Richterliche Rechtspraxis aus wissens-soziologisch-ethnografischer Sicht* (Wiesbaden: VS-Verlag).

Steinbock, A. (1995) *Home and Beyond. Generative Phenomenology after Husserl* (Evanston: Northwestern University Press).

Stetts, J. E. (2005) 'Examining Emotions in Identity Theory', *Social Psychology Quarterly* 68(1), 39–74.

Stetts, J. E. and Harrod, M. M. (2004) 'Verification Across Multiple Identities: The Role of Status', *Social Psychology Quarterly* 67(2), 155–171.

Stewering, R. (2003) 'Die Manie der Assymmetrie. DieTücken "bürgerfre-undlicher" Gerichtsarchitektur am Beispiel des District Courts Münster', *Kritische Justiz* 36, 146–160.

Stokoe, E. and Edwards, D. (2007) ' "Black This, Black That": Racial Insults and Reported Speech in Neighbour Complaints and Police Interrogations', *Discourse & Society* 18(3), 337–372.

Stygall, G. (1994) *Trial Language. Differential Discourse Processing and Discursive Formation* (Amsterdam: John Benjamins).

Sudnow, D. (1964) 'Normal Crimes: Sociological Features of the Penal Code in a Public Defender Office', *Social Problems* 12, 255–276.

Tait, D. and Kennedy, L. (1999) 'Court Perspectives: Architecture, Psychology and Law Reform in Western Australia', *Western Australian Law Commission*, 1017–1100.

Tapper, C. (1999) *Cross and Tapper on Evidence* (London, Edinburgh, Dublin: Butterworths).

Taylor, C. (1989) *Sources of the Self* (Cambridge, MA: Harvard University Press).

Thibaut, J., Walker, L. and Lind, A. (1972) 'Adversary Presentation and Bias in Legal Decision- Making', *Harvard Law Review* 86(2), 386–401.

Tonry, M. (1997) *Sentencing Matters* (Oxford: Oxford University Press).

Tracy, K. and Naughton, J. (2000) 'Institutional Identity Work: A Better Lens', in J. Coupland (ed.) *Small Talk* (London: Longman).

Travers, M. (1992) 'Persuading the Client to Plead Guilty: An Ethnographic Exam-ination of a Routine Morning's Work in the Magistrates' Court', *Manchester Sociology Occasional Papers*, No. 33 (UK: University of Manchester).

Travers, M. (1993) 'Putting Sociology Back into the Sociology of Law', *Law and Society* 20(4), 438–451.

Travers, M. (1997) *The Reality of Law: Work and Talk in a Firm of Criminal Lawyers* (Aldershot: Dartmouth Publishing Co.).

Travers, M. (1999) *The British Immigration Courts. A Study of Law and Politics* (Bristol: Policy Press).

Travers, M. (2006) 'Understanding Talk in Legal Settings: What Law and Society Studies Can Learn from a Conversation Analyst', *Law & Social Inquiry* 31(2), 447–465.

Travers, M. (2007) 'Sentencing in the Children's Court: An Ethnographic Perspectiv', *Youth Justice* 7(1), 21–35.

Travers, M. and Banakar, R. (2002) *An Introduction to Law and Social Theory* (Oxford: Hart Publishing).

Travers, M. and Manzo, J. (eds) (1997) *Law in Action: Ethnomethodological and Conversation Analytic Approaches to Law* (Brookfield: Ashgate).

Ulmer, J. (1994) 'Trial Judges in a Rural Community. Contexts, Organizational Relations, and Interactive Strategies', *Journal of Contemporary Ethnography* 23(1), 79–108.

Valverde, M. (2003) *Law's Dream of a Common Knowledge* (Princeton: Princeton University Press).

Van Kessel, G. (1992) 'Adversary Excesses in the American Criminal Trial', *Notre Dame Law Revue* 67, 403–549.

Van Maanen, J. (1988) *Tales of the field: On Writing Ethnography* (Chicago: The University of Chicago Press).

Vining, J. (1978) *Legal Identitiy* (New Haven: Yale University Press).

Waldenfels, B. (1996) *Order in the Twilight,* David Parent (trans.) (Athens: Ohio University Press).

Walker, A. G. (1986) 'The Verbatim Record: The Myth and the Reality', in S. Fisher (ed.) *Discourse and Institutional Authority* (Norwood: Ablex).

Watson, R. (1990) 'Some Features of the Elicitation of Confessions in Murder Interrogations', in G. Psathas (ed.) *Interaction Competence* (Lanham Maryland: University Press of America).

Watson, R. (1997) 'The Presentation of "Victim" and "Motive" in Discourse: The Case of Police Interrogations and Interviews', in M. Travers and J. F. Manzo (eds) *Law in Action* (Aldershot, England: Dartmouth Publishing Company).

Watson, R. and Sharrock, W. (1988) 'Talk and Police Work: Notes on the Traffic in Information', in H. Coleman (ed.) *Working with Language* (The Hague: Mouton).

Weber, M. (1948) *Essays in Sociology,* H. H. Gerth and C. W. Mills (trans.) (London: Routledge).

Weber, M. (1968) *Economy and Society, Vol. 2,* G. Roth and C. Wittich (eds) (New York: Bedminster Press).

Weiss, R. S. (1994) *Learning from Strangers. The Art and Method of Qualitative Interview Studies* (New York: The Free Press).

Wheeler, S. (1994) 'Capital Fractionalism: The Role of Insolvency Practitioners in Asset Distribution', in Maureen Cain and Christine B. Harrington (eds) *Lawyers in Postmodern World: Translation and Transgression* (Milton Keynes: Open University Press).

Whyte, W. F. (1943) *Street Corner Society* (Chicago: The University of Chicago Press).

Williams, G. (1991) 'When Is Arrest?', *The Modern Law Review* 54(3), 408–417.

Williams, R. and Whalen, M. (1990) 'Describing Trouble: Practical Epistemology in Citizen Calls to the Police', *Language in Society* 19, 465–492.

Winkel, F. W. and Vrij, A. (1998) 'Who is in Need of Victim Support?: The Issue of Accountable, Empirically Validated Selection and Victim Referral', *Expert Evidence* 6, 23–41.

Wishigrad, J. (1992) *Legal Fictions. Short Stories About Attorneys and the Law* (New York: The Overlook Press).

Wolff, S. and Müller, H. (1979) *Kompetente Skepsis.* (Opladen: Westdeutscher Verlag).

Wolff, S. and Müller, H. (1997) *Kompetente Skepsis. Eine konversationsanalytische Untersuchung zur Glaubwürdigkeit in Strafverfahren* (Opladen: Westdeutscher Verlag).

Yngvesson, B. (1988) 'Making Law at the Doorway – The Clerk, the Court, and the Construction of Community in a New-England Town', *Law and Society Review* 22, 409–448.

Zahavi, D. (1999) *Self-awareness and Self-alterity. A Phenomenological Investigation* (Evanston: Northwestern University Press).

Zimmerman, D. (1974) 'Fact as a Practical Accomplishment', in R. Turner (ed.) *Ethnomethodology* (Harmondsworth: Penguin Books Ltd).

Zimmerman, D. (1984) 'Talk and its Occasion: The Case of Calling the Police', in D. Shiffren (ed.) *Meaning, Form and Use in Context: Linguistic Applications. Georgetown Roundtable on Languages and Linguistics* (Washington, D.C.: Georgetown University Press).

Index

Note: letter 'n' followed by locators denotes note numbers.